MEMOIRS

OF

THE CIVIL WAR IN WALES

AND THE MARCHES.

1642—1649.

BY

JOHN ROLAND PHILLIPS
OF LINCOLN'S INN, BARRISTER-AT-LAW.

IN TWO VOLUMES.

VOL. I.

LONDON:
LONGMANS, GREEN, & Co.
1874.

This scarce antiquarian book is included in our special *Legacy Reprint Series*. In the interest of creating a more extensive selection of rare historical book reprints, we have chosen to reproduce this title even though it may possibly have occasional imperfections such as missing and blurred pages, missing text, poor pictures, markings, dark backgrounds and other reproduction issues beyond our control. Because this work is culturally important, we have made it available as a part of our commitment to protecting, preserving and promoting the world's literature. Thank you for your understanding.

TO MY FRIENDS,

THE

MEMBERS OF THE SOUTH WALES CIRCUIT,

I DEDICATE THIS WORK.

PREFACE.

Some years ago, while engaged in an investigation into the history of my native parish, I was anxious to learn whether the Castle, which forms its principal attraction, had been garrisoned during the Civil War. I found that there was no book which could give me the information I wanted, but I discovered that vast materials existed in the boundless waste of the King's Pamphlets at the British Museum, in the State Papers at the Record Office, and in private collections; and that so far as Wales was concerned it was an untrodden field. After some hesitation I resolved to attempt to contribute something towards a history of the Principality during that period. The leisure hours of some years have been devoted to the subject, and the result is now offered to the public, in the belief that it will fill a gap in the History of Wales and the Marches, and that it will not be without some interest to my countrymen. Of the labour which this Work has involved I will not speak. Sufficient it is to say, that every pamphlet and every newspaper of the period,—many thousands in number,—all the memoirs and collections bearing on that period, and all the vast collection of documents at the Record Office, still unindexed, have been carefully overhauled.

To the officials of the British Museum and the Record Office I am indebted for much consideration and civility; and my best thanks are returned to my friends, Joseph Joseph, Esq., F.S.A., Brecon, and Col. Grant Francis, F.S.A., Swansea, for much valuable aid, and for the kindly interest they have evinced in the Work. To Mrs. Myddelton Biddulph of Chirk Castle, and R. Chambre Vaughan, Esq., of Burlton Hall, Shrewsbury, I also return my thanks; and to Dr. Nicholas I must make my acknowledgments for the information I have obtained from his valuable Work, "Annals of Counties and County Families of Wales."

The Temple, June 18, 1874.

MEMOIRS

OF

THE CIVIL WAR IN WALES

AND THE MARCHES.

CHAPTER I.

State of Wales after its conquest—Lord Marchers—Insurrection of Owen Glyndwr—Harsh measures of repression—Social condition in the Middle Ages—Wars of the Roses—Ascension of Henry VII.—Justice to Wales under Henry VIII.—Union with England—Opposition to the division of Wales into shire-ground—The Reformation—Education—The Bible and other books in the Welsh language—Great ignorance—John Penry—Churchyard's "Worthiness of Wales"—Development of the natural resources of the country—Trade and commerce—Roads and travelling—Condition of the towns—And a general survey of the state of the country at the end of the reign of James I.

WALES, after fighting desperately for its independence, had the prudence to submit to a Power which it could no longer resist, and to acquiesce in a Government which, though foreign, did not interfere much with the customs and internal character of the country; for though Edward I., in enacting the *Statutum Walliæ* at Rhyddlan, intended to introduce important changes into the civil government of the Principality, yet, because he had not the machinery to carry out his policy, the ancient laws and customs of the country were permitted to continue: the rule of life of its inhabitants. This continued to be so for some time, and would probably have worked very well had it not been for the conduct of the Lord Marchers. The Norman monarchs, for various reasons, had let loose upon the Principality and the borders a number of powerful subjects to subdue and overawe the Welsh. The success of these hastened what has been called the conquest of Wales, and they were allowed to remain owners of the vast tracts they had won, scarcely subject to any rule. These, paramount in their castles, surrounded with hosts of armed retainers, and backed by the influence of the Court of England, were, in their dealings with the Welsh, unscrupulous and domineering. By them and their descendants the inhabitants were most unjustly and cruelly ill-treated. Their property was confiscated, their rights ignored, and cowed and overawed by the many misfortunes which had befallen their unhappy country, the natives scarcely durst call their lives their own. For a long time they suffered all manner of indignities with a patience which is striking. But the old spirit was at length roused. The bards long sang of the happiness of the days gone bye, and portrayed in vivid colours the misery of their country and its wrongs; and for a long time there had been a smouldering fire of discontent and disaffection. Their sad experiences had taught them that against their persecutors it was useless to appeal to their common King. Their prayers were unheeded; their wrongs remained unredressed, and those against whom they justly complained not only escaped punishment, but found greater favour with their Sovereign. Goaded to desperation, and eager to free their country from a thraldom which had become intolerable, there were thousands ready to take up arms. Only a leader was wanted, active and influential enough to strike for freedom, to kindle the whole country into one insurrectionary flame, and to unite all classes in one common cause. That leader at length appeared in Owen Glyndwr,—a representative of one of the ancient princes,—who, on being despoiled of his property by the rapacious Reginald de Grey, Earl of Ruthin, had appealed in vain to the Court for redress.

Owen took the law into his own hands, resolved to obtain by force what had been denied to him as an applicant of justice. On a memorable fair-day in Ruthin, in the autumn of the year 1400, the first blow was struck. What was doubtless intended as a mere raid to avenge a local wrong, soon assumed greater importance, and when it was found that the King of England espoused the cause of De Grey, the hour which the bards had sung of had arrived. The people made the cause of Owen their own, determined to cast off their bondage and to restore the government of the Principality to a representative of its ancient Royalty.

The struggle was a desperate one. It lasted for many years; and on the part of the Welsh was carried on with a persistence and a strategic skill which taxed the whole power of England, and for some time appeared likely to baffle it. In the end, however, it failed, and Owen, though offered pardon, died an outcast in Herefordshire.

No sooner had the struggle commenced than the antipathy of race began to develop itself. The English Parliament, in its determination to suppress

CHAP. I.
1410-15.

the insurrection and to punish the Welsh, enacted statutes, which for severity are unsurpassed in the history of legislation. To enumerate the pains and penalties would exceed the limit at my command. Intercourse between the two peoples was to be restricted as much as possible. No Welshman was to be capable of purchasing houses or lands in or near any of the cities or towns in the Marches, under pain of forfeiture. Welshmen were disqualified from being citizens or burgesses in any corporate town. Mayoralties, constableships, and all public offices were shut out from them. Suits and actions between Welshmen and Englishmen were to be decided only by English judges and English juries. No child of Welsh parents could be apprenticed to any trade in any city or town within the Kingdom. All meetings were declared unlawful unless licensed by English authority. The manufacture or importation of armour into Wales was prohibited, and the right to carry arms or weapons of any kind was denied. Marriages between Englishmen and Welshwomen were looked upon with disfavour, and an Englishman so misbehaving was to lose all his franchises; while the Welshman who had temerity enough to wed an Englishwoman, or to acquire property in English towns, was liable to extreme penalties. Lewis Glyn Cothi, an eminent Welsh historical poet, whose works, handed down to the present day, are full of interest and beauty, had the audacity to act in contravention of this law by taking to himself for a wife one of the fair daughters of Chester, and by going to live in that highly-dignified city. The Mayor, however, found him out, and with his bailiffs scattered his household gods, and drove the unfortunate bard from the city. What they did with his wife I have not been able to discover. Poor Lewis had no means to retaliate save by his pen, which of a truth he steeped in gall, and thereby has handed down to perpetual infamy, in language most scathing, the memory of that Mayor and his minions.

CHAP. I.
A.D. 1415.

The bards, indeed, as a body were highly obnoxious to the English; for they had exercised a most powerful influence in fanning the flame of insurrection. As enthusiasts they longed to see their beloved land freed from the thraldom of the foreigner. In Owen Glyndwr they saw the deliverer of their country whom the sages had foretold in times long past, and they lauded him to the heavens. Travelling from house to house, the honoured guests wherever they went, they sang their inflammatory songs, and never failed to attend fairs and other gatherings to further their object. An old custom, and a very good one, prevailed in Wales, called *Cymmorthau*, when a whole neighbourhood would turn out to help in agricultural and other undertakings one who needed assistance. During the insurrection these meetings doubtless were often held for no other purpose than to sow disaffection. An act was passed rendering illegal the *Cymmorthau*, and all assemblings of bards, who were designated "rymours and minstralls," and classed with "vagabonds."

The failure of the insurrection reduced the Principality into a far worse state than it was before. Demoralised by their defeat, and crushed by the iron heel of the victor, whose oppression grew in proportion to the weakness of those whom he trampled upon, the entire people were plunged into a state of anarchy and lawlessness. The antipathy of race became more violent, and continual raids upon the Marches afforded the only method of dealing revenge which was left to the Welshman. These raids were of frequent occurrence; and, doubtless, gave rise to the old rhyme which is so slanderous of the Welsh character — "Taffy was a Welshman, &c." The internal condition of the country must have been truly sad. The laity were sunk in the deepest state of degradation. Accustomed to the use of arms during the fifteen years of insurrection, they were not inclined to throw away the sword, and having no enemy to contend with any longer, old feuds between families, which had almost been forgotten, were renewed with the greatest acrimony, and the flow of blood was continuous. Crime prevailed to a degree hitherto unknown. Life had no sanctity, and property no rights. Might alone was right. The chief inhabitants, who occupied the highest position in society, such as it was, were no better than a pack of robbers or bandits. In their depredations murders were of daily occurrence, and theft and sacrilege afforded them the only means to sustain themselves and their numerous retainers. In truth, the *Llawrudd*, or murderer, was one of the favourites amongst their retainers, and ever found choice entertainment at their houses.[1] The natural resources of the country were not developed. Agriculture was neglected. The land was almost barren: for the sword and the fray had superseded the plough and industry. The clergy, also, regular

---

[1] History of the Gwydir Family, by Sir John Wynne.

and secular, were sufferers from the general demoralization. In the remoteness from any centre of civilization, their mountain homes afforded them perfect liberty to do as they list, and to live as they pleased; and when the condition of the laity was such as I have described, the conduct of the clergy was not very narrowly watched. Some of the most sacred rites and doctrines of their Church were utterly ignored. Concubinage was very common. Strype, in his "Memorials," says, that in the diocese of St. David's it was openly permitted upon a payment of tribute to the priest's superior, and that the arrangement was looked upon with favour by the people as affording some protection to their wives and daughters. In this respect the South Walians appear to have had an advantage over their friends in the North, for there are on record many and grave instances of immorality on the part of the clergy. At the Sessions for Carnarvonshire, held at Carnarvon after the Feast of the Conception, in 1499, the matter was before the court; and the record recites that "many and divers vicious priests and clerks within holy orders, within the Principality of North Wales, defile many women, wives and daughters of the Prince's tenants." According to the law then in existence, the husbands and fathers were punished and not the priests, which was adding insult to injury. It was then, however, decided that in future the priests or clerks "so unvirtuously disposed" should be distrained of their goods and lands, and for want of sufficient distress should be imprisoned until satisfaction had been given.[1]

[1] Records of Carnarvon, p. 297.

CHAP. I.

1415-85.

Even amidst all this anarchy the houses possessed some degree of comfort, and the women were acquainted with some amount of female accomplishments. Generous hospitality was then, as it has ever been, a characteristic of the Welsh people. No traveller was at a loss for rude entertainment and kindly welcome. Mead and beer and wine afforded ample drink, while meat and fish were in abundance on their tables. The ladies devoted much of their time to embroidery, and other light household duties, and religious worship found in them the only devotees. To the accomplishments of the women Lewis Glyn Cothi often alludes in his poems; and the old bard himself appears to have been partial to their handiwork, for when the men of Chester had made him "as naked as a fish in water," to use his own expression, he solicited from some of the good ladies his patrons the gift of embroidered bed-coverlets; and, with a familiarity which shows how high the poet was esteemed in those days, he ventures to describe the kind of coverlet he wanted. One was to be of cloth of nine colours, with nine birds embroidered thereon, and nine stags *couchant*. Twelve green leaves, and ten of black and blue, with small images, and sketches of trees and birds, all of maiden's work, was to further beautify the gift.[1]

[1] "Y mae llen i'm naw lliw,
Naw edn ar frethyn ydyw;
Naw o geirw yn eu gorwodd,
Ac a naw ewig un wodd;
Deuddeg o ddail medleilas,
A deg o liw du a glas;
Yr oedd gant o wyrdd a gwyn,
Yr oedd mil rudd a melyn;
Delwau mân, gwaith dwylaw merch,
Derw a llun adar llanerch."

No change of any importance in the condition of the Principality took place until the English throne came to be occupied by a Prince in whose veins ran Welsh blood. It is true, what with the Wars of the Roses, which pretty fully occupied the English, and with the reaction which generally follows too severe measures, the iniquitous Acts of Henry IV. were not carried out in the fulness of their severity. During the early part of the Wars of the Roses the sympathy of the Welsh had been with the House of York; but the great influence of Jasper, Earl of Pembroke, who was in ill-odour at the Court of Richard III., and the knowledge that the representative of the House of Lancaster was the grandson of Owen Tudor and nephew of the Earl of Pembroke, converted the Welsh into Lancastrians. When Henry, Duke of Richmond, and his uncle Jasper, had to flee the English Court, they sought refuge for a time in Merionethshire, and thence, with difficulty, escaped to Brittany. The Earl of Pembroke had been a considerate patron of the Welsh bards. During his exile his praises were sung in house and field in Wales. Lewis Glyn Cothi is full of allusions to him; and the old poet never warms up so much as when he advocates the claims of Pembroke's nephew to the English throne, and invites their appearance in Wales;—an invitation which in due time was responded to. By the aid of Welsh swords the battle of Bosworth was won, Richard III. slain, and Henry, the grandson of Owen Tudor, of Penymynydd, Anglesey, crowned King of England as Henry VII. Though Henry was a selfish man, he was not unmindful of his obligations to his countrymen; and he heaped favours innumerable on Sir Rhys ab Thomas and others. Natives of the Principality flocked to his Court, and found favour there. Their influence rendered obsolete many of the harsh laws to which I have alluded; while the education which they received by a more intimate acquaintance with the outside world had a highly beneficial effect upon the condition of the country generally. But no great scheme for the improvement of Wales was carried out in his reign, or even worked. Justice to Wales was not done till Henry VIII. had been some years on the throne; and then it was chiefly brought about through the untiring zeal for his country's welfare which animated Sir John Price of the Priory, Brecon, a member of the Council of the Court of the Marches. The great curse of Wales had been the Lord Marchers. No one knew this better than Sir John Price; and though something had been done to curtail their power by the establishment of the Council of the Marches at Ludlow, in Edward IV.'s time, their evil influence still continued: the upas tree which poisoned the Principality, and retarded all progress. With a zeal and devotion worthy of the cause, Sir John Price continued to advocate his great scheme, until ultimately he succeeded in destroying the power of the Lord Marchers, and in effecting the real union of England and Wales under one system of law, and one administration of justice. In doing this he had to contend with a compact and determined opposition from those whom he assailed. Henry, however, who, whatever his failings,—and they were, heaven knows, numerous enough,— was a great statesman, saw the many advantages which would accrue to the entire country by destroying a power which trenched upon his own Royal Prerogative, and had done endless mischief to a portion of his kingdom. During the latter part of his reign reform in Wales was the subject which, next to the Reformation, attracted most of his attention. Many statutes were passed, all tending to the same great end—the union of Wales with England, and the improvement of the social condition of the Principality. The preambles to these statutes give curious pictures of the state of the country. The suborning and bribing of juries by friends of accused persons was a common thing, and the acquittal of divers murderers and felons notoriously known had followed as a consequence. To stop this, juries in future were to be placed in custody of a keeper sworn to keep them separate from other persons.[1] South Walians had for a long time been in the habit of crossing the Severn to plunder the worthy people of Gloucestershire and Somersetshire, and then returning with their booty to South Wales and the Forest of Dean, where they were secure from punishment, and the robbed went without a remedy. Owners of ferries and keepers of passages across the estuary were, therefore, to be prohibited from conveying anybody across the Severn in the night-time, under penalty of fine and imprisonment, unless such persons and their habitations were known to them.[2] "The people of Wales and the Marches," according to another statute,[3] "not dreading the good and

---

[1] Stat. 26, Hen. VIII., cap. 4.
[2] Stat. 26, Hen. VIII., cap. 11.
[3] *Ibid*, cap. 6.

wholesome laws and statutes of this realm, have of long time continued and persevered in perpetration and commission of divers and manifold thefts, murders, rebellions, wilful burnings of houses, and other scelerous deeds and abominable malefacts, to the high displeasure of God, inquietation of the King's well-disposed subjects, and disturbance of the public weal."

The principal measures relating to Wales passed in that reign were the 5th and 26th chapters of Statutes 27th Henry, and the 34th and 35th Henry VIII., c. 26. The first of these provided for the appointment of Justices of the Peace in the Counties of Chester, Flint, Anglesey, Carnarvon, Merioneth, Cardigan, Carmarthen, Pembroke, and Glamorgan, who were to administer justice in those counties in the same way as it was done in English shires. The second constituted certain manors and hundreds into new counties, under the names of Brecknock, Radnor, Montgomery, and Denbigh, and annexed certain towns and manors to the counties of Glamorgan, Pembroke, Cardigan, and Merioneth. It provided also for the representation of Wales in the English Parliament: one member for each county, and one burgess for each borough, being shire-town. Some pecuniary rights of the Marches were protected, but it was enacted "that the dominion of Wales shall be, stand, and continue for ever from henceforth incorporated, united, and annexed to and with the realm of England, and that all and singular person and persons born, and to be born, in the said Principality, country, or dominion of Wales, shall have, enjoy, and inherit all and singular freedoms, liberties, rights, privileges, and laws within this realm, and other the King's dominions, as other the King's subjects naturally born within the same have, enjoy, and inherit." It further provided that the laws of England alone should be used in Wales.

And, finally, by the 34th and 35th Henry VIII., c. 26, Wales was divided into twelve shires. The Court of the Marches was to continue. Sessions were to be held in every county twice in every year. These were to be called the Great Sessions of Wales: an arrangement which continued in existence down to the present half century. Justices of the Peace for each county were to be appointed by the Chancellor;—not to exceed eight in each county, and to be of good name and fame. Sheriffs were to be chosen as in England. Gaols to be provided in every county. Trials to be by wager of law; and lands to be held by English tenure.[1]

Thus was Wales finally united with England. We who have participated in the advantages of this union can have no idea what a blessing to Wales must have been produced through the efforts of

---

[1] In the "Cromwell Correspondence," preserved in the Chapter House (State Pap., Henry VIII., i., 454), is a letter from Roland Lee, Bishop of Lichfield, and President of the Council of the Marches to Cromwell. I extract the following from it, to show the kind of opposition which existed against reforms in Wales:—

"Moste harty recommendations promysed. Hit may please you to be advertised that lately I was enfourmed that the Kinges Graces pleasure was, to make Wales shire grounde, and to have Justices of the Peace and off Gaole Delyvery, as in Englande. And forasmoche as I am putt in trusto here, and that by your means and pleasure, I can no lesse doo (my duety remembred) then to declare to you my mynde in oone poincte, specially, as in tryall of fellons. For if they maye comme to their trialles at home, where oone theif shall trye an other as, before the last statute in that part provided, they did, then that as we here have begon is fordon: the experience teacheth the same here dailye. I am sure all this day, ye cannot do the Welshemen more pleasure then to breke that statute. Wolde Gode I were with you oone houre to declare my mynde therin at full. And,

Sir John Price, and a few other devoted men, whose names even have not been handed down to us.

With these beneficial changes came the Reformation, which in the Principality appears to have been very quietly acquiesced in; though, from the tenacity with which the Welsh cling to old institutions and customs, the contrary might have been expected. There were, however, several reasons for this. The vitality of religious worship appears to me to depend, like everything else to a certain extent, on competition, or some momentary cause of enthusiasm. Wherever we find one sort of religion universal among a people, there generally we find the priests careless and the people indifferent. The Crusade, during its continuance, gave life and energy to the Christian Church then universal in western Europe; but the excitement gradually died away, and not before the appearance of Luther on the continent, was there any shaking of the dry bones. These controversies scarcely penetrated into Wales, where everything was stagnant and cold. So that when the Reformation came it

also, for Justices of the Peace and off Gaole Delyvery to be in Wales, I thinke hit not moche expedient; for there be very few Welshemen in Wales above Broknock that may dispende ten pounde lande, and, to say truthe, their discretion [is] lesse then their landes. And, farther, where ther is as yet some beryng of theves by gentlemen, if this saide statute goo forward, ye shall have no other but beryng ther, and lytle justice mynystred; as I doubt not your circumspecte wisedome will considre, as by the demeanours of Meryonethshire and Cardiganshire it dothe appere, which (although they be Shiregroundes) cannot, as yet, be brought to good ordre, and be as ill, as the wourste parte of Wales. Nevertheles, Sir, uppon this my rude intimation I truste ye will considre, and kepe the former statutes provided for the saide countreye of Wales, as well in the premisses as for beryng of wepons and otherwayes; whereby ye shal be assured the goode rule, now begon, herafter to contynue to the pleasure of God, honour and laude of our Soveraigne Lord, the Kinges Majestie, and to your renowned fame in counsailing the same."

found the Welsh masses indifferent, and the priests inactive. Moreover, there is reason to believe that a certain amount of antipathy against the priestcraft prevailed in Wales. For a long time there had been a mortal feud between the bards and the priests. They continually denounced one another, and I fear that the light wit of the bard had greater influence with the populace than the serious wrangles of the clergy. The splendid thrusts of Dafydd ab Gwilym and others, must have possessed a charm for their audience, which comprised persons of all grades, and probably were not without their influence when the separation from Rome was effected. But above all things, the policy of Henry VIII. towards Wales silenced all opposition. The wealthy and powerful were bought over by rich gifts of monastic lands, and the people were naturally led to look upon the Reformation as a part and parcel of the highly beneficial measures which were calculated to do so much for the Principality. It should also be remembered that the promulgation of Protestantism was very gradual. Henry's greatest blow was aimed at the monasteries; he scarcely touched the out-door clergy, and the majority of these continued to minister as they had been wont to do, and with little scruple swallowed the new formulæ.

Up to the Reformation there were no schools in Wales. Of course, I do not mean in very ancient times, when the British had large educational establishments at Bangor-Iscoed, and Lantwit Major. Whatever education the Welsh received in the middle ages, they must have received within the walls of some of the old abbeys or monasteries at the hands of the monks. That some availed themselves of this opportunity is clear, for during those dark days there were men of letters in Wales, whose writings even now abound in many private libraries in the Principality. But the number of educated persons must have been very limited, and ignorance must have covered the country as with a pall. Owen Tudor is said to have introduced to his wife, Queen Catherine, some of his own kinsmen from Wales. Owen himself was a courtier, and he no doubt introduced the very best of his kinsmen. They were all dumb in her presence, for not a word of English could they speak; which caused the Queen to remark, that they were the handsomest dumb-creatures she had ever seen. The story has been often repeated, and whether as a fact it is true or not, matters little; but it clearly represents the ignorance which prevailed even amongst the principal gentry in those days. Before the ascension of Henry VII., very few Welshmen, if any, had the advantages of the University of Oxford. But with the Tudor dynasty a change for the better took place in this respect, and the doors of Oxford were entered by many natives of the Principality. Sir John Price, of whose exertions on behalf of his country notice has already been taken, was educated there, and there must have been many others who had received their education at Oxford. But the rich alone could avail themselves of this, for there were yet no schools in Wales. Henry VIII., by a grant dated 1541, established Christ's College in Brecon. This collegiate institution had been originally founded by Bishop Gower at

Abergwili, and was thence removed to Brecon by Henry VIII., on the recommendation of Bishop Barlow. The King endowed it with some lands belonging to the monastery of St. Nicholas. Edward VI., however, whose endeavours on behalf of education ought to be held in the highest esteem, endowed a school at Shrewsbury, which continues to this day, and has won for itself a high place among the educational institutions of the country. During the reign of Mary matters made no progress; and beyond the burning of Bishop Ferrar at Carmarthen, William Nicholas at Haverfordwest, and Rawlins White, a poor fisherman, at Cardiff, no incident occurred in Wales that I know of. Affairs assumed a very different aspect on the ascension of Elizabeth. The effects of education in the higher classes and in the Church now became manifest. Welshmen were appointed bishops;—men who had the advancement of their country at heart. Dr. Richard Davies was Bishop of St. David's, and Dr. Nicholas Robinson Bishop of Bangor; both eminent men. Dr. Gabriel Goodman, of Ruthin, was Dean of Westminster, and William Salesbury, of Plâs Isaf, Denbighshire, was following the law at Thaives Inn, London. These men used all their influence for the benefit of their country; and, probably, it was through them that an Act was passed by Elizabeth, in 1563, authorizing the translation of the Bible into Welsh. This Act ordained that the Bible, with the Book of Common Prayer, should be translated into Welsh by the 1st of March, 1566, under a penalty of £40 for each of the Bishops of St. David's, St. Asaph, Bangor, Llandaff, and Hereford, who were appointed to edit it. The Act further ordained that a copy of the work when printed should be placed in every parish church and chapel in Wales; but the measure was very defective, for it made no provision as to the cost of the undertaking, and for that reason produced no immediate effect. Private enterprise, however, supplied this defect. William Salesbury, Dr. Richard Davies, and some others, set about the work in earnest, and in 1567 the New Testament was printed. This is known as Salesbury's Testament, and was dedicated to the Queen. Dr. Davies prefixed to it an address to the Welsh, in which he gives by no means a favourable description of the moral state of Wales at the time. "Often in Wales," he says, "the hall of the gentleman is found to be the refuge of thieves. Therefore, I say, that were it not for the arms and the wings of the gentry there would be but little theft in Wales." The expense of printing this book was borne by Humphrey Toy, "dwelling in Paules Churchyard, at the signe of the Helmet," whose mother and grandmother were natives of Wales—the mother carrying on a printing establishment in London. A few books in the Welsh language had been printed before this date, most of them the production of Salesbury's pen. The Book of Common Prayer in the Welsh made its appearance at the same time as the Testament. But the Bible itself was not produced until 1588: the translation of Dr. Morgan, Bishop of St. Asaph, a native of Carnarvonshire. While he was Vicar of Llanrhaidr y Mochnant, he was for some cause or other brought before Dr. Whitgift, Archbishop of Canterbury. By the latter he was encouraged to proceed with the translation of the Bible, a labour which he had already commenced; and in the preface Dr. Morgan confesses that had it not been for the assistance of the Archbishop he would have given up the task, conscious of the difficulties and terrified at the cost of the undertaking. Morgan was assisted also by many other scholarly men, viz.: Dr. Hughes, then Bishop of St. Asaph, Dr. Gabriel Goodman, Dr. David Powell, Archdeacon Prys, and others. Other works now followed in quick succession from the press, either written by Welshmen or relating to Wales, and either in English or Welsh. One of the most important of these was the "History of Cambria," the work of Caradoc of Llancarvan, translated by Humphrey Lloyd, and edited by Dr. David Powell. Soon after, Dr. John David Rhys, a native of Anglesey, published his scholarly work, "Institutes of the Welsh Language." Dr. Goodman, the Dean of Westminster, was a friend and patron to all those who endeavoured to promote the advancement of his native country; and his position as Dean of Westminster afforded him ample opportunities to help in that direction. The cloisters afforded an enlightened home to many Welsh students. Dr. Morgan was a guest there while superintending the printing of the Bible. Camden owed more to Dr. Goodman for his help in the mighty undertaking which resulted in the former's "Britannia," than to any other individual. Born at Ruthin, Dr. Goodman was not unmindful of his native town, and in the year 1595 he established, under a Charter obtained from Elizabeth, a school there, which he endowed very considerably.

Poor John Penry, too, whose sad fate is so well known, did all in his power to promote the interest of the Principality. Address after address, and remonstrance after remonstrance, to the Parliament and others in authority, emanated from his eloquent pen. But he had imbibed Puritanical notions, and found no favour in high quarters. Still his endeavours on behalf of his country place him on the highest pedestal of patriotism, and his unfortunate death, which he suffered for an offence of which I think he was innocent, throws a melancholy halo round his illustrious name. His portraiture of the ignorance of the Welsh, and of their, in his view, spiritual blindness, may be a little overdarkened; but he wrote not without ample cause. In fact, his account is confirmed by several contemporary letters from the bishops and others, one of which, as it is not without considerable interest, I give below.[1]

---

[1] It is a letter from Dr. Robinson, Bishop of Bangor, to Sir William Cecil, afterwards Lord Burleigh, and is preserved in the State Paper Office Dom., Elizabeth 44, § 27 :—

"*In Christo Jesu salutem, pacem, &c.*

"Righte honorable, I thought it some part of my dewtie to certifie your honour touching the state of these shierres wherein I was borne, and where I now life by the Queene's maiesties singular goodnes towardes me. Y*t* in these three shierres called Caernarvon, Anglesey, and Merioneth, through the wisdome and carefull diligence of Mr. George Bromley, Chefe Justice, the people live in much obedience, fredome, and quiet, so that toward their prince they are like to continew faithfull subjects, and among themselves peaceable neighbours.

"But, touching the Welsh peoples receaving of the gospell, I find by my small experience among them here that ignorance contineweth many in the dreggs of superstition, which did grow chefly upon the blindnes of the clergie, joined with the greediness of getting in so bare a country, and also upon the closing up of God's worde from them in an unknown tongue, of the which harmes, though the one be remedied by the great benefite of our

Just by way of contrast to the foregoing overshadowed picture, it may not be out of place here to show what the eye of a poet saw in the condition of Wales at this time. Churchyard appears to have seen only that which was lovely and beautiful, and his praises of the country and its people are painted in words of a roseate hue. The civility of the people he remembered with gratitude, and their honesty he thus describes:—

> They will not strive to royst and take the way
> Of any man that travailes through their lande;
> A greater thing of Wales now I will say:
> Ye may come there, beare purse of gold in hand,
> Or mightie bagges of silver stuffed throwe,
> And no one man dare touch your treasure now,
> Which shows some grace doth rule and guyde them there,
> That doth to God and man such conscience beare;

graciouse Quene and Parleament, yet the other remayneth without hope of redresse: for the most part of the priestes are too olde (they saye) to be put to schole. Upon this inabilitie to teache God's worde (for there are not six y⁴ can preache in y⁶⁶ three shierres) I have found since I came to this countrey images and aulters standing in churches undefaced, lewde and indecent vigils and watches observed, much pilgrimage goyng, many candels sett up to the honour of saintes, some reliques yet carried about, and all the countries full of bedes and knotts, besides diverse other monuments of wilfull serving of God. Of the which abuses some (I thank God) are reformed, and other, my hope is, wyll dayly decaye by the helpe of the worshipfull of the countries who show some better countenance to the Gospell by the godly p'rte of the Chefe Justice, whose counsell and eade I have in such matters; all which (I trust) Almightie God will turne to his owne glorie, and the salvation of his people.

. . . .

"Fare you well in Christe. From my house at Bangor y⁶ 7 of Octob., An. Dm. 1567.

"Your honour's most assured,

"NICHOLAS BANGOR."

While the material prosperity of the country is thus portrayed:—

> Behold besides a further thing to note,
> The best cheape cheare they have that may be found,
> The shot is great when each man pays his groate,
> If all alike the reckoning runneth round.
> There markets good, and victuals nothing deare,[1]
> Each place is filled with plenty all the yeare,
> The ground mannurede the grain doth so encrease,
> That thousands live in wealth and blessed peace.[2]

I am afraid that Churchyard's enthusiasm exaggerated as much on the one hand as the fanaticism of John Penry did on the other, and that the truth lies somewhat between Churchyard's picture and the testimony of Roland Lee, Bishop of Lichfield, Dr. Davies, Bishop of St. Asaph, and John Penry. The country was not so prosperous as Churchyard painted it, though it was nearly as ignorant as set forth by John Penry. How could it be otherwise? For, with the exception of the Collegiate School at Brecon, founded by Henry VIII., and Shrewsbury School, founded by Edward VI., there were no educational seminaries which could remove such ignorance. But the good men who had tasted of the fruit of education, and who took a warm interest in the well-being of their fellow countrymen, were not backward in doing what they could to meet the evil. In the year 1576 a Free School was

---

[1] Of the cheapness of food confirmatory testimony is given by John Taylor, the Water Poet, who made a tour through Wales in 1652. At Carmarthen Taylor says that he could buy the best butter for 2½d. or 3d. the lb.; beef for 1½d. the lb.; salmon, two and a half feet long (big fish !) for 12d.; oysters only a penny a hundred; eggs twelve a penny; pears six a penny. In fact, Taylor says everything was cheap and plentiful, save tobacco pipes.

[2] Worthiness of Wales. Ed. 1587.

founded by Letters Patent of Queen Elizabeth at Carmarthen, through the influence of the unfortunate Earl of Essex, who, along with Richard Davies, the Bishop of St. David's, Sir James Croft, Griffith Rice, and Walter Vaughan, aldermen of the borough, and Robert Toy, one of the burgesses, petitioned the Queen in that behalf. In 1595, Dr. Gabriel Goodman founded, and liberally endowed, a Grammar School at Ruthin, his native place, for which he obtained a Charter from Queen Elizabeth. In this school many men of note have been educated—one of them being Dr. John Williams, Archbishop of York, the last clerical Lord Keeper, whose actions will come under our review during the progress of this work. Dr. John Gwynn, in 1571, endowed two scholarships at St. John's College, Cambridge, by creating a rent-charge of £20 a year on his property near Llanrwst, for the benefit of natives of North Wales, and another scholarship was founded by Dr. Richard Parry, Bishop of St. Asaph, who charged his land at Erbistock with the payment of £6 a year, at Jesus College, Oxford, open to scholars in the diocese of St. Asaph, or from Ruthin Free School. Jesus College, Oxford, had been previously founded for the benefit of Welshmen by Dr. Hugh Price, the son of a butcher at Brecon, who was Treasurer of St. David's. The Charter of Elizabeth, establishing this college, bears date June 25th, 1571. In 1603 one David Hughes, who owned property in Anglesey, endowed a Free School at Beaumaris, which was further enriched by a bequest of £20 a year by Lewis Owen, Serjeant of the Larder to King James I., to found two scholarships in Jesus

College. A Free Grammar School was established at Hawarden 1609, through the liberality of George Ledsham, Steward of the Inner Temple, who bequeathed for that purpose a sum of £300. Thomas Lloyd, of Kilcyffeth, in the County of Pembroke, founded the Grammar School at Haverfordwest in 1614, which he endowed with his property at Haverfordwest, and in the parish of St. Martin, in that county. Though all these schools were intended to be for the benefit of the poor, the intention of the donor in almost every case was soon disregarded; and these educational establishments became the monopoly of the affluent and well-to-do. The masses of the people did not derive much benefit from them, beyond that improvement in their condition which was the natural result of the spread of education among the wealthier classes. The blessings of education did not at all penetrate into the lower strata of society, and when the war broke out between Charles and the Parliament, the body of the people were incapable of forming a correct judgment of the merits of the dispute. Scarcely understanding the duties and rights of citizens, they were at the beck and call of those who occupied a higher rank in life, whom they in many cases implicitly followed.

In a country labouring under so many disadvantages, and torn with so many dissensions, trade and commercial enterprise found no home. During the middle ages no attempt whatever appears to have been made to develop the natural resources of the Principality. Satisfied with the rudest form of agriculture, which produced no more than was consumed, no endeavours were made to improve even the face of the country, or to add to the productiveness of the soil. And, as might have been expected, the wealth of the mineral world was unknown. Coal-mines, however, appear to have been worked to a certain extent in Flintshire at an early period, principally at Bychton and Mostyn. Even as far back as the time of Edward I., the coal mines of Flintshire were in existence;[1] and it is supposed that some use was made of the valuable commodity in which Glamorganshire is so rich.[2]

At the ascension of the House of Tudor, the manufacture of cloth—then called Whites, Russets, and Kennets—was carried on rather extensively, from the wool of the sheep and goats with which the country abounded; and for which a market was found at Shrewsbury and elsewhere. In selling their cottons, I regret to say, the Welsh were suspected of unfair dealing, by representing as superior an inferior quality, and by misrepresenting the quantity of the rolls in which they were usually sold. To protect the purchasers—as if the doctrine of *caveat emptor* ought not to have been applied —Henry VIII. passed certain statutes, which enacted that the "craftily" constructed "roll" should be discontinued, and that in future it should be sold in "plaits or cutlets," on pain of forfeiture.[3] Even the weavers of Cardiganshire, Pembrokeshire, and Carmarthenshire, misrepresented the weight, breadth, and goodness of their friezes and cottons, and a special statute was required to keep them in the line of rectitude and plain dealing.[4]

[1] Pennant.
[2] Wilkin's History of Merthyr Tydfil.
[3] 33 Henry VIII., c. 3.
[4] 34 and 35 Henry VIII., c. 11.

During the reign of Queen Elizabeth, Wales participated in the general progress of the nation. Trade and commerce were extended, and manufactures increased and carried on with an energy and skill hitherto unknown. It was not till that reign that the mineral resources of the country began to be scientifically developed. Up to that time Germany supplied this country with nearly all manufactures of iron. The knowledge of minerals and their adaptability was here a science hidden and unknown. Everything was of foreign workmanship. Elizabeth, far-seeing, forbad the importation of swords, knives, and other articles in iron; and to prevent any inconvenience arising therefrom, but chiefly to encourage the industry and to develop the resources of this country, she invited into this kingdom foreign miners and manufacturers in metal. To these she made liberal grants of mines. The lead mines in Wales were granted to one Daniel Houghsetter. Soon after (in 1567) was established "The Society for the Mines Royal," of which the Earl of Pembroke was the first Governor. The Cardiganshire Lead Mines were let out by these to Sir Hugh Myddelton, who for some time worked them with great energy, bringing profit to himself and contributing very materially to the prosperity of the country; but his time, wealth, and energy, being required to conduct the greatest undertaking of those days — the construction of the New River of London — the Cardiganshire Lead Mines were neglected. Charles I. leased them to Thomas Bushell, one of the Masters of the Mint. Bushell was an enterprising man. Sometime before he had obtained the lease of the

Derbyshire mines. He carried on both undertakings with great ability, and amassed enormous riches. He was further favoured by the King with the right to establish a Mint at Aberystwith. This continued to be worked until the outbreak of the Civil War, when Bushell, in various ways, showed his gratitude to the King, and freely expended his large fortune on his Sovereign's behalf. The Mint was then removed to Shrewsbury, and afterwards to Oxford.

Coal-mines also began to be worked in a more scientific and systematic manner. The coal fields of North Wales supplied Chester and other towns with fuel; and from Glamorganshire an extensive export trade was carried on with Bristol, Gloucester, and other places on the coast of Somersetshire and Devonshire. Bristol then was the great market place for the counties of South Wales, where a ready sale was obtained for all the excess produce of the country. In 1618, coals in Wales had become dear, being 6s. 8d. per chaldron instead of 3s., which occasioned an impost to be levied on exported coals, so as to keep the price down at home.[1]

Agriculture too was improved, and the land made more productive. According to Churchyard, the aspect of the country was pleasing to a degree.

> The ground mannurde, the grain doth so encrease,
> That thousands live in wealth and blessed peace.

And this progress extended over the reigns of Elizabeth and James the First. Corn was raised in great quantities. The Counties of Pembroke and Glamorgan appear to have been the chief

---

[1] State Pap. Dom., James I., vol. xli., § 85.

corn-growing districts of the Principality, while Carmarthen was rich in its cattle and the produce of the dairy. Corn and butter were exported extensively to Bristol. Ireland also afforded a market for the sale of corn.

There was, however, one great obstruction to commercial enterprise: what in itself is the best testimony of the prosperity of the times, viz., the presence of pirates all along the coast. These were chiefly Moors from Spain and Algiers. Sallee appears to have been their head-quarters. Cardiff, in the time of Elizabeth, laboured under the bad odour of being the general resort of pirates, where they were sheltered and protected.[1] Sir John Perrott, who then acted as Admiral of those seas, had ample work to do to repress these robbers. And during the reigns of James and Charles many were the remonstrances and petitions sent up from Wales, demanding further precautions for the protection of commerce.

Another serious drawback arose from the difficulties of inland communication. There were then no railways, nor even canals. The highways afforded the only means of transit, and these were so bad: so ill-constructed, and so indifferently kept, that during the wet season, if not indeed during the greater part of the year, they were impassable to carts and waggons, and could only be traversed on horseback or on foot, and even then not without danger; so that, generally speaking, the only regular means of conveying merchandise from one place to another was by the pack-horse. The discomfort of travelling was under these circumstances very con-

[1] State Pap. Dom., Elizabeth, vol. cxi., § 16, and 112, § 27.

siderable, and patriotic indeed must those worthy men have been who accepted the position of Members of Parliament, when a journey to the metropolis from their distant mountain homes was surrounded with so many inconveniences, and, moreover, beset with no little risk to their lives. Generally, these tedious journeys were performed in the summer time, when advantage was taken of the company of drovers, who carried on some commercial intercourse with London. In a large company there was some security. To an unprotected party mishaps were very likely to occur, for the roads were everywhere infested with highwaymen, who flourished unpunished, to the great terror of all who were called upon to undertake journeys, and who had business to transact at a distance from their homes. The cost of personal travelling in Wales does not appear to have been very heavy. A ten days' journey from Carnarvonshire to South Wales cost no more than fifteen shillings. Eighteenpence covered the outlay of a two days' journey from Tremadoc to Pwllheli, and half-a-crown was sufficient pocket-money for a man who had to travel from the former place to Oswestry and back. These were the expenses of a man who occupied the respectable position of a steward of an extensive estate at the beginning of the seventeenth century. It is, of course, difficult to arrive at an idea as to the entertainment which these modest sums could have commanded. Rude, indeed, it must have been, when the expenses of a four days' stay at Carnarvon amounted to no more than three shillings! One great charge incidental to travelling and visiting was the largesse or vails to servants;

as much as eight shillings were bestowed on the servants at Dolgiog by Sir William Maurice on a visit there.

Glimpses of social life at this time enable us to see that the necessaries of life were not dear, and that housekeeping was comparatively inexpensive. Six chickens cost only fifteenpence. A whole pig could be purchased for twelvepence; but a flitch of cured bacon cost as much as eight shillings. From four shillings and sixpence to five shillings would buy a whole mutton. While a duck could be had for fivepence, a goose fetched four times as much. Fish sufficient for a special occasion, when a distinguished guest was to be entertained, required no greater outlay than ninepence. Oatmeal was sold at sixteen shillings the peck, and wheat was bought at Pwllheli for little over six shillings the "hobbett."[1]

The state of the towns participated in the general progress of the times; but they were still inconsiderable. A glance at the interesting old maps of the Welsh counties, dated 1610, published in Speede's Atlas, giving sketches of the county towns, shows that the towns were at that time of small proportions, comprising a few streets, nearly always within the walls, and occasionally with a few scattered houses in the suburbs. For instance, Newport, Monmouthshire, comprised one principal street, called Monmouth-street. Cardiff comprised a number of mean streets, but the bulk

[1] These particulars are gleaned from an interesting Document in the Peniarth Library, contributed to the *Archæologia Cambrensis* (Original Documents, p. cix.) by Mr. W. W. E. Wynne. Pity it is that other gentlemen who possess such valuable Documents do not follow Mr. Wynne's example, and give them publicity.

of the town was within the walls: Crockherbtown —or Cokkerton, as Speede calls it—was the only part of Cardiff outside the walls. Though Cardiff was the chief town of the shire, and possessed ships which carried on a trade in coal with Bristol and elsewhere, Swansea was even then a more considerable place. Even in 1563 the population of the latter place numbered 1,260, and the parish comprised 180 houses.[1] Swansea also carried on a trade in coal, and there had been established at that place in 1583 a small attempt at copper smelting, forming the nucleus of that enormous branch of industry which has given so unlovely an appearance to Glandwr. Neath was considered the best place in Wales for ship-building;[2] but its trade was naturally small. Insignificant, however, as were the towns, they were not without their attractions; and the rich and wealthy, tired of the loneliness of their country seats in the winter time, sought recreation and social enjoyment in them. The principal gentry generally possessed houses in the chief towns, some of which I think still exist in Chester, at Brecon, and Carnarvon. Their influence there was very great. The mayoralties and other offices of power and honour were generally held by them, and the democratic element which now pervades the towns did not exist in those days, when the bourgeois were every bit as servile and dependent as the rural hinds, and when all political power was in the hands of a few. Of these, those who had received any education at all had either received it at Oxford, or from men who

[1] Dillwyn's History of Swansea; Col. Francis's Charters of Swansea, &c.
[2] Stradling Correspondence.

CHAP. I.
A.D. 1625.

had been educated there, where the obnoxious doctrine of the Divine Right of Kings found its chief stronghold in the reign of James I., and afterwards. Men so educated were not likely to be unprejudiced leaders of the masses in a struggle in which that false doctrine was assailed, and the rights of the people proclaimed. So much of this as is true of the gentry is applicable with far greater force to the clergy; for at that time the doctrine of the Divine Right of Kings found its staunchest advocates within the Church of England. And it was to these alone that the ignorant masses of Wales had to look for guidance. The Welsh laboured under many disadvantages. The few books they possessed in their language were calculated more to befit them for the hereafter than to qualify them for a citizenship of this world. Situated at a great distance from the metropolis, they were ignorant of what was going on in the State; and unacquainted with the English language, they could not profit by the stream of papers and pamphlets which now began to issue from the public press.

CHAPTER II.

1625—1642.

The accession of Charles—His first Parliament called and dissolved—King tries to borrow money on Privy Seals—Another Parliament called—Grievances discussed—Charges against Duke of Buckingham—Parliament dissolved—The country refuses to pay what the Parliament had voted, but not passed—Seaports called upon to furnish ships for war—A loan demanded—Many imprisoned for refusing to pay—They sue to be released on bail—Judges tampered with by Charles—First attempt to levy ship-money—Third Parliament called in 1628—Petition of Rights reluctantly assented to by the King—Parliament prorogued—Buckingham assassinated—High Church divines promoted—General remonstrance against tonnage and poundage, and innovations in religion—Scene in the House of Commons—The Speaker forcibly held down in the chair while protest is made—Parliament dissolved—Prosecution of Members for conduct in Parliament—His Majesty decides on governing without a Parliament—Strafford and Laud—Arbitrary proceedings to raise money—Monopolies—Forest laws—Star Chamber—Prosecution of Dr. Williams Bishop of Lincoln—Prynne's case—Prynne sent to Carnarvon Castle—Is entertained in Chester—High Commission Court—Richard Parry fined for speaking disrespectfully of the Archdeacon of Carmarthen and of Bishops—Puritanism and High Churchism—The Book of Sports—Observance of the Sunday in Wales—Ship-money levied—Effect of Hampden's refusal to pay—Attempt to introduce episcopacy into Scotland fails—Troubles in Scotland—Parliament called after eleven years—Is angrily dissolved—Long Parliament meets—Differences between the King and Parliament—Grow wider and culminate in Civil War.

SUCH was the aspect of social affairs in Wales at the commencement of Charles's reign. To fairly understand the conduct of the Welsh in the momentous struggle which forms the subject of this Work, it will be necessary at the outset to take a cursory glance at matters of common history—the proceedings in Parliament, the arbitrary and unconstitutional acts of the King, the struggles between the King and the

CHAP. II.
A.D. 1625.

Representatives of the People, the growth of Puritanism, the pretensions of the Church of England, the intrigues with the Church of Rome, all which culminated in the final appeal to arms.

This I shall endeavour to do as concisely as possible, though in some instances it will be unavoidable to discuss certain matters in detail.

The accession of Charles was an event of unalloyed pleasure to the great majority of the nation. His virtuous and pure life pleased all men—the uprightness of his character was as yet untarnished by any meanness or duplicity. In fine, no King ever ascended the throne with a better prospect of a peaceful reign than Charles the First. But unfortunately for Charles he had been brought up in a bad school. He was early in life imbued with lofty ideas of the kingly power. James himself had very exaggerated notions of the royal prerogatives, and found courtiers servile enough to flatter him. Notably among these was the Duke of Buckingham, whose influence upon Charles must have been very great. During the Tudor dynasty many encroachments had been made by the Sovereign upon the liberties of the subject. James came to look upon these as his rights, and Charles followed in his father's wake. Moreover, a very obnoxious doctrine was promulgated about this period—that of the divine right of kings. This doctrine obtained its firmest footing in the Church, the clergy of which, having no real ecclesiastical head, were anxious to place the King—its actual head—on the loftiest pedestal. Passive obedience was a natural sequence of this false doctrine, and absurd as it may appear, even this was advocated by many persons of importance. This, too, at a time when a genuine spirit of enquiry was abroad, and when intelligent minds were questioning the legality of many pretensions, which for awhile had been allowed to grow to the derogation of civil and religious liberty.

Charles succeeded to the throne on the 27th day of March, 1625. Within a few days writs were issued to convene a Parliament on the 7th of May. Various circumstances, such as the King's marriage, necessitated some delay, and his first Parliament did not assemble until the 18th day of June. In this Parliament there was rather a strong party of very worthy men, somewhat impressed with the spirit of puritanism, a dislike of the English hierarchy, and a dread of anything that savoured of the Church of Rome. These were exceedingly solicitous for civil liberty. They saw with anxiety the tendency to despotism, which the extension of the royal prerogative under James indicated, and were anxious to retrench excesses and remove grievances, without however, in any way depriving the King of any of his constitutional rights. To do this they resolved to take fair advantage of the King's wants, and determined to grant supplies to the King only on having concessions made on his part in favour of liberty. For Charles's present want they granted him two subsidies (about £120,000) and tonnage and poundage (equivalent to our customs duties) for a year. This Parliament has been much blamed for this very small supply, and the more especially because for some time it had been the practice of Parliaments to vote tonnage and poundage to the King for life. But this clearly arose from no ill-will to Charles personally, nor from any desire to give him annoyance, but simply from a conscientious

CHAP. II.
A.D. 1625.

belief that if reforms were to be secured at all, they could only be done by rendering the Sovereign a little more dependent upon Parliament for money.

A violent plague raged in London at this time; and it became necessary to remove thence. Parliament was prorogued on the 11th of July. On the 1st of August it reassembled at Oxford. Here Charles remonstrated with them on the inadequacy of the supply, asserted his kindly sentiments towards them, but reminded them that the great undertaking they had in hand—viz., the war with Spain—would require much money. Finding that the Commons, instead of augmenting the supplies, persisted in ventilating their grievances, and that they had even commenced an attack upon the royal favourite—the Duke of Buckingham—the King with much ill-humour dissolved the Parliament.

Immediately before this, when these differences with the Parliament were at their height, the King threatened that if he did not find compliance with his desires he would take the government into his own hands and rule the country without a Parliament. This he now essayed. The very day the dissolution took place—a fact which clearly shows the King's desperate resolve—orders from the Council were issued, addressed to the Lord-Lieutenants, to borrow money on Privy Seals from the rich of their counties. The names of those who refused were to be reported to the Council—another fact which shows the absurdity of calling this a loan, when men were to be reported for not doing that which at the best would be but an act of favour and not obligation. This scheme but ill-succeeded. Small was the amount collected, while the dissatisfaction of the people at this stretch of power was intense. In Wales, as in England, it was a failure. In the County of Brecon £105 was advanced by seven persons. Privy Seals had been addressed to nineteen, seven only paid—the rest made excuses.[1] The gentlemen of Cheshire, who were addressed in like manner, were said to "distaste the motion by reason many of them had lent before without repayment." The Deputy-Lieutenants had however "been careful to inform themselves of moneyed men, who employ the same in usury."[2] An inquisition this of the most illegal nature! The people of Herefordshire, Shropshire, and Flintshire, pretended poverty, payment of subsidies, charges for levies of soldiers, and the certainty of a Parliament. The Earl of Northampton could not "without great difficulty persuade men to discover the state of their country" in these counties.[3] Glamorganshire had suffered extensive losses at the hands of Turkish pirates, who had taken their ships (five good barques), trading in butter with France and Ireland, to the utter undoing of many men, and the impoverishment of the whole country—the farmers being even unable to pay their rents, and honest men detained slaves at Sallee imploring the aid of their friends. The Deputy-Lieutenants endeavoured to make a list of persons able to lend, but found them so few and the amounts so small that they preferred representing the state of their poor country.[4] How the project fared in the

[1] Letter of Thomas Price, dated Brecon, June 1626. State Papers Domestic, Charles I., vol. xxx., fol. 85.
[2] Earl Derby to the Council, Oct. 20, 1625. State Pap. Dom., vol. viii.
[3] Earl Northampton to Council from Flint, 11th Jan., 1626. State Pap. Dom., vol. xviii, fol. 33.
[4] State Pap. Dom., vol. xviii., § 5.

CHAP. II.
A.D. 1626.

other Welsh counties I have not been able to discover; but universally it failed.

The necessities of the King were soon, however, more urgent than ever, and, his threat notwithstanding, he was obliged to summon another Parliament. Every effort was made to keep out of the new assembly such men as had been conspicuous in their opposition to the Court in the previous Parliament. By appointing them to the Shrievalty several were incapacitated. But the subterfuge, as events proved, was not successful. It was seen through, and others were returned in the place of the disqualified, who, if they did not possess the abilities, were actuated by the same opposition to tyranny and the same solicitude for the common weal.

The sixth day of February, 1626, witnessed the opening of the new Parliament. Charles fondly hoped that his determined conduct in dissolving the previous Parliament would have a salutary effect upon the new assembly, and could scarcely bring himself to doubt that this Parliament would in the least delay the voting of supplies. But the new assembly was as determined as the old to redress grievances. Nevertheless, they voted a supply of three subsidies, which was afterwards increased to four subsidies and three fifteenths. Even this was a small sum enough, but it was not finally passed—in fact, its grant was made conditional on the redress of grievances, a course which gave great annoyance to the Court. Charles, however, had no choice but to submit, and the Commons proceeded in earnest to discuss their grievances. The Duke of Buckingham, ever unpopular, had now become positively obnoxious to the country. It was he who had plunged the nation into an inglorious war. It was he who had influenced the King in his attempts to abuse the liberties of the people. His removal was absolutely necessary, if anything like harmony was ever to exist between the Sovereign and the Parliament. His impeachment was therefore decided upon. This was the constitutional way of dealing with untrustworthy ministers. But Charles hearing of it, instantly threatened the Commons, stating that he would not allow any of his servants to be questioned by them, especially such as were of eminent place and near to him. The time had gone by to dispute with effect this right of the Commons, and this threat of necessity failed. The Commons demanded a conference with the Lords to discuss the charges against the favourite, and the impeachment was finally decided upon. As soon as the conference was over, the King caused two of the Commons to be cast into the Tower for alleged violence of speech, whereupon the Commons showed a very proper spirit, by proclaiming that until reparation had been done for this indefensible attack upon their privileges, they would do nothing. The Court party in vain tried to frighten them by the bugbear of dissolution. They remained resolute, and soon after the two members were set at liberty and restored to their colleagues. Even the Lords, who had hitherto slept upon their rights, were stimulated by this result to demand that the Earl of Arundel, whose imprisonment was equally illegal, should be discharged, and again the King had ignominiously to give way.

The Parliament were now more than ever bent upon destroying the Duke's influence—Charles on the other hand was determined to afford him his protection. The supply had not yet been voted, and

CHAP. II.
A.D. 1626.

this quarrel rendered it extremely doubtful whether the subsidies would be allowed unless the King granted extraordinary concessions. To avoid this, and also to prevent the adoption by Parliament of a general remonstrance which was in preparation, the royal prerogative was again exercised to dissolve the Parliament. This happened on the 15th of June. The Commons, nevertheless, published their remonstrance, appealing in this way to the public on whose behalf they fought. This the King ordered to be burnt by the common hangman. And Charles on his part appealed to the same public—quite a novel proceeding by the way—by issuing a proclamation explaining the dissolution.

To rule without the intervention of Parliament was consonant with the inclinations and desire of Charles—to feel that he was the sole and absolute master of the situation, for however so short a time, seems to have given him a boyish kind of delight. And were it not for the difficulty of obtaining money to carry on the machinery of State, it is certain he would never summon a Parliament. But the position was a difficult and hazardous one upon which he now resolved to enter. A war was on hand—money was urgently wanted—the Parliament had been dissolved without voting a supply. New expedients were resorted to with the object of obtaining that which the Parliament had refused, and a scheme was adopted which shows that the King clearly misunderstood the character of the nation, or at any rate believed in a simplicity of nature which is astonishing. And it was this. Letters were sent by the Council to the Justices of the Peace of the various counties, stating that the House of Commons had

And the Marches. 41

"unanimously" agreed, which was a fact, to grant a supply of four subsidies and three fifteenths, which would have been granted accordingly, but for the "disordered passion of some members," wherefore the King after admonition was forced to dissolve the Parliament—that the necessity for the supply still continuing, the King "desired his loving subjects to be a law unto themselves, and to grant that which, if it had passed as was intended, they would have been compellable unto."[1] The Justices were therefore ordered to call the people together, and to exhort them to grant a supply equal to the King's wants. The pretext for this demand was that the country was threatened with an invasion, which however had no foundation in fact. In London, and throughout England, the people were assembled to consider the matter, and everywhere the payment was objected to. The loving subjects appealed to did not care to tax themselves, even though the Judges were influenced to persuade the people of the legality of the thing. It was all in vain. As in England so in the Principality, much murmuring took place. The Justices did their duty by calling together the people, but the result was far from reassuring to Charles, and he would have done well had he taken to heart the lesson which this affair taught him. The County of Pembroke was called together on the 29th of July at Haverfordwest. The letter was read. Many objections were made, the people were backward, further time was required to consider what answer to make.[2] The adjourned meeting took place on the 8th of August, when the

CHAP. II.
A.D. 1626.

[1] State Pap. Dom., vol. 31, § 30.
[2] Letter from H. West, 29th July. State Pap. Dom., vol. 32, § 66.

inhabitants excused themselves from making a voluntary supply, on the ground of the heavy burdens which had already been imposed upon them, and their diminished means; but they added that it would have "ministered no small comfort to their hearts, if by course of Parliament this supply had been added to their former burdens, although thereby they had ever so much wanted."[1] The Monmouthshire people met at Usk, on the 25th day of August, "and utterly refused to pay the subsidies, except they were granted by Act of Parliament." A clear and bold answer this. Moreover, they sent back the King's letter, as if they did not wish to harbour amongst themselves even the slightest memento of such illegality.[2] The answer of the Carmarthenshire people was to the effect that they "were ready to supply his Majesty's wants according to the usual and ancient custom."[3] In the other counties, in all probability, the application failed in like manner.

Vessels were wanted to carry on the war. Charles called upon the seaport towns to furnish him with them. In this he kept himself strictly within limits, for the call was made only on maritime districts. There were many precedents for this, but the demand on this occasion was in excess of any in previous reigns. The City of London alone was required to furnish twenty ships. Upon complaining that Elizabeth had not required so many when threatened with the Armada, the Corporation was curtly told that "precedents in former times were obedience and not direction." I have not been able to discover what

---

[1] State Pap. Dom., vol. 33, § 57.
[2] Letter of Justices to Council. State Pap. Dom., vol. 34, § 30.
[3] *Ibid.* September 15. State Pap. Dom., vol. 35, § 97.

demand was made upon the Welsh seaports, save from the few replies which exist, and from which it is apparent that the demand was looked upon as excessive. No alacrity to obey is anywhere manifest. The County of Carmarthen was called upon to supply a vessel of thirty tons. The people begged to be excused. Their county they said "was an inland county with only a few creeks, in which there was no such ship." Some pressure, probably, was brought to bear upon them, for by another letter (of the 15th of September) they again re-assert that they had no vessel of that size, but had assessed themselves in a sum equivalent to its value.[1] The Justices of Monmouth, writing from Newport on the 24th July, had to confess that "having inquired what ships belong to any port in that county they cannot find that there is anyone.[2] Curious this, that Monmouth, which now boasts a large seaport town in Newport, should have been in the time of Charles without a single ship of thirty tons; or, indeed, if we are to believe the Justices literally, without a single ship of any size whatever. The Pembrokeshire people were also called upon to furnish a pinnace. Whether it was intended that the entire county should contribute is not quite clear, though it seems as if such were the case. Sir John Lewis loses no time to write to Sir John Wogan to say that he thinks the charge was to be borne by those parts of the county adjoining Milford Haven.[3] Sir John Lewis here raises the whole question of ship money, a question which was before long to assume serious importance, and to occupy a prominent place in the

[1] State Pap. Dom., vol. 39, § 98. [2] *Ibid*, vol 32, § 29.
[3] *Ibid*, vol. 32, § 66.

affairs of the country. This furnishing of a ship appears to have been considered a serious imposition by the Pembrokeshire men. They tried to get their good neighbours of Cardiganshire to go halves with them, but the proposal was declined, and the Justices of Pembrokeshire were compelled to inform the Council that they had been unable to furnish the pinnace which was required of them.[1]

The attempt to persuade the people to pay what the Parliament had voted but not passed, having failed, as we have already seen, Charles and his councillors had to devise some other scheme to obtain money wherewith to carry on the government. A general loan was decided upon, notwithstanding the declared illegality of such a thing. Letters were sent to the Lord-Lieutenants, and Commissioners were appointed to collect the loan in each county. Accompanying those letters were private instructions for them to assess the amount each man had to pay on the last subsidy. They were told to treat with each person separately, and should any refuse to lend, they were to be examined on oath as to their reasons, and who (if any) instigated their refusing, and with what design. They were to admit of no excuse, and the names of such as proved obstinate they were to report to the Council. For a good example they were themselves asked to lend freely, and at the outset to seek the loan from such as were deemed most likely to be willing to give the money, so that by the appearance of their names on the list others less willing might be induced to lend. In the King's public declaration for the loan it was said that the urgency of the occasion would not admit

[1] State Pap. Dom., vol. 36, § 19, Sept. 19, 1626.

of the calling of Parliament, and that this loan should not be drawn into a precedent. By which means it was endeavoured to avoid the suspicion which was on the increase in the public mind, that the King intended to govern without Parliaments. Moreover, "on the word of a Prince," he promised to repay all such sums as should be lent, so soon as he should in any way be enabled so to do. But further instructions—private of course—ordered the Commissioners of the loan to bind over all refractory persons to appear at the Council Table. Afterwards, fearing that there would be a great number in this category, another letter was sent to say it was not the King's intention to have the Council troubled with every ordinary person, but only with those whom the Commissioners should think fit. However, that no one should escape, they were instructed that "for the rest who refuse to assist with their purses it is the King's pleasure that they should do so with their persons," and these were to be bound over to appear in the Military Yard, near St. Martin's in the Fields, "to be enrolled amongst the soldiers to be employed in the King's service."[1] And this was called a loan! It certainly is not the usual way to borrow. It is true Charles promised to pay, but it would be weakness to place too much reliance on his word. At any rate, throughout his career as King, it is difficult to discover that he once kept faith. Many opposed this loan throughout the country, and were dealt with in the summary manner above indicated. Terrified at the consequences of a refusal, and wanting organization which alone enables a resistance to be successfully

[1] State Pap. Dom., vol. 38, § 23, under date Oct. 20, 1626.

CHAP. II.
A.D. 1627.

carried out, the country generally gave in. In Wales, as elsewhere, there was, however, a great deal of grumbling. At Haverfordwest the inhabitants required "much persuasion," but yielded, "and to avoid the great hazard [probably from highway robbers] of conveying the money to London at two separate times," they agreed to pay the whole at once.[1] In the County of Pembroke very few persons made default, and those were poor or absent.[2] From Carmarthenshire it was reported as early as February 21 (in a letter from Golden Grove) that the subsidy men "with all cheerful and dutiful hearts had paid, and the Commissioners had freely condescended to do the same."[3] Probably the only instance on record where a tax was paid with a cheerful heart! The Cardiganshire people showed a somewhat less obsequious front. They alleged a decay in their estates, their present disability, and "their fear that the unusual demand might be drawn into a precedent," evidently doubting Charles's promise to the contrary. One hundred and ninety-four positively refused, and a list of them was duly sent to the Council. The sum levied in Cardiganshire was £200.[4] Radnorshire probably is the only county in the Kingdom which actually boasted of having agreed to the loan "without a negative voice." This statement, however, which appears in a letter dated the 12th of June,[5] appears to have been premature, for in September the names of five persons, who, being of sufficient estate in that county, had refused, were sent to the Council.

[1] State Pap. Dom., vol. 57, § 3, March 13th, and vol. 58, § 12, March 24, 1627.
[2] *Ibid*, vol. 73, § 6, August 1st.   [3] *Ibid*, vol. 54, § 54.
[4] *Ibid*, vol. 54, § 74.   [5] *Ibid*, vol. 66, § 73.

The loan succeeded better than could have been expected—nearly the whole amount demanded was collected. Charles had too little foresight, or was too much engrossed with his own high notions of the prerogative, to observe the feeling of the nation upon the illegality of the imposition and the outrageous manner in which those who refused to pay were treated. Many men of position were brought before the Council, and were ruthlessly cast into prison. Five of these claimed the protection of the law, and claimed to be discharged on bail— the clear and undisputed right of every Englishman. But with Charles the privileges and liberties of the subject were of no consideration, and in his zeal to overthrow them he was unprincipled enough to tamper with the Judges and to pollute the very fountain of justice. The Judges at this time were more open to corrupt and venal influence than now. They held their office only during the King's pleasure. Now they hold office for life, and are removable by Parliament only for grave misconduct. The demand of the prisoners was of course, under such circumstances, refused. This was a direct blow at liberty. Already the King did as he liked with the property of the subject: now it would appear their persons were also to be at his disposal. Every enactment for the protection of liberty from the Great Charter downwards, which our forefathers had wrested from unwilling Sovereigns, was now trampled upon and ignored. Step by step Charles pursued his blind and infatuated course, goading his people to a resistance which, if it was a long time ripening into rebellion, was destined to sweep away from the English throne not only himself but the House he belonged to.

After all this abuse of power, money was as much wanted as ever. The war in which the King foolishly persisted exhausted everything. Charles was afraid to try another loan, and it was difficult to discover any fresh expedient. Ancient muniments were diligently searched to find out some forgotten precedent. The Council were moving heaven and earth for some new method. In the last extremity —all things else failing—they were forced to confess that a Parliament must be called. To this the King showed great unwillingness. He abominated the very name of Parliament, he said. But nothing else could be done, and the writs were issued. Still Charles loved the crooked path. Even while the writs were out, the Council was urged to discover some plan wherewith to obtain money. Commissioners were appointed to do so by "imposition and otherwise," as they should think fit. Even the levying of ship-money, and that too in its very worst form, was not only debated, as Hallam says,[1] but actually resolved upon. This is a fact which seems to have been overlooked in common history—at all events, I have nowhere seen it mentioned. On the 11th of February, 1628, the King writes to the Sheriff, Deputy-Lieutenant, and Justices of the Peace of the County of Anglesea—"The King of Denmark is in such great distress, that without present means the Sound will be lost, the English garrison in Stade will be broken up, our eastland trade and the staple of Hamburgh be gotten from us; besides, Spain and France are joined to root out our religion, their Admirals are endeavouring to block up Rochelle, and have a store of landsmen ready on the coast of

[1] Constitutional Hist., i., p. 388.

Brittany to invade us. The fleet in preparation cannot stay safely for a Parliament, but writs are issued, and if the persons addressed make the supply which is the subject of this letter, the King will go on with the Parliament; if not, he must think of some more speedy way. The great business of setting out ships, which used to be charged on the port towns and neighbouring shires, is too heavy for them alone, therefore the Council have cast up the whole charge of the fleet, and have divided it proportionably among all the counties." The sum to be levied in Anglesea was £111, which was to be paid in before the 1st of March. This letter was accompanied by another from the Council, recommending them "to divide the county among them, and so settle the business speedily."[1] Cardiganshire was to contribute £330, Carmarthenshire £411, Glamorganshire £672, Merionethshire £136. Similar letters were most probably sent to the other shires, though I have found no traces of them. Here was at any rate an undisguised attempt to raise ship-money in its most illegal form. What the result was I have not discovered. Even at this early date, it is clear that Charles hesitated at nothing which extended his own arbitrary power. Though the Parliament was summoned, and the elections actually going on, he manifested so little faith in the Parliament, that he and his advisers were constantaneously with the elections carrying out unconstitutional schemes to force money from the nation.

On the 17th March, 1628, Charles's third Parliament met. When the writs were issued, the King, as an act of grace, and to conciliate the people,

---

[1] State Pap. Dom., vol. 92, §§ 88 and 89.

CHAP. II.
A.D. 1628.

ordered the prison doors to be thrown open. Many who had suffered long imprisonment for asserting their rights—the common rights of all—were released. Of these no less than twenty-seven entered Parliament: elected by the people as a protest against the abuses of the times. These, by their sad experience, thoroughly understood the tendencies of the Court. And they appeared at Westminster with an earnest resolution to fight the battle of freedom against despotism. It would be idle to expect them to forget their own sufferings; in fact, the great majority of the elected were determined to place if possible the public liberties on a firm and clear footing. The King's speech on opening Parliament cannot well be surpassed for indiscretion. While soliciting aid his behaviour was imperious, and his language at least threatening. If they should not do their duties in "contributing what the State needed, he should; in discharge of his conscience, use those other means which God had put into his hands to save that which the follies of some particular men may otherwise hazard to lose." Notwithstanding this, the first intercourse between the King and the Commons was friendly, though the latter were resolved to put an end to encroachments upon their privileges, and to create some limit to the Royal Prerogative. The King's wants and their own grievances were at one and the same time considered, and within a fortnight of the opening a large subsidy was unanimously voted. Charles was delighted, and fancied that his threat had availed. But no Act had as yet been passed for the grant, and before this was to take place there would have to be a considerable redress of grievances. Both Lords and

Commons were now united in the wish to have their rights satisfactorily established by a lawful declaration. Charles hearing of the conferences between the two Houses, went to Westminster, and declared before Parliament that he was willing to acknowledge the inviolability of the Great Charter and other ancient statutes, and asked them to accept his royal word. The Lords were willing to accept this, but the Commons did not evince the same faith in the royal word. The trampling upon the popular rights had been too great; their persons and their property had been illegally dealt with; loans had been imposed upon them in the face of Acts of Parliament, for refusing to pay many had suffered imprisonment; soldiers had been billeted in private houses; and martial law had been everywhere applied, against the whole tenour of the law. By the Bill which they had prepared, and which to all posterity will be known by the sacred name Petition of Rights, all these were once more in terms declared illegal; and to this the Commons were resolved to obtain the King's assent. Charles resisted it as much as possible, did all he could to evade it, threatened he would not even receive it. It was useless for the Lords to suggest a compromise, the Commons had made up their minds. It was presented to Charles. He returned a long equivocal assent, instead of using the formal words by which English kings have ever assented to Bills. The formal assent was demanded, and a remonstrance was discussed. Remonstrances in this reign were very frequent. Nothing the King disliked more. Charles sent word that the Commons should not meddle thenceforth with the affairs of State. The House was in no mood to brook such an insult.

CHAP. II.
A.D. 1628.

A wild scene occurred, strong language was used; Buckingham was openly accused as the sole cause of the quarrel. The Speaker of the House was mean enough to slink away and inform the King of this. The latter became in his turn alarmed, sent an explanatory message, and seeing that the Bill for the subsidies had not passed he reluctantly gave his assent to the Petition of Rights in the usual form.

The public joy was intense,—bonfires were lit, and bells rung throughout the metropolis and elsewhere. The supplies were at once passed. All that the Commons wanted had not yet however been effected. There were other grievances to be remedied. Buckingham was still the chief adviser of the King. Tonnage and poundage had been levied without Parliamentary consent. Two remonstrances directed against these things were prepared but not presented, for the King, anxious to have a respite from further contention, prorogued the Parliament.

In the interim the Duke of Buckingham was assassinated by a fanatic of the name of Felton, who believed himself to be an instrument in the hand of Heaven to rid the country of that bad man. The King by no means took this to heart; he was simply irritated, and continued to pursue his old course. The enemies of the Parliament, the upholders of the divine right, and preachers of passive obedience, had favours heaped upon them. Such as were obnoxious to the people found favour with the King. Dr. Laud, who a couple of years before this time was Bishop of St. David's, was translated from Winchester to the see of London. Dr. Mainwaring, whose intemperate zeal in his advocacy of the divine right had evoked the censure of Parliament, was promoted to a rich living. This man actually asserted in a sermon, which was published with Laud's license—Abbot, the Archbishop, within whose province it was, had refused to grant his license, and for his refusal had been suspended—that the King was not bound to observe the laws of the land, that he could, without any consent of Parliament, impose loans and levy taxes, and that the obstinate would not only be lawfully subjected to penalties, but would incur eternal damnation. In 1635, a few years later, this very divine was made Bishop of St. David's, and in that capacity he will probably pass under our review hereafter.

Before the Houses had separated it had been resolved that the Petition of Rights, with the King's final assent, should be printed and dispersed all over the country. The Bill was accordingly printed, but the very next day after the prorogation, the King's printer received instructions to destroy all the copies, and to print instead the Petition with the King's first answer attached to it. A more disgraceful act cannot well be imagined, and the folly of it passes all understanding.

The Parliament reassembled in January. They satisfied themselves as to the cause of this gross breach of faith, but hushed it up as if ashamed of the transaction. Now was heard for the first time in Parliament the voice of that ill-dressed, uncouth man from the Fens, whose destiny was to be so closely connected with the period we are entering upon— Oliver Cromwell. The subject of his maiden speech was to protest against the preferment of Dr. Mainwaring, whom the House of Lords had a little before the adjournment voted incapable of any ecclesiastical

CHAP. II.
A.D. 1629.

promotion. Civil and religious grievances were once more taken into consideration. The King's right to the everlasting tonnage and poundage was once more denied, and Popery and innovations in the Church were held decidedly obnoxious by the majority of the Commons, whom a puritanical bias pervaded. The terrible remonstrance was again about to be resorted to, directed against all such grievances. Charles on this occasion exceeded himself. He enjoined the Speaker not to put it to the House. Such an interference, if allowed, would be simply fatal to Parliament. The House adjourned for a week in a very angry mood. On their reassembling the Speaker again refused to put the vote, and having announced that the House stood adjourned by King's command till the 10th of March, was about to leave the chair, when several Members rushed forward, held him forcibly in his place, when a formal protest was put to the House and carried. This protest declared against innovations in the Church, against the levying of tonnage and poundage, and denounced all such as voluntarily paid the impost as "betrayers of the liberties of England, and enemies to the same." The King was informed of what was going on. He dispatched a messenger to the Sergeant-at-Arms to remove the mace, but the messenger was denied admittance, and the Sergeant himself was detained. Another messenger was sent to dissolve the Parliament, but found the doors locked. Furious at this, Charles actually ordered the Captain of the Guards to go and break open the doors, but before he could execute his commission the resolution was passed, and the Commons had dispersed.

Dissolution of course instantly followed. A few

days later the King published a proclamation justifying himself, attributing everything to "some vipers who must look for their reward," and in the most open manner threatening anyone who presumed to prescribe to him any time again for the calling of a Parliament.

The "vipers" soon met with their reward. Several members were apprehended and cast into the Tower. They claimed to be admitted to bail. The judges were again tampered with. The application naturally failed. Heavy fines were inflicted—some of them refused to pay, preferring to remain in prison; and one of them, Sir John Elliot, an upright and honourable man, died there.

Charles thus once more felt himself free and untrammelled, able to pursue his despotism without any fear of remonstrances—an absolute sovereign. His courtiers, deluded with the idea that without a Parliament they would flourish better, flattered him. The victory of the High Church was complete, and the puritanical opposition at least for a time rendered powerless.

His Majesty's threat against public interference on the question of calling a Parliament was effectual. The country, contented in the main to pursue their industries and trade, submitted to many illegalities and wrongs. At the outset, too, the impositions were not very heavy, for the war with France and Spain was suddenly terminated. The expenses of the State was thereby much reduced, and the country for a while enjoyed the benefit of this.

The two great councillors of Charles at this time were Strafford and Laud. The Earl of Strafford, while yet a Commoner, had been in Charles's first and second Parliaments, one of the most determined opponents of the Court party. Some attribute this to a personal hatred of Buckingham, rather than to any convictions of the sacredness of the cause he then advocated. When Buckingham was assassinated, Charles found no difficulty in winning over Sir Thomas Wentworth to his side. Haughty, able, and ambitious, this apostate soon sold his old friends, the popular party, and, like all apostates, he became as assiduous now to extend the Prerogative as during his early Parliamentary career he had been strenuous to curtail it. He became the object of much popular hatred. In his capacity of adviser to the King, in the offices of Lord President of the North, and afterwards Lord-Lieutenant of Ireland, he was guilty of acts which can bear no palliation. Laud, less able than the former, was every bit as earnest to serve the King. Disinterested so far as personal ambition went, his great object was to elevate the Church into the loftiest possible position and to extend the Royal Prerogative, by which alone the object of his life could be secured. A cruel, hard-hearted man, his chief delight was to punish and oppress those who differed from him, or who stood in his way. A pious man withal. He appears to be infatuated with the belief that the best way to promote the end he had in view was by the cruel persecution and oppression of the Puritans. These two laboured hard and incessantly, entirely devoted, as they were, to the work, to promote the same evil end—to make the King absolute, and the Church independent of popular whims. Simple and not frivolous, they were disliked by the courtiers; time-servers and persecutors, they were hated by the people. Both were deadly enemies of liberty, which they tried their utmost to subvert. Both in the end came to the block.

With such men for his advisers, there was not much difficulty experienced in finding means to conduct the government without the aid of a Parliament. Every species of oppression was resorted to; the abuses of former times were converted into royal privileges; the Prerogative was declared absolute, unquestionable. No one dare lift his voice against the injustice perpetrated, dreading the terrible judgments of illegal tribunals, which now usurped the jurisdiction of the ordinary courts of law. Tonnage and poundage with greater rigour than ever was now levied—for refusing to pay merchants were fined and imprisoned. In direct violation of well-known statutes, innumerable monopolies in trade were openly granted, giving exclusive rights to favourites and companies to trade in various commodities, to the injury of commerce and the impoverishment of the country; and this for the sole object of having the fine which each monopolist paid on receiving his charter. On more than one occasion Charles was base enough to grant two monopolies of the same thing to two distinct grantees, so as to receive double fines, without any regard whatever to the inexcusable dishonesty of the transaction. The Forest Laws were revived to the disturbance of the rights of property, which had been uninterruptedly enjoyed for scores, and even hundreds of years. One forest was thus enlarged from six to sixty miles. Alleged encroachers were heavily fined—£12,000, £19,000, and even £20,000 in some instances were thus inflicted. This was done by the odious exercise of authority by the Court of Star Chamber—a tribunal which from the iniquity of its sentences and the illegality of its acts was perhaps the most objectionable feature in a reign which was altogether cruel, vindictive, and unjust. The Courts of Law were not pliant enough to satisfy the ill-will and wants of the King, and his two great advisers. The judges of these Courts, though often weak and submissive, could not always be counted upon; for occasionally, either from a dread of public vengeance, or from a conscientiousness which was not always manifest, the Common Law judges stood up in defence of public rights. The Star Chamber, however, worked better, was far less technical, and not bound by precedents; moreover, Strafford and Laud were all powerful there. It assumed a most extended jurisdiction over persons and property, and, in excess of all previous precedents, heard and decided a vast number of criminal cases. The object, as Hallam says, was twofold—to accustom the people to acts of despotism by a tribunal more immediately connected with the Crown, and to bring money into the exchequer by means of fines and forfeitures. "Those who inflicted the punishment reaped the gain, and sat like famished birds of prey, with keen eyes and bended talons, eager to supply for a moment, by some wretch's ruin, the craving emptiness of the exchequer."[1] Not merely satisfied by ruining persons in their estates, it dealt out the most cruel corporal punishments and torture to those who were brave enough to disobey its mandates, or to deny its jurisdiction. Ears were ordered to be lopped, noses to be slit, cheeks to be branded with hot iron.

[1] Const. Hist., ii., 35.

Men were dragged through the streets tied to carts, and whipped and pilloried. Perpetual and solitary imprisonment, too, was sometimes ordered. It would be beyond the scope of this Work to enter into anything like a detailed account of the many atrocities committed by this Court, and chiefly at the instigation of Laud; but there are some cases which, inasmuch as they in some sense concern Wales and Welshmen, should not be omitted.

Dr. John Williams, Bishop of Lincoln, a native of Denbighshire (and of whom I shall have more to say anon), in James's time, had acquired such a position and influence as enabled him to secure the preferment of Laud. Laud, by tact and intrigues, soon supplanted him at Court. And now that the Bishop of Lincoln somewhat favoured the Puritans, this serpent, whom he had as it were warmed in his own bosom, now turned upon him, and with great vindictiveness harrassed and persecuted the very man to whom he owed everything. For merely receiving some letters from one Osbadilston, a master of Westminster School, in which Laud was called by a nickname, which letters Dr. Williams had never shown—the mere concealment of such letters being declared an offence—Williams was ordered to pay a penalty of £5,000 to the King, and £3,000 to Laud. He was further to be imprisoned during pleasure, and to make a humble submission. Osbadilston had a heavier judgment. In addition to a heavier fine and imprisonment, he was ordered to be placed in the pillory in front of his own school, and to have his ears nailed to it. The latter made his escape, but Williams, like a stout Briton, refusing to tender the required apology, was cast into the Tower, and there remained until he was released at the beginning of the Long Parliament.

William Prynne, a barrister of Lincoln's Inn, a gloomy Puritan, wrote a long-winded book upon the stage—a fearfully dull and heavy, though learned work—in which he classed all actors and actresses as depraved characters. The Queen, a short time after its publication, acted a part in a play at Court, and by an extraordinary stretch of the imagination, Prynne's book was looked upon as an attack upon the Queen. Peter Heylin, a Chaplain of Laud, was the ferret who dragged this allusion to light. Heylin, by no means a truthful character, and an intense hater of all things puritanical, appears in several cases to have been Laud's bloodhound in the persecution of the Puritans. And to me it is a matter of regret to have to acknowledge him as a Welshman. He was a member of the family of that name settled at Llanymynech, in the north of Montgomeryshire, a few miles to the south of Oswestry. A very different man from his uncle, Rowland Heylin, Alderman and Sheriff of London, who, in conjunction with Sir Thomas Myddelton, was the instrument of publishing the first popular edition of the Bible in Welsh, for the benefit of his countrymen. This work, produced at great expense, borne by these two worthy men, was published in 1630, in small quarto.[1] Prynne was ordered to pay £5,000 fine, to stand twice in the pillory, to have both his ears cropped, and to suffer perpetual imprisonment. Prynne employed his time in gaol to write a bitter attack upon Episcopacy. So did two other men named Burton and Bastwick, the

[1] Rowland's Cambrian Bibliography, p. 109.

one a divine, and the other a physician. The three were brought before the Star Chamber. The proceedings against them were of the most outrageous character. They were not even allowed to speak in their own defence. Laud himself spoke for over two hours against them. Prynne, too, was reviled for the croppiness of his ears. £5,000 fine was imposed upon each of them, they were to lose their ears, and to be imprisoned for their lives; and to prevent any further offending, writing materials were forbidden them. On the 30th of June, 1637, the sentence was carried into effect. Crowds of sympathizing people assembled round the pillory, and the sufferers were looked upon as martyrs, which they undoubtedly were. Burton and Bastwick were sent to Launceston and Lancaster Castles respectively, and on the 27th July, the Warden of the Fleet handed William Prynne to three keepers named Ralph Evans, John Witch, and John Maynard, who were under orders to take him to Carnarvon Castle, with instructions to allow no persons to speak to him on the road. Travelling in those days was slow, though the time of the year was favourable. On his way from the Fleet prison to Barnet, the streets and fair country lanes were thronged with people, who wept bitter tears at the sight of the brave Puritan, who, for defending and advocating a cause dear to many of them, had suffered such indignities. Many as he passed fell upon their knees and prayed for him. All wished him God speed. Of course, it was intended by sending him to so distant a place as Carnarvon Castle to put him in such a position as would prevent his annoying those in power any more. Perhaps, too, it was hoped that by sending him thus through the heart of the country as an example of the manifestation of power, to strike awe into the people. If any such hopes prevailed, they were soon dispelled, for their appearance everywhere elicited nothing but the deepest sympathy for the sufferers, and the strongest condemnation of their cruel persecutors. Prynne's progress more especially evoked the most sincere good-will towards him. In every town and village through which he passed he was greeted by the populace — in several places entertained—for the keepers were easily bribed. The journey commenced on Thursday the 27th of July. By Saturday night they had come to Coventry. Three times the next day Prynne went to church. In the evening many came to salute him. At Chester they stayed two nights;—divers men and women resorted there to him. He went into a stationer's shop there and bought a copy of a Welsh Bible and Prayer Book — doubtless a copy of the very edition to which I have just alluded. On Friday night they came to Carnarvon. The gaoler there could not speak English, so they went to the Under-Sheriff, who, however, would not be prepared to receive the prisoner until the Monday following. The news soon reached the Council of the dangerous sympathy everywhere exhibited towards Prynne, and the Attorney-General was instructed to thoroughly investigate the matter. Maynard, one of the keepers, was by him examined. He admitted that much sympathy had been manifested, and that their charge was in some places entertained; but he tried to convince the questioner that the persons were of mean quality, asserting especially that at Chester no aldermen or men of quality had resorted to him. Further, he confessed that they, the keepers, had been given 26s. at Barnet, 12d. a piece at Coventry, and about three ounces of tobacco at Chester, and that "they who gave the same desired the keepers to be as kind to him as they might."[1] But Maynard's story was not true in all respects; at any rate, with regard to the prisoner's reception at Chester, for several persons of quality were implicated in it. Puritanism was evidently strong in the quaint old city at this time. One of the sheriffs of the city, Calvin Bruen—mark the name—was brought before the Council for entertaining Prynne.[2] Mr. Peter Ince, a stationer there, was taken before the High Commission Court at York.[3] These with others were fined heavily, some £500, some £300, others £250. Bruen made a public submission at the Town Hall, and Peter Ince went humbly on his knees before the Bishop in the Cathedral. Two however, Mr. Peter Lee and Mr. Richard Golborne, suffered their bonds to be estreated rather than perform such humiliating conditions. In the following year four portraits of Prynne painted at Chester were burnt at the High Cross in the presence of the Magistracy.[4] In consequence of so much sympathy, even the remote fortress on the Welsh coast was not deemed secure enough for Prynne. He was removed soon after to the Isle of Jersey, where he remained until liberated by the Long Parliament.

Another Court, the proceedings in which were of the most infamous character, was the Court of High Commission, which had cognizance of all spiritual affairs, and was presided over by bishops. There were two branches of this Court—one for the

---

[1] State Pap. Dom., vol. 368, § 14.
[2] Ibid, vol. 367, §§ 18 and 101.
[3] Ibid, vol. 370, § 31.
[4] Ormerod's Cheshire, i, p. 203.

CHAP. II.
1629-40.

Archbishopric of Canterbury, the other for York. Laud was the great strength of this Court. He was its head, as in fact he was at the head of all affairs in England at this time, for Strafford had enough to do in Ireland, where he was Viceroy. This Court punished with extraordinary vindictiveness those who were brought before it, and the slightest thing was enough to bring a person within its dreadful jurisdiction. To utter one word against the Episcopacy, to show the slightest opposition to the ecclesiastical policy of the Archbishop, or to speak disrespectfully of any of the dignitaries of the Church, was an offence in the eyes of the judges of this Court which called for the most tremendous punishment. I have no space, even if I had the desire, to enumerate instances to substantiate this. One case, however, is especially interesting, inasmuch as it affects a Welshman, and because it shows that even in the distant recesses of mountainous Wales a spirit of enquiry was abroad, and a tone of liberalism was beginning to prevail. Richard Parry, of Llanvallteg, in the County of Carmarthen, was charged with having created a disturbance in his parish church, by causing the sexton to arrest a person who was present there during divine service,—with having on another occasion exclaimed, after having received the bread in the sacrament, "some devil is in my knee,"—with having told his rector, Roger Phillips, "I am a better preacher than thou, and I care not a straw for thee." Moreover, he was alleged to have said of the Archdeacon of Carmarthen, or his official, who had sent out process against him, that he hoped he would be hanged, which was a little illiberal. But the gist of his offence was this—that he had the impiety to say that "if he were king, there should be no Bishop in the land, but every Doctor should have £100 a year, and every Master of Arts £20 or £30,"—adding, "What good do bishops do in the land?" Considering what very little good the bishops did in Wales at this time, for they were mere creatures of Laud, and considering also the blind ignorance which prevailed for want of schools, the name of Richard Parry deserves some praise for protesting against the neglect of his country. It is quite certain the endowment of a number of Masters of Arts at even the small salaries suggested, would have been far more conducive to the intellectual and even the moral advancement of the people, than the efforts of the bishops to introduce absurd innovations into the Church, and to suppress by rigour and injustice all those who differed from them, or questioned the legality of their pretensions. For this very grave offence poor Parry was ordered to pay a fine of £2,000 to the King, and to make a submission, both in his parish church of Llanvallteg, and in the cathedral of his diocese, at St. David's.[1]

Puritanism at this time pervaded English society very extensively, more especially among the middle classes; and even in the higher classes there was a strong dislike to the pretensions of the Episcopacy and the High Church party. When Abbot was Archbishop of Canterbury, many persons imbued with puritanical ideas entered the Church, and were presented to livings. Laud hated these, and was bent upon effecting a clear uniformity within the Church, and so far as persecution could do,

[1] Acts of High Commission Court in 1634 and 1635. In State Pap. Dom.

to suppress Puritanism even outside the Church. All those who occupied pulpits, and who resisted the innovations which the Archbishop introduced into the ceremonial of the Church, were relentlessly turned adrift, and persecuted. Thus deprived of their livings, they travelled from place to place, preaching and expounding the scriptures to their followers secretly, in uninhabited houses, barns, caves, and elsewhere. But persecution with its lynx-eyes followed them wherever they went. Many were taken by the rich whose sympathies were that way inclined, into their houses as chaplains and tutors in their families. Laud, however, would not permit this. They were proscribed everywhere, and many sought shelter from oppression on foreign soil. Among these was Roger Williams, the great apostle of toleration—one of the most gifted men ever born in Wales. He afterwards settled at Rhode Island, and was in fact the founder of that colony. The pilgrim fathers had already made a settlement in the far West, and had formed the nucleus of that Great Power beyond the Atlantic, where religious freedom and civil liberty have since prevailed. They were now forbidden to leave the country. One precious boat-load, with Cromwell and Hampden, was thus detained. Probably this came afterwards to be regretted by Charles and Laud. Not allowed to exercise religious worship at home, prevented from seeking refuge abroad, the persecution of the Puritans could not very well go farther.

One of the distinctive characteristics of the Puritans was a strict observance of the Sunday, by them called the Sabbath, or the Lord's Day. This they placed on the same footing as the Jewish

Sabbath—a day of cessation from all worldly work, and from everything save the exercise of religion. To ascertain who were puritanical, James I., at the instigation of some bishops, issued a proclamation, to be read in all the churches, permitting all manner of sports to be played after divine service on Sunday. This was however abandoned, through the strenuous opposition of Archbishop Abbott. Laud, different in every respect from his predecessor, in his many endeavours to harass the Puritans, bethought himself of this unused proclamation. And the Book of Sports was soon after published. To the Puritan, who looked upon things in general from a gloomy and strict point of view, sports and all amusements even on week days were abominable enough, but sports on the Sabbath, and in obedience to an order from the pulpit, was the grossest impiety. They resisted it to the death. Many of the clergy refused to read the order. These were at once summoned before the Court of High Commission. Even in the Principality a few openly protested against this, and refused to promulgate the proclamation from the pulpit. William Wroth, rector of Llanvaches, William Erbury, vicar of Cardiff, and Walter Cradock, his curate, were prominent in their resistance, and felt the power of the High Commission Court. They were fined and expelled their livings. They afterwards became the founders of Dissent in Wales.

But if we are to believe, and I see no reason to doubt, the account which the worthy Vicar of Llandovery—Vicar Pritchard—and other contemporary authorities give, it would appear that in Wales there was scarcely any necessity for the promulgation of any such order, for without it the people enjoyed to the fulness of their hearts all kinds of games and sports. The Sunday, indeed, was the day of all others for games; and the parish churchyard shared with the old tennis court or castle green the doubtful advantage of being the scene for athletic sports on the Sunday afternoon.

> "Dydd i feddwi, dydd i fowlian,
> Dydd i ddawnsio, dydd i loetran;
> Dydd i hwrian a gwylhersu,
> Yw'r dydd Sabboth gan y Cymry." [1]

The parsons as a rule cared but little for the spiritual welfare of their parishioners, but they never missed the games of a Sunday afternoon. To the few precise clergy this conduct was exceedingly objectionable. They did their utmost to put it down, but the Book of Sports had in it what was more captivating for the young than the austerities of the Puritan, so that their influence was not very great. The excellent Vicar, however, hit upon far happier tactics of opposition, and instead of waging a sullen and mortal war with the proclivities of youth, he rather humoured them. Knowing the Welshman's natural love for music, the Vicar set to writing hymns, which he set to music. The hymns were sung in his church every Sunday afternoon, and were soon the means of clearing his churchyard of the gamesters and reprobates. The strict Puritans, however, could allow of no middle course like this. They were morose fanatics, whom success rendered less tolerant, and whom persecution made more desperate, but nevertheless deeply pious

---

[1] Pritchard's Canwyll y Cymry.

and honest. But the game-playing parson was a far greater favourite than his sour-faced rival in the hills of Wales at this time, and so continued to be for many years, to the near destruction of the Church in the Principality. The effect, however, of this most foolish move of the High Church party was quite the reverse of what Laud anticipated. Persecution only stirs people to a deeper resistance, and surrounds the persecuted with a host of sympathisers and recruits. Coupling the relentless harassing of the Puritans with the favour openly shown to the Roman Catholics, and the tendency of the High Church party towards Rome, the people saw in Laud's acts nothing less than what to the great majority of them appeared the source of the greatest danger. The nation at heart was Protestant. Nothing could change this. No rigours, no fines.

In the middle of these persecutions—notwithstanding that the fines inflicted by the Star Chamber and the Court of High Commission amounted to nearly six millions sterling, which ought to have poured into the exchequer,—money was urgently wanted. The exchequer was quite low. Clarendon states that the way in which the fines were levied and applied, instead of being of any benefit to the King was the reverse, for their infliction made him enemies, and the money never came into his hands. With such bad management, no wonder the exchequer was low. Every method had been tried—every expedient had been made. There was nothing to do but to try once more the questionable plan of levying ship-money. As mentioned in a former page, there were some precedents for levying such a tax

CHAP. II.
1629-40.

upon the seaport towns; but in no previous reign had inland counties been assessed for the purpose of erecting a fleet. Moreover, the levying of ship-money even upon the maritime towns had only taken place when the country was in actual danger, when it was threatened with foreign invasion. The credit of inventing this new mode of obtaining money is attributed to Noy, the Attorney-General, "a man of venal diligence and prostituted learning."[1] But at this particular period there was no justification whatever for this demand upon the country. We were at profound peace with all the world. There was not the slightest shadow of danger threatening the country. The sole object was to obtain money; it never was intended to construct a navy. In former times the ships were supplied direct by the towns upon which the tax was imposed. Now the money was to be paid in to a duly-appointed treasurer. In fact, money and not ships was what was wanted. In the month of August, 1635, Noy's scheme was put in full force. Writs from the Council were issued to the Sheriffs of the several counties, ordering them to levy in their respective counties the sums set out by the Council. The total sum to be collected in this way amounted to a little over £200,000. Some counties were to contribute no less a sum than £10,000. Yorkshire, for instance. Wales was to pay £9,000, of which £5,000 was charged to South Wales, and the rest to North Wales. Of the £5,000 to be levied in the southern division, Brecknockshire had to contribute £933, Cardiganshire £654, Carmarthenshire £760, Glamorganshire £1,449,

[1] Hallam's Const. Hist., ii., 12.

Pembrokeshire £713 10s, and Radnorshire £490 10s; while the £4,000 to be raised in North Wales was apportioned thus: Anglesey £448, Carnarvonshire £447, Denbighshire £1,117, Flintshire £738 14s., Merionethshire £416, and Montgomeryshire £833 6s. The burden to be borne by the chief towns in the several counties was specified in the instructions; the remainder was to be assessed upon the county generally. To this illegal impost, strange to say, there seems to have been little or no objection raised in the Principality. Whether it was that the people, now long accustomed to arbitrary government, and despairing of ever again being governed in a constitutional manner, blindly acquiesced in it: or whether, most of the Welsh counties having a seaboard, they thought it was an equitable taxation: or whether they actually believed that the money so charged upon them would be employed in the construction of a navy to protect the coast from the raids of the Turkish and Moorish pirates, who at this period infested these seas and paralysed commercial enterprise, it is now impossible to discover. Of course, the generality of the people were far too ignorant to comprehend the illegal character of the impost, and merely followed the example set them by the higher and educated classes in paying it. That these did as a rule pay the tax is clear, and that too without anything like a serious objection to it on principle. There were, however, many objections made to the magnitude of the assessment. For instance, Cardiganshire was, as before stated, called upon to pay £654. This was characterized as unfair in a letter addressed by Sir John Lewis and others to Hector

Phillips, the high-sheriff. In all similar assessments, they said, they had hitherto been charged only the half of what the Counties of Carmarthen and Pembroke were charged with. The High-Sheriff was therefore asked to respite the levy, and to tender the exceptions to the Council, which he did;[1] but without effect. The County of Flint made a similar complaint. Ever since the time of Queen Elizabeth they had never been asked to pay more than half what Montgomeryshire and Denbighshire had to pay. The Council is petitioned to abate the charge, on the ground that their county was a poor one in comparison with others in North Wales.[2] In November, the bailiffs of Shrewsbury complain of an excessive charge—notwithstanding their town had lately been greatly impoverished by the plague, which made the burden all the more unbearable.[3] From Haverfordwest, also, a petition was sent. That ancient town was called upon to pay £65 10s. The Council were sorry for them, and "would have liked it very well," if the Mayor and Sheriff had met in time and had agreed to have the town rated in a lesser sum; but now it was too late to disturb the assessment, as such a course "would bring great prejudice to the service." They were, therefore, requested to pay up "with all convenient speed," but they were consoled by the promise that it should not be a precedent on any future occasion.[4] The diligence of the Sheriff of Glamorganshire, and the readiness of the people of that county to pay, was such as to be a subject of discussion in the Council on the 23rd of December.

---

[1] State Pap. Dom., vol. 298, § 32. Letter dated Cardigan, Sept. 21.
[2] *Ibid*, vol. 300, § 9. Letter from Justices of Flint, Oct. 20, from Flint.
[3] *Ibid*, vol. 302, § 130.
[4] *Ibid*, vol. 304, § 80. Letter from Council of 20th December.

The King commanded the Council to inform the Sheriff that his Majesty had taken "especial notice of his forwardness" in collecting the £1,449 charged upon the county.[1] This letter must have added considerably to the Sheriff's enjoyment of his Christmas holidays. In like manner the expeditiousness of the Sheriff of Cheshire was highly commended. This man was anxious even to exceed the arbitrary instructions of the Council, and wished he had the power to put the constables and others upon their oath, the better to "discover men's estates."[2] The Sheriff of Denbighshire was not so energetic — Hugh Lloyd of Foxhall;—indeed, he did not pay in the amount until the 7th of the November following. But it was not entirely his fault. Full six weeks before, he handed over the money to drovers to be conveyed to London. But the sickness which prevailed in the Metropolis had deterred them, and they had returned without paying. Few or none travelled to London in those days, he says, save the drovers, wherefore he begged to be tolerated until All Saints. To propitiate the authorities, he begs Nicholas, the Secretary of State, whom he addresses, to accept of one piece as a token of his love.[3] In Merionethshire, the bailiffs had to be employed. Matters do not appear to have gone on so peaceably there as elsewhere, and we find men in high position at variance. One poor man, named Humphrey Tudor, was assessed in eightpence, which he would not or could not pay—more probably the former. Two of the collectors appointed by the High-Sheriff—Evan Evans of Tanybwlch—distrained

[1] State Pap. Dom., vol. 305, § 15.
[2] *Ibid*, vol. 305, § 19.
[3] *Ibid*, vol. 331, § 20. and vol. 335, § 72.

upon him. Griffith Lloyd, a justice of the peace, he doubtless of Maesyneuadd, on the matter being brought to his knowledge, granted his warrant for the apprehension of the two collectors, whereupon Evans, the high-sheriff, accused Lloyd before the Council of the Marches of hindering the service, by encouraging the non-payment of the tax. Lloyd calls this a false accusation, and satisfactorily explains his conduct to the Council, who thereupon find that he had been presented maliciously.[1] In Pembrokeshire the money was collected without any difficulty; but a sum of £43 had not been paid in the October following. Application was made to the county for it. John Wogan of Wiston, the then sheriff, sends answer. The whole contribution had been paid to the Sheriff, his predecessor, and the sum in dispute would have been long ago duly paid to the Council had it not been that the High-Sheriff, about the 1st of the preceding February, on his journey to London, was drowned, with divers others, at Ensham Ferry, and the unpaid balance of the ship-money had gone to the bottom. The Town of Pembroke, which, in the apportionment made by the Council, was called upon to pay £10, complained bitterly of the High-Sheriff, who, in his eagerness to lighten the burden upon the county, had added nearly four pounds to their assessment, from which trifling circumstance it might be inferred that the objection was deeper than appears on the surface.

The letters sent from Wales relating to the payment of the ship-money, such as have been just referred to, disclose many interesting facts, which throw some light on the condition of the country at that period.

[1] State Pap. Dom., vol. 350, § 12.

The difficulties of communication with London appear to have been very great. Nearly all the sheriffs beg to be excused from having to attend personally to pay the money. From some places leave is asked to send the whole assessment in one sum. Many dangers beset travellers; the roads were bad, and infested with robbers. The drovers who went up in gangs to London in the summer months afforded the safest means of transmitting large sums of money. From Shrewsbury, however, it would appear that a carrier went up thence to London once a fortnight. There seems to have been very little gold in the country. The whole of the Denbighshire ship-money levied in 1636, amounting to nearly twelve hundred pounds, was collected entirely in silver, and could not possibly be exchanged for gold in that county. Carmarthenshire, a purely agricultural county—for then Llanelly was a village, and the industries of Carmarthen were unknown—depended entirely on the sale of sheep and cattle, and these sales only took place in the summer time. The collection of money at any other season was, therefore, extremely difficult. Pembrokeshire and Glamorganshire were chiefly corn-growing counties. The western counties found a sale for their commodities—corn and butter—at Bristol, then as now the great emporium of the west. St. James's fair was the chief season for transacting business of this kind.

Upon the whole, this first general assessment of ship-money in Wales occasioned no real opposition; and with a few isolated instances, matters were carried on smoothly enough throughout England also.

CHAP. II.
1629-40.

Encouraged by the general submissiveness of the people, and by the important addition it made to a needy exchequer, and as if either convinced that the spirit of the nation had been entirely crushed out, or regardless of all opposition, fresh writs for ship-money were again issued in October, 1636, without any legal pretence whatsoever.

The second call upon the Welsh counties was for the same amount as the previous demand. From all accounts, the same submission was manifested. The illegality of the impost even now does not appear to have aroused any serious opposition to the task of collecting the money. Hampden was still in prison;—his trial had not yet commenced. In England, however, his example was followed by many others; but the same spirit had not penetrated into the Principality. Not, I believe, because the Welsh cared less for their rights than their neighbours, but because they were at a greater distance from the source of public opinion, knew little of what was going on in the world outside their own hills, and also because they dared not question the right of the King, seeing that the judges everywhere at the assizes had declared the perfect legality of the imposition.

At length the trial of Hampden was commenced. It had been delayed as long as possible. Indeed, not until Charles had by base means and out of the basest motives obtained the favourable opinion of all the judges upon the case, had he dared to confront this worthy man in a court of justice. The trial lasted thirteen days. It was conducted with eminent ability on both sides. The judges took time to consider their judgment. The public attention had now been directly called to the nature of the issue, and the judgment of the Court was looked forward to with marked anxiety. The result is well known. Hampden was condemned to pay, ship-money was declared legal, and the King victorious. The judges, however, were not unanimous. Eight supported the Royal Prerogative, and on reasoning which was subversive of all constitutional government. The other four, notwithstanding their signatures to the opinion which the King extracted from them, as if pricked by their conscience and actuated by a sense of the responsibility of their oaths, gave judgment for Hampden. Charles, though victor, gained nothing by this judgment. With four judges to back them, the opposers of ship-money everywhere took heart, and the further payment of the tax was everywhere resisted.

Even in Wales it was not easy now to collect the money. In Cardiganshire the people would not pay at all. Their goods were distrained, but nobody would buy, and they remained in the hands of the High Sheriff. Sir Richard Pryse, the sheriff, was in sore trouble. He knew not what to do. Money he could not obtain. In his distress he writes to the Council, "What was he to do?" From Cheshire and Flintshire, from Shrewsbury and Haverfordwest, complaints were sent up instead of cash. In Hereford the plague came to hand as an excuse. No collectors would venture near the infected places. Even Radnorshire—that county which boasted of its readiness to pay illegal exactions—was backward. The Sheriff found no money, he said, but a great deal of illness. The substance of the county had been exhausted in supporting its poor. And so with

CHAP. II.
1629-40.

various excuses there was everywhere a manifest determination on the part of the public to evade paying any more ship-money. One curious little memorandum of Mr. Secretary Nicholas, dated February 16th, 1639, some months after Hampden's trial and the issue of fresh writs, again shows the County of Glamorgan in a peculiar light. "This week," he says, "the Mayor of Doncaster has paid £40 and Glamorganshire £420, upon writs issued in 1638, which is the first money I have heard of having been collected by virtue of these writs."

But Charles was not destined to have everything in his own way, and about this time he met with a rebuff from a very unexpected quarter. At the instigation of Laud, the King became anxious to establish Episcopacy in Scotland. The form of religion which prevailed in Scotland was that known by the name Presbyterianism. Some attempts were made by James to introduce Episcopacy into Scotland, but the attempt did not prove very successful. The whole country was too Calvinistic, and held the memory of John Knox too dear to give in. Charles, like his father, had been constantly aiming to overthrow Scotch Presbyterianism, and matters in this respect looked more hopeful about this time than it had done in the preceding reign. Bishops had been introduced there, and their power and influence had increased; they held high offices, and formed an important element in the Council. At length, Laud and his master resolved to introduce the English Liturgy into that incongenial soil, and with force, too, if need be. On Sunday, the 23rd of July, 1637, at St. Giles Kirk, Edinburgh, the attempt was made to introduce the Liturgy. It was too much. To hear prayers said, and canticles sung—savouring strong of Rome—in the very church, and from the very pulpit, wherein John Knox, "the first apostle of the Scottish Reformation," had thundered against sin and Satan, and had often transfixed his audience with his wild fiery eloquence! The Bishop of Edinburgh officiated, robed in all his canonicals. A wild scene ensued. An old woman, Jenny Geddes by name, hurled her three-legged-stool at his head. "'Let us read the collect of the day,' said the pretended Bishop from amid his tippets. 'De'il colic the wame of thee!' answered Jenny, hurling her stool at his head, 'thou foul thief, wilt thou say mass at my lug?' 'A Pape, a Pape!' cried others, 'stane him.' In fact, the service could not go on at all. . . . Now, on small signal, the hour was come. All Edinburgh, all Scotland; behind that, all England and Ireland, rose into unappeasable commotion on the flight of this stool of Jenny's; and his Grace of Canterbury, and King Charles himself, and many others, had lost their heads before there could be peace again."[1] In an incredible short space of time the whole of Scotland was in commotion. From north and south, from east and west, from field and workshop, the people flocked in innumerable masses to Edinburgh. They menaced the authorities, insulted the bishops, and though dispersed for a while, returned in greater numbers, with a firmer determination to resist the King's policy. It was not now the common people only: men of position and of rank joined the populace, and became their leaders; and that there may be no mistake as to their purpose, they bound

[1] Carlyle's Letters of Cromwell.

CHAP. II.
1629–40.

themselves by a solemn league to defend their country and their religion to the death. This Covenant was received throughout the country with the wildest enthusiasm. It was carried from village to village by swift messengers, and in less than six weeks the entire people were firmly united in one cause.

Charles amazed at this spirit of opposition, at once made up his mind to use force; and though he sent the Marquis of Hamilton to treat with the insurgents, it was not with any hope of effecting a conciliation, but merely to cause a little delay, so that he might prepare for a determined attack. Meanwhile, therefore, active preparations for war were being carried on. A general levy was made. Wales had to contribute 1,160 men.[1] These were to join the King at York. Herefordshire was to send 150, Shropshire 300, and Monmouth 150. In Cheshire no levy was made; but some of the Cheshire men volunteered.[2]

At length, the King, with an army under the command of the Earl of Essex, set out for Scotland. The Scots, who knew of the preparations, were on the alert. With an army of 30,000 they were already advanced to the borders. The two armies confronted one another, and the soldiers fraternized. No blood was spilt: a treaty was entered into at Berwick on the 18th June, 1639.

Both parties, however, were conscious that no lasting peace had been secured, and each distrustful

[1] These were made up thus: Anglesey 100, Brecon 100, Cardigan 50, Carmarthen 100, Carnarvon 50, Denbigh 250, Flint 60, Glamorgan 100, Merioneth 50, Montgomery 100, Pembroke 150, and Radnor 50.—State Pap. Dom.

[2] Letter of Thos. Wilbraham (Harl. MSS. 2135, fol. 22), vol. ii, p. 33.

of the other, evaded the strict terms of the treaty. Strafford was in Ireland. He was sent for. He, with Laud, soon inculcated their principle of "thorough" upon Charles, and war to the knife was now declared to be the sole remedy to remove this canker-worm of disaffection. The Scots meanwhile were busily preparing, and were in communication with the disaffected and persecuted in England, whose sympathies were naturally with the Scotch, whose cause was really their own.

But Charles had no money to carry on the war. Afraid of awakening the opposition of his subjects by any fresh impost, for the recently-delivered judgment in the ship-money case had exasperated them to the quick, he resolved to issue writs for a Parliament at Westminster, calculating upon their assistance, and half assured of arousing their zeal by a discovery which he had just made, that the Scots had been negotiating for the help of the King of France.

The country was surprised at being once more called upon to elect representatives to Parliament. It had nearly given up all hopes of ever again being governed constitutionally. The opportunity was not lost. Many members were returned whose principles were directly opposed to the arbitrary conduct of the King.

The 13th day of April, 1640, after a lapse of over eleven years, saw the empty seats at Westminster once again occupied by the constitutional representatives of the people. Of course, Charles's sole object was to obtain money to go to war with the Scotch. Their letter to the French King, which had come into his hands through

CHAP. II.
1640.

treachery, was placed before them, but scarcely any notice was taken of it, and the Commons proceeded to consider the many grievances of the country, as if the atmosphere was not laden with schemes of war and blood. Charles was urgent, and the House of Lords, with unpardonable obsequiousness, suggested to the Lower House that supply ought to precede grievances—a suggestion which evoked from the sturdy Commons a resolution that it was a breach of privilege. The King next tried by promises to conciliate them. He was willing to forego the levying of ship-money in future without the consent of Parliament, if they would only grant him twelve subsidies payable in three years. But the House was in no mood to accept the mere word of Charles: they were resolved to have the question settled once for all—aye or no —was ship-money legal? They were not, however, unwilling to make a suitable grant to the King. Indeed, they were actually discussing it, when a courtier stated that unless the whole sum demanded was granted it would be useless labour to prolong the discussion, for the King had said he would accept no less. This view was confirmed by the Attorney-General. The House was not going tamely to submit to this interference with their dearest privilege,—an adjournment till next day was at once decided upon; but when the next day came the benches were once more empty. The King had angrily dissolved the Parliament.

Charles regretted his precipitancy before the evening was over. He wanted to throw the blame on others, and denied that he had ever made the statement which Vane had reported. It was nevertheless true. He also enquired whether the dissolution could not be recalled. But this could not be.

Once more did Charles pursue his own course, regardless of consequences. Loans were again requested. Strafford set a good example—lending himself £20,000. Others followed, and £300,000 is said to have been thus got in. Those who refused were forced. Even ship-money was collected. Members for speaking freely in Parliament were imprisoned and their houses searched. The Chairman of the Committee of the House, whose duty it was to open petitions, was sent to the Tower for refusing to show such petitions.

The war at Scotland was at once to be renewed. Charles accompanied by Strafford advanced to York. The Scotch had already crossed the frontier, and were in England even before Charles got to York. This war having been chiefly brought about by Laud's attempt to force Episcopacy upon the unwilling Scotch, the sympathies of the English Puritans were entirely against the war, and Laud became more obnoxious than ever. His palace at Lambeth was attacked by the populace; and himself had to seek shelter at Whitehall from the infuriate mob. Everywhere in the streets of London were heard the cries "No bishops," "No High Commission," and the same feeling spread throughout the country. The unpopularity of the war was so great that there was no secret made of the sympathy with the Scotch; indeed, there is ample reason to believe that they were very much encouraged in their resistance by correspondence with the leaders of the Puritans in England. Strafford, however, bent on his resolve, advanced towards the enemy, but disaffection soon began to manifest itself in his ranks. The sight of the opposite camp, where praying and psalm singing was going on, struck the simple-minded soldiers with awe, which made them dread a conflict in which they thought they would be fighting against their very God. No fighting could take place under such circumstances. Strafford's last hope here perished, his last card had been thrown. Ignominiously he had to beat a retreat to York. Charles himself grew moody. All around him he saw clear, unmistakeable signs of his own unpopularity. The soldiers mutinied. The popular excitement was at white heat. Peace was demanded—and a Parliament. The King summoned together a great council of the Peers—an institution which had been in abeyance for many generations —whom he might consult as to what was to be done. Just before they met—September 24—two important petitions reached him, one from the City of London, the other signed by twelve of the most popular of the nobility. These decided him to call a Parliament. When the Peers assembled they were informed of this decision. Writs were at once issued. The elections were carried on amidst the wildest excitement. In many places Court nominees were started: Court influence was used to the utmost, but it availed little. The popular candidates were men who needed no Court support. They were everywhere victorious, and the generality of those elected were men honestly resolved to maintain their liberties, and to prune and trim the ungainly growth of the Royal Prerogative.

On the 3rd of November, 1640, the Parliament met. It was destined to be the most memorable that ever assembled at Westminster. It was obliged to do many equivocal acts, and doubtless committed some grave errors. But it cannot be denied that it had the interests of the nation dearly at heart, and impartial judges will have no difficulty in conceding that posterity is more indebted to the Long Parliament for the civil and religious liberty which is now enjoyed in this country, than to any other preceding or subsequent Parliament, for it firmly established the charters of liberty which had been created theretofore, and was the dawn of a nobler policy of government, which has enabled this country to stand foremost in the world.

CHAP. II.
1640.

For twelve years had Charles ruled the country with an iron hand, and in the most arbitrary manner. The Church had done its utmost to uphold the King in his pretensions, and venal and criminal advisers had exercised their greatest ingenuity in suggesting means to subvert the constitution. For all this there was a day of retribution, and it was at hand. The men returned to Parliament had been sent thither by excited constituencies to act a part and to fight for a principle. That principle was to secure the government of this country upon a just and constitutional basis, to restore the sacred rights of the people, and to ensure their permanence. Not forgetting the sudden and unjustifiable dissolution of the last Parliament, the same moderation in debates could scarcely be anticipated by any one who observed the excitement at the elections. It was evident that the Commons thus assembled were fired with a firm resolution to cope with Charles. Not a man was there who was not anxious to put a period to the condition of things which had prevailed for so long a time. Charles's arbitrary conduct found no advocate in Parliament—no apologist even. The greatest unanimity prevailed with regard to measures which were deemed necessary to limit the Prerogative and to ensure sufficient guarantees for the future; and no division of consequence occurred to disturb this harmony until the question of sacrificing Strafford came to be discussed. Against his impeachment in the ordinary way, and against the impeachment of Laud, which was about the earliest proceeding of Parliament, not a voice was raised; and amid the exultations of the people these two were cast into the Tower to abide the time when they should be called upon to answer for their deeds.

With a greater sense of security, the redress of grievances was now proceeded with. Ship-money was declared illegal. The irrepressible tonnage and poundage was placed beyond a doubt. The Star Chamber, which had been the accursed instrument of tyranny, was abolished; and justice was done to its victims, so far as could be, by their release. The High Commission Court, and the Council of the North, were for ever swept away; and the same fate befel the Court of the Council of the Marches in Wales, a tribunal which, though established with a laudable object, yet, through the general corruption of the period, had become an iniquitous instrument of oppression and injustice to such as were unfortunate enough to be brought within its clutches.

Meanwhile the impeachment of Strafford was being slowly proceeded with, and in face of the difficulty of bringing home to him the commission of acts clearly illegal, there was a likelihood of his escaping altogether. The popular leaders in the Commons, who were bent on his destruction, prepared a Bill of Attainder against him, convinced that morally he deserved the severest punishment. But on this question, which perhaps can be justified only by absolute necessity, there was a difference of opinion, and the harmony and unanimity which had hitherto prevailed in the Commons was at an end. Strafford had many friends in the House, who, though they would not shield him from an impeachment on legal proof, objected to a measure in its nature oppressive, and which was also persisted in contemporaneously with the trial before the Lords. A warm discussion was followed by a division, and the Bill of Attainder was carried by an overwhelming majority. Strafford was doomed. Some sixty members voted against the Bill. In the course of the night bills were posted up on the walls throughout the City and in Westminster, with the names of the opposition, who were denounced as "Straffordians" and "betrayers of their country," and held up to public odium. Several Welsh members appear in this category. The two Griffithses, father and son, Members for Beaumaris and the County of Carnarvon respectively; Mr. Herbert, the member for Cardiff; Mr. Price,—without doubt Herbert Price, the representative of Brecon; Mr. Orlando Bridgman, of Chester; and Mr. Newport, of Shrewsbury. And Mr. Vaughan—John Vaughan, of Trawscoed, afterwards Chief Justice Vaughan after the Restoration,—was absent, "but whose good-will for the Lord Strafford was known."[1]

One more important measure was passed, which prescribed the calling of a Parliament within three years at the most of a dissolution. And this was not to be left to the King. If writs were not issued under the Great Seal within the period of three years, other methods, authorised by the Act, were to be resorted to, the ultimate right being vested in the people themselves, who might assemble of their own motion to elect representatives.

To all these measures of reform Charles was very loth to give his assent. It was his invariable practice to resist reforms, unless demanded in a menacing tone, or as an equivalent for money. However, it must be admitted that he made many valuable concessions, some of them trenching, too, on his undoubted prerogative, but which were really called for. For the Commons could place no faith in him. Hence they granted only temporary subsidies, convinced that if they did otherwise the King would soon dispense with their services and return to his old ways. Even the Act prescribing triennial Parliaments was not considered a sufficient guarantee. For we find on the very day that Charles placed his signature to the warrant to execute Strafford—an act which he had sworn he never would do—he assented to a measure which deprived him of the power to dissolve that Parliament at all without their own consent: a most extraordinary

---

[1] Two lists are preserved, one in Rushworth, vol. i., part iii., 248; the other in the Harl. MSS., 4931, fol. 86. These differ a little, but the names above given appear in both, with the exception of the reference to Mr. Vaughan, which appears in Rushworth only.

measure, unconstitutional to say the least of it, and excusable only on the ground of Charles's continual ill-faith

In August, 1641, the King visited Scotland, where he openly relinquished all intentions of establishing Episcopacy there. While there he collected certain evidence implicating, it is said, some of the popular leaders in the Commons in the late insurrection in Scotland; and at once, without consulting any of his more worthy councillors, he resolved to act upon this when opportunity should offer.

The Parliament also adjourned for a short period. On re-assembling, certain vague rumours as to an attempt by the King to seize Argyle and Hamilton, who were active in the Scotch rising, prepared the Puritan leaders for a similar attempt upon them. Under this fear a guard was demanded, and the City Militia came to protect the Houses. On the King's return—which was in great state—he withdrew this guard, and removed the Earl of Essex from military command.

Religious questions were now agitating the public, and formed subjects of much discussion in Parliament. The freedom of the press since the assembling of the Long Parliament gave birth to a host of pamphlets, many of them turning upon the persecution of the Puritans. The bishops were especially odious. Petitions for the removal of the bishops from the House of Lords were followed by petitions for the total abolition of Episcopacy. But opinion in Parliament was very much divided on these questions, and heated debates took place.

CHAP. II.
1641.

At this very juncture, when the populace were much excited with these questions, came like a thunder-clap the alarming news that the Catholics in Ireland had risen, and had in one day massacred in the most inhuman manner, and with a deliberate design, the entire body of the Protestants in Ulster and elsewhere in that distracted country. Details of the atrocities were published, and produced the deepest revulsion of feeling, inciting to a most bitter and mortal hatred of Popery. Charles, though himself a Protestant, had too long concurred in Laud's attempts to introduce into the English Church a sort of bastard imitation of Rome to be above suspicion. His wife was a professed Catholic, surrounded by priests of that faith. His animosity to the Puritans had too long and too severely been felt to be forgotten. His moderation towards the Catholics was marked, and even favours had been conferred by him upon them; and the lukewarmness with which he listened to the cry for retaliation upon the Irish Catholics, which now issued from the very heart of the nation;—all these facts tended to impress upon the unthinking multitude, mad with excitement and alarmed by fears, that Charles himself was at the bottom of all. And this received confirmation when it was boasted by the Irish that they had the King's warrant, though this was a forgery. Before we find fault with these people we should endeavour to consider all the surroundings of the case. If we do so their acts are intelligible, their fears well grounded, their anger justified.

Around Westminster tumultuous assemblies gathered daily—crying for revenge. The sight of a bishop was the occasion for a riot. John Williams, of Lincoln, though but recently released from the prison into which the Star Chamber had cast him, was roughly handled by the mob—had his gown torn off his back as he essayed to pass to the Lords. The cry against the bishops grew in intensity. Alarmed, several of them withdrew themselves from Parliament, and issued a foolish protest, declaring—what was really most absurd—that their forced absence would nullify all the proceedings of the Parliament. This suicidal step soon recoiled upon its authors, and the twelve bishops who signed the protest had ample time to repent in prison. Of these, three were Welshmen. The first signature was that of Williams; Dr. John Owen, Bishop of St. Asaph, and Dr. Morgan Owen, Bishop of Llandaff, were the two others. When called before the Lords to hear the impeachment, Dr. Williams simply begged for time to answer; and once more he saw the gates of a prison closing upon his eventful life. St. Asaph said he signed it "for matter of form, because the rest of his brethren had done so—that thoughts of treason were far from his heart"—moreover, he "desired their lordships' favour and compassion." The Bishop of Llandaff stated it had been done "through ignorance and indiscretion—that he had no design to overthrow the fundamental laws of the land."[1]

The turmoil, both within and without Westminster Hall, was now daily increasing. Outside two large parties attended regularly—the cavaliers, with a swaggering military air, from Whitehall; the apprentice boys and others from the City. Conflicts were of frequent occurrence, and some bloodshed

[1] Parliamentary Hist., ii., 996.

CHAP. II.
1641.

even. Within very little business was done, for the excitement was too intense. The bishops were excluded. War with Ireland was resolved upon, but not with that activity which might have been expected, for the principal subject which concerned Parliament was to make preparations for their own safety—conscious that this turbulence could not go on long and this division continue without violence.

At this time Charles foolishly, unless with a sinister object, removed from the Lieutenantship of the Tower of London Sir William Balfour, a man devoted to the Commons, and appointed in his stead Sir Thomas Lunsford, a man of no principle and an outlaw, one of the most noisy and threatening of the cavaliers who frequented Whitehall. The object of having such an unworthy instrument at the Tower was instantly understood by the Commons. This created much noise: even an attack upon the Tower by the apprentice boys was threatened. Charles had to cancel the appointment. Sir John Byron was thereupon appointed. Even his appointment was not pleasing to the Commons. This Sir John Byron will hereafter figure in these pages chiefly in connection with North Wales. Lunsford, too, will turn up sometime hence in Monmouthshire.

The year (1641) was drawing to a close amid vague rumours of approaching danger. In the Parliament and in the City people whispered in bated breath. The cavaliers were swarming in Whitehall. The Commons once more demanded a guard. It was on the last day of the year. Three days after the King sent his reply. It was a denial. Whereupon the Commons ordered the Lord Mayor to keep the militia on foot and to guard the City.

The year ended gloomily. The clouds were fast gathering and darkening, and the storm ripening. It broke forth on the very day that the King's answer was sent. On that memorable day Charles, without the knowledge of any of his more worthy ministers, though he had a few days before promised them to take no step of importance without first consulting them, sent his Attorney-General, Sir Edward Herbert, to the House of Commons to impeach five of its members for high treason. These were Pym, Holles, Hampden, Haslerig, and Strode. The Sergeant-at-Arms was sent to the Commons to arrest them. He was ordered to retire; and they promised to send an answer on the morrow. That day, however, the King in person, accompanied to the very door by several hundreds of armed men, went to the House to seize their persons. But he was baulked; the accused were not there, for the Commons, informed but a few minutes before his actual entry that he was on his way thither, had prevailed upon them to withdraw. The King was very angry, and the Commons were excited. They voted that after so enormous a breach of privilege, until a trusty guard was appointed to protect them from such perils, and until reparation was made, they could not sit in safety, and adjourned for six days. A committee of the whole House was, however, appointed to consider what had best be done. This committee sat in the Guildhall—the City being unanimously with them, and its entire armed force placed at their disposal. The accused had sought refuge there when they escaped from the House.

To the City Charles proceeded the next day to demand their surrender. On his way thither and back to Whitehall, threatening cries alone assailed his ears. The mob which had shouted "all hail" to him some months back on his passage through the City now cursed and menaced him. But his journey was in vain. The City was by no means inclined to surrender the accused, who openly attended the meetings of the Committee. Charles was now helpless. And the energy of the Commons, the resolution of the City, and the attitude of the populace, silenced the cavaliers, who scarcely durst show themselves.

On the 10th of January the House was to resume its sittings, and it had been arranged that the five members should be brought back in triumph to Westminster. Being informed of this, and afraid of violence, the King quitted London. He was fated never to return save to have his career terminated by the axe of the executioner.

After this fatal attempt to aim a deadly blow at the most sacred right and privilege of Parliament, any confidence in the King was now quite out of the question; and self-protection became the primary consideration. This could never be secured until the King was reduced to a position of helplessness and dependence, the Royal Prerogative reduced to the lowest possible limit, and the Parliament made really the supreme power in the State. Who can blame the popular leaders in this assembly if, after all this duplicity and faithlessness, they insisted upon the curtailment of prerogatives which had ever been acknowledged? It was now clear that all accommodation with the King was almost impossible, and that no sense of security could be felt until the King was shorn of all power to do mischief. There was no desire to remove him from the kingship—no thought even of such a thing.

An army was at this time wanted to put down the insurrection in Ireland. Charles seemed anxious to obtain such an army, but the Commons viewed matters in a different aspect: not that they were at all less desirous to protect the Irish Protestants and to punish the perpetrators of the dreadful massacre, but because they were afraid that such a power in the hand of the King would be turned against them to their destruction. And hence they required guarantees that this great military power should be within their control. Thus arose the question of the Militia. The Parliament required that at least for a time, until confidence had been restored, that the command of the militia in the various counties should be given to men to be nominated by the Parliament, such as they had confidence in. The appointment of lord-lieutenants had hitherto belonged to the sovereign. The King resisted this encroachment obstinately, and declined giving his assent to a measure depriving him of this right. The men nominated by the Commons in February, 1642, were such as the King could hardly object to. The majority of them, when the sword was actually appealed to, went over to the King, a fact which goes far to show that at this time war was not thought of by the Parliament. The names were the names of those in whom the Parliament had confidence, and they were not chosen, as some suppose, because they were inimical to the King. Of those who were nominated for the Welsh and border counties, several afterwards proved themselves most zealous royalists—Lord Strange for Cheshire, Lord Dacres for Hereford, Lord Littleton for Shropshire and Radnor, and the Earl of Carbery for Cardigan and Carmarthen. The Lord Philip Herbert for Monmouth, Brecon, and Glamorgan; the Earl of Pembroke for Carnarvon and Merioneth, the Earl of Northumerland for Pembrokeshire, Haverfordwest, and Anglesey; the Lord Fielding for Denbigh and Flint, and the Earl of Essex for Montgomery, on the other hand, threw in their lot with the Parliament.

Charles, however, was not inclined to give up prerogatives which he valued so much. Even before the ordinance for the militia had been presented to him he had made up his mind for war. The Queen had already quitted the country for Holland, with the crown jewels to pawn for the purchase of arms. The King saw her off at Dover towards the end of February, and then avoiding London passed by slow marches through the country to York. The ordinance for the militia was presented to him on the road. He refused to assent to it. He was also asked to return to London, but he continued his journey northwards, and arrived at York towards the middle of March.

Negotiations between the King and Parliament now commenced, and continued without interruption throughout that spring. Message after message went between them, and Commissioners from either party were constantly on the road between the metropolis and York. From these negotiations neither side could hardly have expected any good to come. It was nothing more than a controversy between two disputing parties freely indulging in accusation and recrimination—neither hoping to convince the other, but both endeavouring to gain the better in the estimation of the general public. "Law pleadings," as Carlyle says, "of both parties before the great tribunal of the English nation, each party striving to prove itself right and within the verge of the law." The Parliament upon good ground accused Charles of illegal conduct, for he had over and over again trampled upon the liberties of the people in a manner which no other sovereign had ever done before; but recently he had made many concessions—concessions which, however, viewed in the light of his last attempt to be above the law, could not be deemed safe. In insisting on guarantees and further pledges of good faith the Parliament were only carrying out what common sense dictated; but when they declared and insisted that the Parliament could make enactments without the assent of the King they also were in the wrong, and rightly enough accused of illegal conduct by Charles. These disputes were argued at great length and with much ability. The arguments, contained in the proclamations of the King and the solemn declarations of Parliament, were all published for the public benefit.

The Press at this period assumed greater vigour than it had ever done before. From London and from York—from the former more especially—were issued countless pamphlets bearing upon every conceivable question—religious and political. Subjects were discussed with an earnestness and thoroughness, and with a sense of freedom which had never before been witnessed. Newspapers, too, started up in great profusion: not the kind of papers we now have the advantage daily to peruse, but small book-like publications of between twelve and twenty pages, containing on the whole a creditable amount of news, which was supplied by "our own correspondents," then irreverently called "scouts," stationed at various places of interest. These were scattered all over the country. They were bought with eagerness, and read with avidity. It was the interest of both parties to disseminate them. In this respect Wales was at a great disadvantage. All these publications were in English—a language but little understood in the Principality. The commerce of thought was on that account difficult. The appeal to public opinion in Wales could not be as direct as in the English counties. I have never discovered a single sheet of printed matter in the Welsh language which in any way bore on the disputes between King and Parliament. The masses in Wales, therefore, had to follow the example of those above them, and to accept as gospel truth what they were told by such as were educated; and the latter were, of course, confined to the clergy and gentry. The influence of these has always been great, but it is ever in proportion to the ignorance and dependence of a people. The ignorance of the Welsh at this time was intense. This, I think, I have already conclusively shown. They were even "as moles who had no eyes," as one of the old newspapers justly remarks. The clergy and gentry had, therefore, all the greater influence, and whatever side they took the populace blindly followed. It is true that there were some poetasters in the Principality at the time, but the sons of song were mere retainers of the wealthy, which only increased the influence of the latter. In the struggle which ensued this should not be lost sight of, for it will in a great measure serve as a key whereby we may the more reasonably account for the part which Wales played.

Failing to obtain the King's assent to the Militia Bill, the Parliament resolved to carry out their measure independent of him. They nominated deputy-lieutenants and appointed commissioners for every county, and these were to "settle" the Militia. Against these appointments Charles issued his declaration, maintaining that he alone had the power. This the Parliament denied. During June, July, and August they issued orders to their Commissioners to put their powers in execution—to assemble and train the Militia. The King, too, issued his Commissions of Array, in which he commanded certain persons nominated for each county to call out and drill the trained bands and other military forces of their several counties. The Parliament in their turn declared the Commissions of Array to be against the law and the liberty and property of the subject, and denounced all who should act under them as "betrayers of the peace of the Kingdom." Another discussion ensued; proclamation and declaration followed each other with rapidity—the King maintaining the lawfulness of the Commission, the Parliament declaring the contrary. Some of those named by the King in the Array were friends of the Parliament, and disobeyed the royal mandate, while some of those nominated by the Parliament to settle the Militia went over to the King.

Early in July the Parliament, with much solemnity, discussed the question of War. There was only one voice raised against it in the Commons, and that was the voice of a friend of the Parliament; for most of the Royalist members of the House had withdrawn, and were either in attendance upon the King at York, or busily making preparations for the worse in their respective counties and boroughs. On the 12th July a vote passed for raising an army. The Earl of Essex was appointed General-in-Chief of all the Parliament's forces, the Earl of Bedford General of the Horse.

About the beginning of August the King appointed the Marquis of Hertford Lieutenant-General for the western counties of England, where his influence was very great, and also for Monmouthshire, Herefordshire, and the six counties of South Wales. He was entrusted with power to order the Commissioners of Array to levy forces, to train and arm them, and to conduct and lead them against all enemies—rebels and traitors—in any of the said counties.[1]

The Parliament also began to take active steps. Warrants and commissions were issued to its most prominent supporters in Wales, giving them full power to raise forces and to suppress any forces raised under colour of a defence or guard for the King, against whose person the Parliament declared, as was true, that they had no evil intent. Two of these warrants have been handed down—one to the Commissioners for the County of Pembroke,[2]

---

[1] Rushworth, pt. iii., vol. i., 672.
[2] Lord's Journals, v. 364. See also vol. ii., Document No. ii.

and the other to Sir William Brereton, and the Deputy-Lieutenants for Cheshire.[1]

During the heat of those summer months the country was stirred to its very depths, and earnest preparations for war were being made. With a strange inconsistency each party professed the most peaceable desires, and yet both parties were busily engaged in preparing for hostilities. The Commissioners of the Array on the one hand, and the Commissioners for the Militia on the other, were carrying out the object for which they were respectively appointed, and every county in the Kingdom was torn into two factions. Wherever the Parliament had a zealous member, he was dispatched to his constituency to use all his influence on behalf of the Parliament. Sir William Brereton, one of the members for Cheshire, Sir John Corbet in Shropshire, Sir Thomas Myddelton in Denbighshire, Sir Hugh Owen in the borough of Pembroke, were among those who were so engaged. But by far the greater majority of the Welsh members were of the King's party. Many of these, too, went down to their mountain homes and busied themselves for the cause which they had made their own. As might have been expected in a struggle so momentous party spirit ran very high, much ill-feeling prevailed, and many bickerings took place between the contentients. On the eighth day of August Sir William Brereton, whose zealous opposition to the King is attributed by Clarendon to his well-known aversion to the Established Church and its government,[2] had come down to

---
[1] King's Pamphlets, Brit. Mus., No. 68, § 37.
[2] Hist. Rebellion, ii., p. 510.

Chester, where the people were much divided. We have already seen a glimpse of the Puritan element breaking forth on Prynne's passage through the quaint old city.[1] Moreover, very early in July the citizens had declared against the Array, on the ground that "as God and the fundamental laws of this Kingdom have joined his Majesty and the Parliament together," so they could "not agree to a disjointed obedience."[2] On the day in question Brereton had caused a drum to be beat publicly in the streets for the Parliament. There were in the city at that time many Royalists—men of position and influence. It was the custom of the nobility and gentry in those days—and, indeed, until railways rendered communication with the metropolis easy, it prevailed generally in Wales— to spend some portion of their time every year in the city or county town nearest to their habitations. Very convenient for social purposes this custom was. Thus there were in Chester a number of houses occupied by the wealthy. Earl Derby, Earl Rivers, Lord Cholmondeley, and others, were amongst the number. Their influence, of course, was considerable, and being Royalists they ordered the constables to put a stop to the drumbeating. A serious tumult ensued. Brereton and his friends, Alderman Edwards and Henry Birkenhead, who accompanied the drum, had to seek shelter from the violence of the mob.[3] The Mayor had some difficulty in quieting the riot. Sir William was taken before the city authorities at

---

[1] Ante p. 63.
[2] King's Pamphlets 68—29. See Document No. iii , vol. ii., p. 8.
[3] Randle Holmes' MSS., Harl. 2125, fol. 313.

the Pentice—the Guildhall of Chester—but was discharged.[1] In South Wales the influence of the Marquis of Worcester was very great, especially in Monmouthshire—where he was an almost "universal landlord," as one old tract has it. Throughout the war he continued the most lavish supporter of the King, and spared neither men nor money to aid his cause. Too advanced in years for much activity, the actual exercise of his influence devolved upon his son, the Lord Herbert—who, as Earl of Glamorgan, hereafter plays a conspicuous part. The Worcester family were Roman Catholics, and therefore in obloquy at the time, which must have very much diminished their influence. And there were many who were energetic in destroying, or at any rate neutralizing that influence. Most powerful in this respect was the Earl of Pembroke, whose possessions in Monmouthshire and Glamorganshire were extensive. He and his were from the beginning strenuous adherents of Parliament. In Brecknockshire, Herbert Price, of the Priory, was influential on the King's side, as were the Earl of Carbery and his brother, Sir Henry Vaughan, in Carmarthenshire, Sir John Stepney in Pembrokeshire, and, though in a less active manner, John Vaughan of Trawscoed,—who became Chief Justice Vaughan soon after the Restoration,—in Cardiganshire. Sir Hugh Owen and his son Arthur had a large following on the Parliament side in the town of Pembroke, which from the beginning manifested an opposition to the King. In North Wales the royal interest very much preponderated. There were the Bulkeleys in Anglesey, John Owen

[1] Ormerod's History of Cheshire, i., 203.

(afterwards Sir John) of Cleneney, and the Griffithses in Carnarvonshire, the Salisburys—chief of them old "hosanau gleision" (blue stockings)—and the Wynnes in Denbighshire, and the Mostyns in Flintshire. Others there were of less note who were equally busy on either side.

Addresses containing strong expressions of loyalty were got up in several counties, and sent to the King at York. That from Flint has come down to us.[1] The tone of these addresses was calculated to afford encouragement to the King, in whom the petitioners appear to place boundless faith. The good people of Flint, in acknowledging that they rested "thoroughly persuaded of the sincerity and constancy" of Charles's resolution to maintain the privileges of Parliament and the liberties of the subject in their integrity, manifest a faith noticeable from its simplicity, and which is difficult to comprehend, unless we charitably suppose them to be ignorant of the character of the Sovereign whom they addressed.

[1] K. P. 67–3. See also Document No. i., vol. ii.

CHAPTER III.

1642.

Charles quits York—Sets up his Standard at Nottingham and formally declares War—Parliament declines to negotiate with him—Strength of their forces—Charles resolves to go to Shrewsbury—Preparations there—The town sends him an invitation—The King arrives there—Proceeds to Chester—Prince Rupert arrives at Shrewsbury—Attacks a detachment of Essex's army near Worcester—Charles quits Chester—Visits Wrexham—Addresses the people there and returns to Shrewsbury—Where a Mint is established—And a Press—Growth of Newspapers—Liberality of the Welsh—State of South Wales—Marquis of Hertford defeated in the West, crosses the Channel and occupies Cardiff Castle—Aided by the Marquis of Worcester he raises forces in Glamorganshire and Monmouthshire—Prince Charles visits Raglan—Disaffection amongst the soldiers at Shrewsbury—Charles explains his conduct to them and the people—His second visit to Wrexham—Inactivity of Essex—The King departs from Shrewsbury, intending to advance to London—Battle of Edgehill—Some account of the Welsh there—Charles goes to Oxford—Thence to Reading, whence his soldiers scour the country—Parliament opens fresh negotiations—Cessation of arms—Perfidy of Charles—Battle of Brentford—Oxford made winter quarters—Marquis of Hertford and his Welsh forces intend to join the King there—Defeated at Tewkesbury—And at Hereford—Condition of Shrewsbury and Chester after the departure of the King—Cheshire agrees upon Articles of Neutrality—Agreement repudiated by the Parliament—Declaration of the Shropshire gentry—A glimpse of South Wales.

WITH such assurances of loyal zeal, and such expressions of confidence reaching him at York from all parts of the country, Charles felt himself in a position to take some active measures to assert his rights. He was stirred the more to this by the energetic preparations which the Parliament was making. Hitherto Charles himself had been the most backward and the most hesitating. His

CHAP III.
1642.

partisans everywhere were far more eager. Throughout the country they were moving in all directions. Private houses were strengthened, castles which had half tumbled down fortified, towns put in a posture of defence, arms burnished up, and ammunition and accoutrements of war brought into magazines. In many places the over-zeal of the Royalists had, as at Chester, resulted in the effusion of blood. They were also, at this early stage of the conflict, more daring than their opponents, better organized, and less scrupulous. They ransacked houses, plundered villages, oftentimes caring very little whom they robbed—friends or opponents—their sole aim being to obtain booty. A large quantity of clothing intended for the Protestant soldiers in Ireland was sent by order of the Parliament by way of Chester. A party of cavaliers coming upon the convoy in the neighbourhood of Coventry, seized the clothing and made off with it. These indiscretions on the part of the King's friends were calculated seriously to damage his cause. To counteract this, to keep his party in order, and, moreover, to enlist by his presence the loyal support of the country, Charles quitted York, and, passing through Leicester, Derby, and Lincoln, arrived at Nottingham. His progress was not, perhaps, so enthusiastic as had been anticipated, still the nobility came out to meet him; the people did him homage. His conduct on these occasions was such as to evoke the good-will of his subjects, and was marked with much gentleness and humility; while his professions of loyalty to the laws of the land, and of his fidelity to the Protestant cause, were calculated to make him appear in the right and his opponents in the wrong.

Up to this both parties showed great indecision. As if anxious for peace, yet knowing that peace was impossible, each party delayed resorting to open hostilities. Both appeared averse to initiate the reign of terror and bloodshed—each desirous to have cause to call the other the aggressor. It was too terrible a suspense to last long.

Encouraged by the loyalty which he had witnessed in his progress from York to Nottingham, and by the arrival of some arms from abroad which the Queen had purchased with the fruit of the pawned jewels, Charles at length resolved to call his subjects to arms by a formal Declaration of War. On the 23rd day of August the Royal Standard was set up at Nottingham, under circumstances which were by no means reassuring, and which many considered as ominous of the result of the struggle which was so unhappily commenced. In fact, so downcast were those surrounding the King, that they prevailed upon him, within a few days of the setting up of the Standard, to open fresh negotiations with the Parliament with a view to avoid hostilities. But the Parliament were in no mood just then for further messages. For they had been very successful in obtaining men and money. Already the Earl of Essex was engaged in drilling and training large numbers, and fresh recruits kept constantly streaming in. On the 7th of September he quitted London at the head of a large army, amidst the greatest enthusiasm. Thousands of citizens accompanied them a part of the way, and fervently wished them God-speed. They

CHAP. III.
1642.

reached Northampton, and were there much increased. The Parliamentary army by this time is said to have numbered between fifteen and twenty thousand men. The King had nothing like this. He was not in a position to offer fight, the attempt to renew negotiations with Westminster had failed, and he was advised to quit a place where he was surrounded with so much danger. Anxious as he was to be near London he was too weak to proceed thither.

Nottingham was quitted and Derby was reached. While there Charles heard from the loyalists of Shrewsbury that that town was entirely at his disposal. On the 4th of September Charles had sent his commission to Mr. Francis Ottley, ordering him to raise 200 foot soldiers in Shropshire, and with all possible speed to conduct them to Shrewsbury. This commission seems to have been carried out so well that the Puritans in that town, though considerable in number and influence, were silenced, and the Town Council, which but a short time before had agreed to maintain a neutrality, were eager to promise the King if he came to Shrewsbury "the best entertainment the troublesome times afford." There were many reasons to induce the King to remove to Shrewsbury. Its position was pleasant: it was on the borders of North Wales, where the Royalists could count upon a great majority. Moreover, the river Severn, which winds itself round the base of the picturesque old town, would prove of great service. The King, therefore, resolved to go thither. The invitation of the town was alone wanting. The Town Council agreed upon that on the 15th day of September. On that very day Charles signed a warrant calling upon the Commissioners of Array for the County of Carnarvon to raise the trained bands of that county, and such volunteers as they could persuade to come, and with all possible speed to bring them to Shrewsbury, "to our Royal Standard there." And as an incentive to the loyalty of the Welsh people, they were told that they would be appointed as a guard to the Prince of Wales.[1]

Immediately upon the receipt of the invitation from the municipal authorities of Shrewsbury, Derby was quitted. Stafford was reached on the 18th, Wellington the next day. The King's forces at this time are variously estimated. That they were not very strong is the universal testimony. Probably not exceeding, horse and foot, eight thousand. At Wellington, in the presence of all his soldiers, Charles made that memorable protestation, in which he vowed his loyalty to the laws, and his fidelity to the Protestant religion. This protestation was read in every church throughout the Kingdom where a Royalist clergyman ministered.

On Tuesday, the twentieth day of September, Shrewsbury was reached. The Salopians no doubt gave the King a warm reception, and an enthusiastic entertainment, spending freely a considerable sum of money. Charles stayed at the Council House. Wednesday and Thursday were in all probability spent in inspecting the preparations which Francis Ottley, now created a Knight, had made for the defence of that town. On Friday the King went to Chester, where his presence at this time

[1] See Appendix to Williams's Tourist's Guide to Carnarvonshire.

was much needed, not only to encourage his adherents, but to discountenance his opponents, who were rather strong in point of numbers and influence in the quaint old city. Charles took with him to Chester only a small body of soldiers, the bulk of his army being left behind in Shrewsbury. He was accompanied on this journey by Prince Charles, now a lad of about twelve years. The royal party halted for refreshments at Whitchurch, and thence continued their march, reaching Chester that evening. Some distance outside Chester they were met by the leading men of the county, who had come forth at the head of detachments of followers to accord a welcome to their Sovereign. Mr. Richard Egerton of Ridley, at the head of some six hundred musketeers, met him at Milton Green. At Halton Heath, the Earl Rivers and Lord Cholmondeley showed to advantage with a considerable body of retainers. They received the King with a royal salute. Sir Thomas Aston, with the Sheriff of the county, and other gentlemen, awaited him on Rowton Heath.[1] All these with their forces joined the King in his progress, so that Charles made his entry into Chester at the head of a somewhat imposing body. The Mayor and Aldermen also, with all the civic authorities in their various coloured robes of office, the numerous trade guilds with their insignia, had all turned out to accord him welcome. At the Bars, at the top of Eastgate-street, which marked the limits of their jurisdiction, a platform had been erected for the Mayor and Sheriffs. The Recorder was there too with an address. The Sword of the

---

[1] King's Pamphlets 75—3. See vol. ii., Document iv. A., p. 10.

City was in due form presented to the King, who graciously handed it back again to the Mayor. The address was duly read, but one eye-witness says that the shouting was so great that he doubted whether his Majesty heard one word of it. This ceremony over, the whole company, in great state and with much pomp, marched through the principal street, which was lined with soldiers, towards the Bishop's Palace, where the King was to stay.[1] The next day Charles was employed in making an inspection of the works for the defence of the city, which already had been in progress for several weeks. The gentlemen who had opposed the Array had all been marked men. And as Charles always loved to punish his enemies they were brought before him. Sir Richard Wilbraham, Sir Thomas Delves, Mr. Philip Mainwaring of Badley, Mr. Birkenhead, the Protonotary, and his son Henry, were among these. They were all placed in custody, and removed afterwards to Shrewsbury.

The Sunday was a day of excitement in the quiet city. The soldiers thronged the streets, the people enjoyed the sight. Crowds from the neighbourhood came in eager to catch a glimpse of the King. Even in the churches the general excitement prevailed, for in all of them the King's declaration was read. Monday was again devoted to an inspection of the works, and in conferences as to future movements. The city presented to the King the sum of two hundred pounds, and to the Prince of Wales half that amount. A smaller sum it is said than had been expected, but still

[1] K. P. 75—25. See vol. ii., Document iv. B., C., and F., pp. 11—15.

CHAP. III.
1642.

a considerable sum in those days. From the Welsh counties arrived several regiments of trained bands and recruits. Among the commanders of these were Capt. Roger Mostyn and Capt. Salisbury. The Lord Grandison also came with a considerable force of well-armed men, having on his way successfully attacked the little town of Nantwich in Cheshire. Nantwich from the very first had shown an unmistakeable preference for the Parliament. What with the Puritan clergyman at Acton, close by, and the gentlemen whom we have just seen suffering from Charles's displeasure, who resided in its immediate neighbourhood, the town of Nantwich had been much influenced for the Parliament. Of this attack by Lord Grandison there are several accounts. All agree that the town was given up without any serious resistance, but as to the after-conduct of the soldiers the accounts differ. One relator would have us believe that frightful atrocities were perpetrated. Another gives a more temperate account of the affair. Probably, the town met with no worse fate than such places generally do when invaded by a host of men not very scrupulous, somewhat hostile, and not under the most strict discipline.[1]

While the King was at Chester the Princes Rupert and Maurice came to Shrewsbury. Sons of the King of Bohemia, by Elizabeth, the eldest daughter of James I., they were the nephews of Charles; and given to military life, they had come over to offer their assistance. High command was naturally bestowed on both brothers. Of these, Prince Rupert was destined to become by far the

[1] K. P. 75—25. Vol. ii., Doc iv. D. and note.

more famous. He was at this time quite young, but possessed an energy of character and a military daring which soon won for him considerable notoriety. Maurice, on the other hand, was slow and heavy, lacking no courage, but wanting in the energy and resolution which characterised his brother. The Earl of Essex, who had at a distance followed the King on his westward march, was at this period approaching Worcester. Prince Rupert, who was eager for an exploit, went to that city at the head of a considerable force. On the 24th of September the advanced detachment of Essex's army came in sight of the city. In number these were not considerable, and their quality was not of the best. The opportunity was too inviting to be resisted, and the Prince made a most dashing attack upon them, and with success. The Parliamentary soldiers, under the command of Col. Sandys, were discomfited; many of them, Col. Sandys included, were wounded; and several were taken prisoners, some of them of note: Edward Wingate, Member of Parliament for Saint Albans, being among them. He held a captain's commission in the Parliament's army. This exploit, dashing as it was, produced no result beyond the momentary annoyance, for on the approach of the Earl of Essex with the main body of his army, Rupert withdrew from Worcester, taking with him Captain Wingate as a prisoner. If the letter which was shortly after published, purporting to have been written by Capt. Wingate from Ludlow, is genuine, Prince Rupert was guilty of conduct, unsoldierly and dishonourable, for, not satisfied with dealing out ribald taunts to the defenceless prisoner, finding the latter bold and courageous enough even in

CHAP. III.
1642.

that extremity to defend his and the Parliament's conduct, he caused him to be stripped of his clothing and to be mounted on horseback naked at the head of the army. To me such conduct seems almost incredible, though I am afraid there was some truth in it. Rupert, passing through Ludlow and Bridgnorth, retreated to Shrewsbury. Essex stationed himself at Worcester.

From Chester orders were sent to the leading men, the Commissioners of Array and others, in the several counties of North Wales, calling upon them to conduct the trained bands into Shrewsbury, and to use all possible efforts to levy money for their support. On the 25th Charles wrote to the Commissioners for the County of Carnarvon, directing them to pay the money thus collected by them into the hands of John Owen, of Cleneney—"one of our colonels."[1] This John Owen will hereafter come often before us. He was one of the staunchest Royalists in North Wales. He fought for the King with a pertinacity which cannot but be admired, and his unswerving fidelity to his sovereign brought him under the shadow of the scaffold.

On Tuesday, the 27th, Charles departed from Chester. Making a slight detour he called at Wrexham, where the inhabitants of Denbighshire and Flintshire had been summoned to meet him. A large number assembled, whom the King addressed at great length, justifying his conduct, throwing all the blame on his enemies, and explaining the capture by his partisans of the clothing intended by the Parliament for the soldiers in Ireland.[2]

---

[1] See Appendix to Williams's Tourist's Guide to Carnarvonshire.
[2] Rushworth, pt 3, vol. ii., p. 21, and Document iv. x., vol. ii., p. 20.

How this meeting passed off is a matter which rests unknown. Probably the reception which the King met with in Wrexham, which was then the chief town in North Wales, was a hearty and a satisfactory one. His entertainer on the occasion was Mr. Richard Lloyd, who was then the Attorney-General for North Wales, a man whose zeal and energy on behalf of the King became afterwards so displeasing to the Parliament that his name was included in the list of persons who, in the negotiations in 1647 with the King, were demanded to be excepted from pardon.

Shrewsbury was once more reached. Here Charles found his army considerably increased by new contingents which had arrived in his absence, some under Prince Rupert, and others from the several counties of North Wales. The town was full of soldiers, and the neighbourhood was heavily taxed for free quarters; for the soldiers were billeted everywhere upon the inhabitants, who suffered not only the material losses which such charges entailed, but had to endure indignities and illusage from an undisciplined and unfriendly soldiery. Complaints from them hardly availed, and only added to the complications. Soon, too, dissensions arose among the soldiers, to the embarrassment of those in power over them, leading to difficulties which at one time threatened even a disruption of the forces there. Money was very much wanted. The payment of the soldiers was greatly in arrear, which naturally created dissatisfaction. Add to these the fact that many of the soldiers were deeply influenced by persons who were notoriously disaffected to the King, and

CHAP. III.
1642.

the difficulties of the situation are apparent.[1] Nevertheless, they were all tided over.

A Mint was established at Shrewsbury under the superintendence of Thomas Bushell, the lessee of the Cardiganshire Silver Mines. Bushell had succeeded Sir Hugh Myddelton, of the New River Company, in the farming of these mines. He appears to have carried them on with great spirit and energy. Some years before this he had obtained a royal grant enabling him to establish a Mint at Aberystwith. The coins there made are now very scarce. Bushell appears to have been warmly attached to the King's cause. From a letter of Charles to him it appears that at the very outset of the war he raised a body of Derbyshire miners as a Life Guard for the King, when the Lord-Lieutenant of that county refused to do anything for his Sovereign. Various other acts of loyalty are enumerated in the letter in question, which reflectively show the state of affairs in Shrewsbury at this time. The soldiers were sorely in want of clothing. Bushell provided them with ample materials. They had no lead to make shot. Bushell supplied one hundred tons without being paid one farthing, when the King hitherto had had to pay twenty pounds a ton. Guns for mounting on the walls were wanted both at Chester and at Shrewsbury. He furnished them at a great strait. His credit was good with merchants abroad, and it was freely used for the advancement of the royal cause. He was also of an inventive turn of mind. To encourage the soldiers to acts of bravery, he invented silver badges to reward

[1] King's Pamphlets, 77—4. Vol. ii., Document iv. G., p. 19.

the forlorn hope, and supplied them at his own cost. Of all the officers of the Mint in London, there was only one besides Bushell who adopted the King's cause.[1]

But a Mint without silver and gold was of little use. On Michaelmas Eve a large meeting was held in a field outside the town. The King spoke, and appealed for help. He was fighting, not merely for himself, but for their liberties. He had been deprived of means to do so effectually by the sharp practice of the Parliament. His circumstances, he said, were then straitened. Nevertheless, he would sacrifice his own plate for the common weal. It should be at once melted down, and converted into money. Would others—his loving subjects—follow his example? Such was the issue which Charles placed before the assembly. The appeal in a measure succeeded. Many freely sacrificed their plate and brought in to the common stock what they could spare. The Catholics preeminently showed a liberal disposition. Clarendon commends the generosity of the Salopians and their neighbours, and compares their liberality with the stinginess and closeness of the other places where the King had been at. Plate and money, he said, were brought in voluntarily in such quantities that the army was full and constantly paid.[2] The noble historian evidently draws a little upon his imagination, or what is more likely, he wrote the passage I have just quoted years after the event, when he had no greater authority than a mere impression on his mind; for it is manifest that there was a

[1] Caxt. Harl. Antiq., iii. B., 61; and Vol. ii., Doc. vii. B., p. 31.
[2] Clarendon's Rebellion.

lack of resources. The soldiers could with difficulty be kept from breaking out into open mutiny because of their irregular payments; and they were left much to help themselves, which they did by an indiscriminate sacking and plundering of houses, where there was any likelihood of booty, often indifferent whether the houses belonged to friends or foes. One fruitful source of money at Shrewsbury appears to have been the selling of dignities and titles. Sir Richard Newport of High Ercal is said to have paid six thousand pounds for a peerage. For a purse of gold Thomas Lyster of Routon was knighted.[1] If every man who was knighted here and elsewhere during the war presented Charles with a purse of gold it must have produced a rather considerable sum of money. The town presented Prince Charles with one hundred pounds, and to the Duke of York they gave sixty.

A Press, too, was established at Shrewsbury, whence were issued pamphlets, declarations, and packets of news. The Parliament possessed a great advantage over the Royalists in the matter of printing. Outside London at this period I do not suppose there were half-a-dozen presses throughout the Kingdom. The consequence was that the Parliament had almost a monopoly. Their pamphlets were more numerous: their newspapers were almost countless, while Charles had to rest contented with an irregular and will-o'-the-wisp-like appearance of *Mercurius Aulicus*, and an occasional broadside. Charles complained of this in his speech at Wrexham, when he requested the Sheriffs to distribute copies of his protestation. This was

[1] Owen and Blakeway's Shrewsbury.

the period when the Newspaper Press obtained a firm footing in this country. Very different, of course, to the newspapers we have now the advantage of, but still carried on with a wonderful amount of public spirit and enterprise. Even some of these had their "special correspondents" following the two camps. The passion and the prejudices of the readers of these papers required stimulating and exciting matter to read, and the demand created a supply of exceedingly virulent and vigorous writing. The times were, however, times of great excitement, when the whole country was stirred to its very depths by the importance of the struggle, and this consideration condones to a great extent the exaggerations which we discover in these early newspapers. At this particular period their mission seems to have been to inflame the public mind against their respective opponents. The Parliament advocates gave publicity to matters which were calculated to instil into the minds of the Puritans a deadly hatred to the King and his party. From Shrewsbury came many a news-letter which had this object. In one of them it was stated that the King's soldiers had crucifixes hanging around their necks, that they openly drank a health to Phelim O'Neale, the villainous instigator of the massacre of the Irish Protestants; and what was worse than all, that the cavaliers "ravished the wife of a very discreet, moderate, able, and godly minister in Shropshire."[1]

South Wales at this time was free from that feverish excitement which the King's presence occasioned in North Wales and the borders. The

[1] Special Passages, No. 9, p. 70. (K.P. 77—31.)

King's partisans were, however, energetic in influencing the populace, in collecting arms, and in training men. Notably among these was the Lord Herbert, the eldest son of the Marquis of Worcester. The extensiveness of his father's possession and his great wealth,—for the the Marquis was supposed to be the richest man in England,—gave him very great influence and power. The Earl Carbery, who, from all accounts, was popular in the western counties, was also active. The Lord Herbert's religion debarred him at this early period from receiving a commission; for Charles was afraid as yet to give to the Parliament a further cause of outcry against him. Already he had suffered enough from the charge of favouring the Roman Catholics: it was inexpedient to set at defiance popular indignation. Moreover, many of Charles's chief advisers were as opposed to the Catholics as the Puritans themselves, though, probably, on different grounds. The Lord Herbert was eager for command, and was rather sore because it was not given him; still he was active in promoting the interest of his King, with whom he was personally a favourite. South Wales was not destined to continue long in a quiet peaceful state, for on the very day Charles made his first entry into Chester the town of Cardiff was the scene of bustle and confusion. We have already seen that the Marquis of Hertford has been appointed Lieutenant-General for the West of England and for South Wales. The Earl of Bedford represented the Parliament in the west. Between these broils and skirmishes had already taken place. But for a while there had been a cessation of hostilities, owing to their maintaining a distance between one another. About the middle of September they had an encounter near Sherborne, in Dorsetshire. The Royalists having the worst of it, were forced to retreat to Minehead, in Glo'stershire, whither the Earl of Bedford pursued them. Failing to get admission into the fortress there, the Marquis availed himself of some coalships in the port, and crossed the channel to Cardiff. At this time the most important place in Cardiff was its castle, the property of the Earl of Pembroke. The Earl of Pembroke was a staunch Parliamentarian, and continued true to the cause till his death. Owing to his opposition, Charles ordered the castle to be seized, as well as all the other possessions of the Earl. The person entrusted with this was William Herbert, who lived at the Friars, Cardiff, a zealous Royalist, and a cousin of William Herbert of Cogan Peel, the representative of Cardiff in the Long Parliament, but who met with his death in the battle of Edgehill. Power was also given to William Herbert to collect the rents of the Earl of Pembroke, full instructions as to which from the King may yet be seen by the curious among the letters of the period in the Record Office. When the Marquis of Hertford came over with a great company of the leading Royalists of the west, he and his men were gladly admitted into the castle, and there does not appear to have been any real opposition to this. Though a pamphlet issued at the time, entitled "A true and joyful relation of a famous and remarkable victory obtained by the inhabitants of Glamorganshire, in Wales, against the Marquis of Hertford and the cavaliers, who had taken the Castle of Cardiff," states that the country people, fearing plundering, attacked him, killing a number of his soldiers,[1] I am inclined to look upon this, in the absence of corroboration, as fiction. There was no organization on the part of the Parliament. The Militia Ordinance had never been put in execution in the county.[2] The leading men of the county were all the other way, and it is simply impossible that a mob should be organized to give battle with effect in so short a time. In another place it is stated that the Earl of Bedford had followed the Marquis across the channel, had effected an entry into Cardiff, and was fortifying the town for the Parliament. This, too, has no better authority than the mere uncorroborated assertion of one of the newspapers, for which I am inclined to look upon it as unsatisfactory. Probably, the Earl of Bedford was quite satisfied with his success in the west. Besides, there is sufficient testimony that the Marquis remained at Cardiff and in Monmouthshire for some weeks, carrying out his commission in that neighbourhood by levying men for the war. In this he was aided by the Marquis of Worcester, who spent large sums of money for that purpose. The Earl of Glamorgan, in after years, asserted that £8,000 was thus spent, and that his father lent a further sum of £2,000 to the Marquis of Hertford.[3] And this, too, notwithstanding the natural jealousy which Lord Herbert felt at the presence of the Marquis of Hertford with a com-

---

[1] King's Pamphlets, 75—31. See vol. ii., Document v., p. 23.
[2] Symond's Diary. See vol. ii., Document lxxvii., p. 262.
[3] Warburton's Prince Rupert, iii., 524.

mission, which he thought should have been his own. The loyalty of the old Marquis of Worcester was too sincere to be affected by any consideration like that. The situation was, however, a delicate one, and some differences did exist between the Lords Herbert and Hertford. Clarendon is very savage about this, more so, perhaps, than was justifiable. Speaking of the differences between the two noblemen, he says that the Lord Herbert, out of his vanity to magnify his own power, had not shown that regard to the position of the other which he should have had; and maintains, that the Lord Herbert would have advanced the King's service far more, if he had contributed his full assistance to another who more popularly might have borne such command.[1] What detracted from Lord Herbert's popularity was his religion.

While the King was busily endeavouring to further his cause between Shrewsbury and Chester, he sent his son, Prince Charles, to Raglan. There he was received with all the pomp and state which the wealth of his entertainer could enable him to do. The whole country was glad to have an opportunity of paying homage to their Sovereign, in the person of his son, who, moreover, was Prince of Wales. Boy though he was, he represented Royalty, and evoked that enthusiasm which generally attends the progress of princes among their subjects. An address of welcome was delivered to him by one Sir Hugh Vaughan. A banquet was prepared in his honour, and presents of various kinds were brought to him by the loyal in those parts, which seems to have been highly gratifying

[1] Clarendon's Rebellion, ii., 522.

to the boy-prince. It was certainly a politic move on the part of the King to send his son on this journey. The Welsh had seen but little of their princes hitherto, since that farce at Rhuddlan, when Edward I. foisted upon the credulous Welsh a baby-prince as a true-born Prince of Wales. Nor have they since that time been much better off. The young Prince was, however, amply repaid for his visit. He met with nothing but kindness, and he must have done some good to his father's cause. On his way back he passed through Radnorshire. The country people everywhere greeted him with tokens of affection, and loaded him with presents.[1]

The King still continued at Shrewsbury. The position of that town as head-quarters entailed upon the whole neighbourhood great inconvenience. The presence of large bodies of soldiers in quiet country villages was by no means welcome. Conducting themselves with great swagger, resorting to violence wherever their exaggerated demands were not complied with, the whole country around suffered immensely. Complaints were daily made, but the suffering was not abated;—on the contrary, was enhanced by the fresh reinforcements which continued to pour in. Even the Royalists had cause to complain, and became less enthusiastic for a cause which cost them so much. The soldiers themselves had but an indifferent time of it. Clarendon notwithstanding, it is clear they were not regularly paid. They had to look out for food and forage. Overwhelmed with complaints from the country-people, and threatened with sedition amongst

[1] See vol. ii., Document vi., p. 26.

the ranks, the King must have been perturbed at this aspect of affairs. The soldiers were again and again mustered to hear addresses from and on behalf of the King—on Merville Heath and elsewhere. The people, too, were convened. Their complaints were too serious to be glossed over. Civilians and soldiers were promised a better state of things shortly. A large meeting was held outside the town on Saturday, the 8th of October, at which Endymion Porter, the Member for Droitwich, was the chief spokesman. The King himself was present. Porter spoke at great length, and made various propositions. These were not quite satisfactory to the assembly. The leaders of the people had a meeting at the George Hotel in the town, and came to an adverse decision; and declared to the King in very plain terms that he was acting foolishly.[1]

On the 7th of October, Charles visited Wrexham for the second time. He went there to meet some Commissioners from Chester and the adjacent towns. On this occasion he knighted his Attorney-General, Mr. Richard Lloyd, whose guest he had been on the previous visit.[2] He returned the same night to Shrewsbury. A pathetic story is told of him on this visit. Lloyd pressed him to stay over night, pointing out to him the length of the journey, which was something like forty miles, and the inclemency of the weather. But Charles was not to be persuaded. "Gentlemen," said he, "go you and take your rests; for you have houses and homes to go to, and beds of your own to lodge in; and God grant you may long enjoy them. I am deprived

[1] Owen and Blakeway's Shrewsbury.
[2] Harl. MSS. 2125, fol. 313.

of these comforts. I must attend to my present affairs, and return this night to the place whence I came."[1]

All this while the Earl of Essex, with the Parliamentary army, had been lying in a state of utter inactivity at Worcester and in the neighbourhood—much to the disgust of his party generally. Encouraged by this want of energy and resolution, and also eager to afford employment to his soldiers, whose disaffection was growing daily, the King finally resolved to quit Shrewsbury and to advance towards London. His forces now amounted to about 16,000 in number—having been quite doubled during the stay at Shrewsbury. At the head of this Charles marched out of Shrewsbury on the evening of the 12th of October,[2] in the direction of Bridgnorth, where they stayed three days. Here was a rendezvous of the whole army, which Clarendon says "appeared very cheerful," notwithstanding their want of arms and clothing. Charles stayed at the castle, and was the guest of Sir Thomas Whitmore, of Apley. Some preparations for the evil days that were coming were already commenced at Bridgnorth. "The gates had been repaired and made strong with chains and otherwise, posts and chains had been placed at the ends of several streets,"—a primitive method, certainly, of putting a town in a "posture of defence." The Earl of Essex appears to have been ignorant of this movement—at any rate, he allowed Charles a start of three days before he made the slightest preparation to follow. In London, as might be expected, the

---

[1] Quoted in Ormerod's Cheshire, vol. i., xxxv.
[2] *Iter Carolinum.*

greatest consternation followed the announcement that the King, far in advance of Essex, was on his way to the metropolis. Steps were at once taken for the defence of the City. Threatened with a common danger, money flowed in freely; and no difficulty was experienced in calling out the militia, and willing hands speedily raised fortifications.

Whilst this was going on in London, Essex overtook Charles near Keynton, in Warwickshire—at the base of Edgehill. It was on Sunday, the 23rd of October, that the hostile armies came in sight of one another. The King's army was by far the better manned. It contained more men of position and of honour, and was characterized with a greater *esprit de corps* than an army consisting, to use Cromwell's own words, of "a set of poor tapsters and town-apprentice people." Both parties were eager for a battle; and the conflict was commenced about two o'clock. Prince Rupert distinguished himself as much with his recklessness as with that dash and vigour which characterized his military actions. At the very outset he dashed through the Parliamentary cavalry, which at the first firing had been weakened by the desertion of a whole regiment commanded by Sir Faithful (mark the name!) Fortescue. The cavalry were thrown into the wildest confusion, and were hotly chased by Rupert, who pursued them for over two miles—in fact, until his pursuit was checked by the approach of Hampden's regiment, coming up for the first time with the Parliamentary cavalry. Rupert meanwhile was unconscious of the disaster which had befallen the King's infantry in his absence. When he returned he found them utterly routed, and their Commander-in-Chief, the Earl of Lindsey, wounded. No power could again induce them to make a charge, while Hampden's arrival brought back confidence to the Parliament's ranks. Darkness put a stop to further fighting. Both armies passed the night on the field of battle, and in the morning each claimed the victory. The Parliament had lost more in number: the King more distinguished men and officers. The royal army was thinned also by the desertion in great numbers of faint-hearted volunteers.

At the battle of Edgehill a great number of Welshmen were engaged. A body of Welsh, under Col. Salesbury, formed the only troop of infantry reserve.[1] Sir Edward Stradling is said to have brought from North Wales to Shrewsbury a thousand men. And Col. John Owen, of Cleneney, was probably present with his regiment from Anglesey and Carnarvonshire. All these were, more or less, sadly equipped. A contemporary MSS., speaking of them, says: "Arms were the great deficiency, and the men stood up in the same garments in which they left their native fields; and with scythes, pitchforks, and even sickles in their hands, they cheerfully took the field, and literally like reapers descend[ed] to that harvest of death."[2] One Robert Evans, writing to Mr. Grenville, the High-Sheriff of Bucks, states that Col. Salesbury ("my countryman," as he calls him,) "hath 1,200 poor Welsh vermin, the offscouring of the nation."[3] In addition to this, a large number of the influential families of

---

[1] Warburton's Prince Rupert.
[2] Harl. MSS., 6844.
[3] Nugent's Life of Hampden, ii., p.

Wales were represented at this battle. Some holding commissions, others acting as volunteers. Of these, William Herbert, of Cogan Peel, the Member for Cardiff, was slain, and Sir Edward Stradling, of St. Donat's Castle, taken prisoner. Of the conduct of the Welsh at this battle different accounts are given. Warburton, probably upon the authority of documents which he had before him while writing his life of Rupert, states that the Welshmen, seeing the success of Rupert's impetuous charge, became fired with the spirit of battle, and with their "cudgels fought bravely, and proved themselves most valorous."[1] Clarendon, on the other hand, would lead us to believe that their conduct was not so praiseworthy, and that at any rate an imputation had been cast upon them, and their courage questioned.[2] And this is the view which seems manifestly supported by the satires to which they became subjected from unfriendly pens.[3] Whatever was the conduct of the Welsh on this occasion, it should not be forgotten that they were raw and undisciplined, scandalously deficient in arms, having nothing better than scythes and pitchforks; incapable therefore of effecting any brilliant action, or of resisting the onslaught of properly-armed forces. Even if many of them deserted, they only did so in company with hundreds of others, when Hampden's forces came up fresh and victorious, and when demoralization seems to have seized the royal army. The battle was not renewed the next morning.

From Edgehill the King and his forces went

---

[1] Life of Prince Rupert, ii., 36.
[2] Hist. of Rebellion, iii , 327.
[3] King's Pamphlets, 85—20. See Vol. ii., Document ix, p. 36.

to Oxford. There the Royal head-quarters were formed. Their resolution was to advance as quickly as possible upon London; and being again in advance of the Earl of Essex, they were scattered all over the country, around Abingdon, Henley, and elsewhere. These towns fell into their hands without any show of resistance. The town of Reading, garrisoned by the Parliament, was deserted at the appearance of a handful of cavaliers. From Oxford, therefore, the head-quarters were removed to Reading. Thence Rupert, reckless and restless, scoured the whole country, even to the very suburbs of London, frightening the Parliament, and plundering the people, whence he soon obtained the not inappropriate designation of Prince Robber. The Parliament, alarmed at the audacity of the enemy and the inactivity of their own forces, sent propositions for peace. After a show of opposition on the part of the King to certain of the negotiators, negotiations were opened. By this time the King was at Colnbrook, within fifteen miles of London. The Parliament in good faith ordered Essex to suspend hostilities; but Charles, with that perfidiousness which was his curse, notwithstanding that the negotiations were pending, moved onwards towards London, and had it not been for the greatest alacrity on the part of the Parliamentary leaders, would, beyond a doubt, have entered the metropolis. At Brentford was stationed a regiment of soldiers under the command of Denzil Holles. Rupert came against them at the head of his cavalry. But the preparations which had been made to resist an attack, the redoubts raised and barricades set up, proved an unsurmountable barrier to the horse.

Retreating with them, Rupert changed his tactics, and renewed the attack with a body of infantry. Hampden and Lord Brook had come to the rescue of Holles; but Rupert's infantry, who were none other than the wild Welshmen, brought to the field by Salesbury, Stradling, and others, burning to redeem themselves from the imputation which had been cast upon them at Edgehill—these "gallant mountaineers" rushed upon the barricades, tore them in pieces, and pushed through, causing the Parliamentary troops, after sustaining considerable loss, to retire in confusion. The Earl of Essex, who was in the House of Lords when the news of the attack came, hastened to the spot, but only in time to find the cavaliers in possession, and his own soldiers dispersed and dispirited.

London was once more terrified at the danger which threatened it, but far more indignant at the faithlessness of the King. The Parliament, taking advantage of these feelings, called forth fresh levies of the militia and volunteers; and within two days of the battle of Brentford, the Earl of Essex, in the presence of members of both Houses, and a crowd of spectators, reviewed an army of twenty-four thousand men at Turnham Green.

The King, dreading an attack, withdrew to Oxford with his troops, and rested there for the winter; and the Parliamentary army, against the advice of Hampden, and others of an energetic turn of mind, rested also for the winter.

Meanwhile, the Marquis of Hertford, aided by the influence of the House of Worcester and other loyalists in Monmouthshire and Glamorganshire, was very successful in raising an army for the King.

CHAP. III.
1642.

Rumours had it that he had got together ten thousand men;[1] but this seems an exaggeration: though probably not very far beyond the mark, for an account of their opponents' estimated them at about seven thousand. These were said to have been well armed at the expense of the House of Raglan, and were not allowed, like the Welsh at Edgehill, with their scythes and pitchforks, "literally like reapers to descend to the harvest of death." The Marquis intended to conduct them to Oxford as soon as possible, where they would prove a valuable acquisition. About the 4th of November, the Marquis, with his brother, Lord Seymour, and Lord Herbert, quitted Cardiff Castle (which from the first had been the head quarters); and with colours flying and drums beating, set forth on their journey to join the King. Descending to the banks of the Severn, and keeping along them, they passed into Herefordshire. The City of Hereford at this time was garrisoned for the Parliament under the command of the Earl of Stamford, the Lord-Lieutenant of that county and of Gloucestershire. Hearing of the approach of the Welsh, he called in the trained bands of the county and adjoining parts, with the intention of obstructing their passage. But instead of proceeding by Hereford, the Marquis and the Welsh crossed the Severn, turned southwards, and made for Tewkesbury. The Earl Stamford followed with about four thousand men, and on Wednesday, the 16th November, came upon them on Tewkesbury Plain. The charge was commenced by the Marquis, who rushed on at the head of about five hundred horse, all trained men, being those who

---

[1] Ellis's Orig. Letters, 2nd Series, vol. iii., p. 303.

had escaped with him from Devonshire. The enemy found it difficult to bear the brunt of so furious a charge; but ultimately did. The Welsh foot, under Lord Seymour, then came on; but these were unaccustomed to war and could hardly use their muskets, so that they fell in whole ranks. Seymour himself had his horse shot under him. The Parliamentary army had also with them two field pieces, with which they decimated the "poor half-armed Welshmen."[1] Being utterly baffled by an enemy of superior training, they took to flight, in spite of Lord Herbert's persuasions. The horse under the Marquis still endeavoured to stem the tide of adversity, but they were fairly beaten, and the day proved disastrous to the Royalists. Two thousand five hundred men were slain on that dreadful day, and twelve hundred prisoners were made. Of the slain the vast majority were the unfortunate Welsh. A large pit was dug, and friends and foes found a common grave on Tewkesbury Plain. The prisoners, saving such as were officers, having been reproved for their conduct and made sensible and sorry for their error, were sent home in peace. The vanquished Marquis, the Lord Herbert, and others, with what remained of their forces, beat a retreat, crossed the Severn, and got again into South Wales; while the Earl of Stamford returned to Hereford.[2]

Notwithstanding this great disaster, the Marquis of Hertford, in less than a fortnight, viz., on the 27th November, attempts an attack upon Hereford.

[1] True News of Herefordshire. (K. P. 83—28.) See vol. ii., Document x., p. 38.
[2] *Ibid.*

Earl Stamford's force on this occasion only numbered some fifteen hundred strong. Here, again, the unfortunate Welsh were most thoroughly beaten, and, it is said, that something like another two thousand of them fell upon this occasion. This defeat was as thorough in its nature as the other, and were it not for the minute circumstantiality of my authority,[1] I should be inclined to look upon it as a different account of the former transaction. If they are accounts of distinct conflicts, it is clear that the Marquis of Hertford recruited, while in South Wales, a body of nearly twelve thousand men, which exceeds even the rumour of ten thousand, to which allusion has already been made.

The Earl of Stamford soon after this quitted Herefordshire for Gloucester, where his presence was needed, seeing that that city was perfectly naked. Whereupon Herefordshire fell into the hands of the Royalists.[2]

Leaving the Marquis of Hertford repairing his losses, we will now take a glance at matters in North Wales and the borders.

When Charles left Shrewsbury for Edgehill, he drafted away with him all the available forces, leaving the town in a perfectly undefended state, without any pretence of a garrison, and entrusting everything to the loyalty of its inhabitants.[3] Shortly after, however, Sir Francis Ottley was made Governor, and under his influence important preparations were made for the security of the town. The castle

---

[1] True Relation of a most blessed Victory obtained against the Marquis of Hertford. (K. P. 83—44.)

[2] Somer's Tracts, vol. v., 506.

[3] Clarendon's Rebellion, ii., 510.

walls were repaired; the gates and town walls put in order; a body of men trained for its defence, and a watch kept at night. The Town Council voted a sum of £200 towards purchasing two pieces of ordnance.[1] This activity of the Royalists silenced the large and by no means uninfluential party within the town, who were decided friends of the Parliament. So much so, that Arthur Trevor, writing on the last day of December, 1642, says of the people of Shrewsbury, that they were "one and all his Majesty's good subjects."[2]

Chester was left in the same defenceless state. There, too, similar activity soon characterised the King's party. Mr. Orlando Bridgman, son of the Bishop there,—he who after the Restoration became Lord Chancellor,—assumed the governorship of the city, and rode imperiously over the quiet and timid civic authorities.[3] Lord Kilmurry, Mr. Francis Gamul, one of the aldermen, and more especially the Lady Cholmondeley, without whom, it was said, nothing could be done, gave influence and power to this dictatorship; and in face of the danger which threatened the open city, owing to its nearness to Manchester, where the Parliamentary party was very strong, probably the shopkeepers of Chester were rather glad than otherwise to see some steps being taken to defend the town, were it only from plundering, and without being inclined to question the authority. Mud walls were cast up, the walls —which are yet the most perfect in England—were repaired, and other preparations carried out to secure

[1] Owen and Blakeway's Shrewsbury.
[2] Trevor to Ormond, December 31, 1642. Carte's Collection of Letters, i., p. 14.
[3] The Unfaithfulness of the Cavaliers, &c. (K. P. 89–37.) See vol. ii., Document xiii., p. 46.

the city against any sudden attack. The Commissioners of Array were also recruiting men for its defence. By the 17th of December they had got into the city three hundred horse and six hundred foot.[1]

These preparations were not at all uncalled for, for Cheshire was threatened with considerable danger. Sir William Brereton, one of the members for the county, was known to be in London forming an army for the reduction of that county to the obedience of the Parliament. Manchester, "the very London of these parts," as was said by Arthur Trevor, was also ready at any time to aid any attempt in that direction. And as it was clear, that even if these within would be able to defend the city, such combined forces would devastate the whole county, and bring ruin upon those who had quitted their houses in the county to seek refuge in the town. A desire for pacification began to show itself, and was taken up with energy. Through the solicitation of Sir Richard Wilbraham, whose sympathies were for the Parliament, a meeting was arranged to take place between representatives of the Commissioners of Array and of the Committee of the Militia to discuss terms of neutrality. The meeting came off, after some slight hitch, at Bunbury, and an agreement was arranged, whereby it was articled that there should be an absolute cessation of arms; that the prisoners on both sides should be released; the fortifications of Chester, Nantwich, Slopford, and Knutsford, demolished; that goods which had been plundered be restored; and that both parties should obtain

---

[1] The latest Printed News. (K. P. 88—8.)

the ratification of the Articles from the King and the Parliament respectively. Lord Kilmurry and Mr. Orlando Bridgman represented the Royalists, while Mr. Marbury and Mr. Henry Mainwaring attended on behalf of the Deputy-Lieutenants.¹ This agreement, concluded on the 23rd of December, on grounds which commend themselves to all who have an aversion to the shedding of human blood, was, however, impracticable under the circumstances. There could be no *imperium in imperio* at this desperate season; and Cheshire, if it sought the protection must bear the burdens of government. The Parliament, without any hesitation, repudiated the agreement as inexpedient, and characterised its adoption as setting a bad example. What the King thought of it I know not. Arthur Trevor, who was always about the Court, and well posted in the views which prevailed there, confessed that he "did not like this kind of measuring out of treason by the month," alluding probably to the provisional character of the Articles.

Very different in their conduct were the Salopians. The friends of the King there boldly declared their resolution to stand by him and to defend themselves. The leading men of the county subscribed an agreement, whereby they engaged themselves to raise and maintain troops for the defence of the King and their country; and nominated Sir Vincent Corbet as commander-in-chief of such forces.² This was on the 20th of December. By the end of that month they had raised two thousand dragoons for that service.³

---

¹ Harl. MSS. 2135, fol. 87. Vol. ii., Document xii., p. 44.
² Wiltshire's Resolution, &c. (K. P. 86—22.) Vol. ii., Document xi., p. 42.
³ Arthur Trevor's letter (already quoted) to Marquis of Ormond.

CHAPTER IV.

1643.

The state of parties at the beginning of 1643—Sir W. Brereton in Cheshire—Defeats Sir Thomas Aston and the Chester cavaliers at Nantwich—A skirmish at Torperley—The battle of Middlewich—Sir Thomas Aston routed—The dispute between Lord Herbert and the Marquis of Hertford settled—The Marquis quits Wales with his Welsh army—Arrives at Burford—Suggests an attack upon Cirencester—That town taken and plundered—Aided by Rupert, summons Gloucester, which refuses to yield—The Lord Herbert raises an army and appears before Gloucester—Is totally routed, and main body of his army made prisoners by Sir William Waller—Clarendon's strictures on the disaster—Waller pursues the Welsh but fails to overtake them, takes Chepstow and Monmouth, and has to cut his way back to Gloucester through Prince Maurice's army sent to encompass him—Waller takes Hereford—A glimpse of imperial affairs during the spring—Reading is taken by the Parliament—Brereton's successes in Cheshire—The Lord Capel, the King's Lieut.-General for that county and North Wales is dismayed—The Earl of Denbigh and Colonel Mytton—Conflicts between Capel and Brereton—Sir Thomas Myddelton appointed by the Parliament Lieut.-General of North Wales—Earl of Carbery in Pembrokeshire and Carmarthenshire—Is impeached—Others implicated—Parliamentary reverses in the West—Waller defeated—Bristol taken—Gloucester besieged—Consternation in London—Raising of siege of Gloucester—Help of the Scotch—The Covenant—Difficulties of Lord Capel—Sir Thomas Myddelton arrives in Wales—Wem garrisoned by the Parliament—Naval fight at Milford Haven—The Earl Carbery garrisons Tenby and Haverfordwest,—Declaration of loyalty by Mayor and Aldermen of Haverfordwest—Battle at Wem—Valour of the women—Lord Capel worsted—Brereton and Myddelton enter North Wales—Take Holt, Wrexham, Hawarden, Flint, Mostyn, and Holywell—Chester blocked—Denbigh Castle summoned—Cessation of arms in Ireland—Irish forces land in North Wales—Brereton and Myddelton obliged to retreat into Cheshire—Siege of Hawarden—North Wales freed from the Roundheads—Distress of Brereton.

THE position of the Royalists in Wales and the Marches at the beginning of 1643 was such as to satisfy the staunchest of the King's adherents. They had everything their own way nearly. At Raglan Castle the Marquis of Worcester had placed a strong garrison, while the Lord Herbert and his forces swept the Forest of Dean without molestation. Hereford was garrisoned for the King, with Sir William Coningsby for its governor, backed by all the influence of Lord Scudamore of Holme Lacy. In Cardiff Castle William Herbert of the Friars had placed a garrison. Sir Michael Wodehouse occupied Ludlow. Through the exertions of Sir Francis Ottley and the Shropshire cavaliers, Shrewsbury was made secure. Nearly every post on the banks of the Severn was occupied. The Castles of Shrawarden, Caus, and Apley, were all manned. At Oswestry, Col. Lloyd of Llanwrda headed a force strong enough to command that important pass. The passages across the Dee were all in their hands. And Chester completed this chain, which was sufficient in all reason to protect Wales in its loyalty. Ruthin, which belonged to Sir Thomas Myddelton, and Chirk Castle also, were possessed by the Royalists. Under the influence of John Williams, once Bishop of Lincoln, then Lord Keeper, and now Archbishop of York, but debarred from the exercise of his spiritual functions by the whirligig of events, Conway Castle from nearly a ruin was made strong and defensible; while the zeal of Mr. Thomas Bulkeley of Baron Hill rendered Beaumaris Castle a tower of strength.

For the Parliament, on the other hand, there was anything but an encouraging prospect in Wales. Pembroke was the only town in the Principality which had actually declared for the Parliament. That town appears to have been leavened with disaffection to a certain extent. John Poyer, the Mayor, was pre-eminently the most active at this place for the Parliament: a man of considerable public spirit, who had risen from the ranks to fill the most important civic post in his native town; and given somewhat, if any credit is to be given to the stories of the time, to his cups and Presbyterianism. He found an able coadjutor in William Laugharne, a son of John Laugharne of St. Brides, who, having served as a page to the Earl of Essex, made choice of a military life for his calling. These were backed, too, by Sir Hugh Owen of Orielton, the Member for Haverfordwest, whose influence at Pembroke was considerable. In Cheshire, however, the Parliamentary party were strong enough to declare themselves, and were taking active measures to prepare for the conflict. Nantwich was their headquarters. All around that town resided men of position and influence whose sympathies were entirely with the Parliament. Some of them had suffered for manifesting a little kindly interest in poor ear-cropped Prynne. But foremost in influencing these was Sir William Brereton, one of the knights for the shire. He having received a commission from the Parliament, had been during that Christmastide engaged in raising forces in London; and was, towards the middle of January, said to be on his way to his native county. This gave courage to his friends. The cavaliers hearing of it, and thinking to steal a march upon him, sent out from Chester a large force, commanded by Sir Thomas Aston, for the purpose of capturing Nantwich and of dispersing the Roundheads there. But in this they were foiled, for Sir William being on the 28th come to Congleton heard of their intention, and lost not t in pushing forward to the assistan

His drakes or quarter-cannons settled the day. The cavaliers beat a disorderly retreat, in which a large number of them were made prisoners, while a large accession of horse and arms fell into the hands of the victors. Sir Thomas Aston with difficulty got away, while Sir Vincent Corbet (he who had been nominated to the command of the Shropshire forces in the engagement of the leading men of that county, which has been already referred to), crawled away on all-fours lest he should be discovered. Brereton, whose letters show him to be a man of great religious fervour, acknowledged his indebtedness for the victory, not to the power of flesh, but to the Lord of Hosts, and set apart a day of solemn thanksgiving. After which they fell to the managing of the weighty affairs of the county—in calling out the militia, summoning all persons between sixteen and sixty years of age, and in casting up mud walls and digging trenches around Nantwich.[1]

In managing these "weighty affairs" they were often disturbed, for the Royalists in Chester were by no means cowed with the defeat they had experienced. Even within a few days after, all the horse and foot in the city, which had been brought together by the Earl of Derby, Viscount Molyneux, Viscount Cholmondeley, Earl Rivers, Sir John Savage, and others, set out towards Nantwich under the command of Alderman Edwards. They did no good, but returned with some loss after a fruitless outing.[2] Why an alderman should have been appointed to the command is a mystery—Alderman Edwards of all persons, for his name was always associated with

shire's Successe. (K. P. 99—6.) See vol. ii., Document xiv., p. 49.
[2] 25, fol. 315.

CHAP. IV.
1648.

those who had a tendency to befriend the other side.

During January, Col. Mostyn and others brought into Chester a large number of Welshmen to assist in the defence of the city. Hot-headed and enthusiastic, like Welshmen of all time, they were eager for a fray; and finding no chance of fighting a real enemy, they gave vent to their loyalty in an attack upon a house called the Nunnery or Noons —the town-house, in fact, of Sir William Brereton. They sacked the house, smashed the windows, stripped off the lead and gutters, carried away the furniture, selling whatever was saleable for a small value, and committing to the flames what they could not so dispose of. Their officers had no hand in this outrage, and were powerless to control them. And they did not desist from this wanton act until Sir Orlando Bridgman and some of the city officials interfered. It is to the credit of the city authorities that they caused to be taken back all they could discover.[1] In the city at this time lived many who were suspected of having strong sympathies with the Parliament. Their houses were searched, such arms as were found therein were seized, and they themselves, in many instances, placed in custody within the castle. Many of these went quietly out of the city, leaving house and home, rather than sacrifice their consciences. They were gladly welcomed at Nantwich.

It was not often that the Royalists now ventured out of Chester, for their opponents were daily gaining strength and confidence; and whenever they did venture outside the walls, they seldom

[1] Harl. MSS., *supra*.

returned without a skirmish. On the 21st of February a conflict of this kind occurred at Torperley, a village midway between Chester and Nantwich. Warrants had been issued by Sir Wm. Brereton, summoning all persons liable to serve on the militia to meet at Torperley on that day. The Commissioners of Array, on learning this, sent out their warrants also, calling a meeting at the same time and place. The day came, and with it brought to quiet Torperley the Array, represented by a large body of soldiers under the command of Sir Nicholas Byron (whom Charles had lately sent down to Chester to be Governor there). The militia, too, fifteen hundred strong, under Brereton, came betimes to the place. The Royalists came first, and choose their ground to advantage. The militia posted themselves on Tilston Hill. The fighting which followed produced no other result than obstructing the recruiting which was contemplated.[1]

The issue of the next battle between these hostile bodies was not so undecided. By the beginning of March the whole of the salt district of Cheshire was in the hands of the Parliament; and great preparations were being made to render the principal places secure by fortifications. On the 11th of that month the largest force which had yet issued out of Chester came to Middlewich. They were exceedingly strong in foot soldiers, most of whom were Welshmen, under the command of Col. Ellis[2] and Major Gilmore. Sir Thomas Aston

[1] Cheshire's Success, *supra.*
[2] Col. Ellis was of Gwesnewydd, near Wrexham. By command of the King he had taken possession of Chirk Castle in 1642, which was soon afterwards placed under the governorship of Sir Thomas Hanmer.

CHAP. IV.
1642.

commanded the horse. The next day was Sunday. Partial as was the Puritan to a strict observance of the Sabbath, even in his view there were times when work and not repose was to be. And it was so now, the urgency of the occasion did not permit of delay, and Sir William Brereton occupied himself the whole day in preparing for the morrow, when an attack was a certainty, and in annoying the enemy by frequent alarms. Sir William was then at Northwich, superintending the fortifications going on there. The body of his forces was at Nantwich. Messages were sent thither ordering them to join with the Nantwich forces on Monday morning. The battle, however, had been raging for some hours before these appeared. When they did come they brought victory with them. The Royalists could not stand the attack of the reinforcement, and were driven back from the streets into the church, where they were "wedged up like billets in a wood-pile, no one man at his arms." All in the church were captured. No less than five hundred prisoners were made: among them were Colonel Ellis, Major Gilmore, some eleven captains, and a number of other officers. Horses, arms, and ammunition in great quantity fell into the hands of the Parliamentarians. The Royalists were utterly routed. Sir Thomas Aston gives a graphic picture of the entire want of discipline, if not even the cowardice, of the men engaged. The footmen, principally Welsh, dropped their arms

Being taken prisoner at this battle of Middlewich, he continued in custody until the September following. After his release he was placed by Lord Capel chief in command in Counties of Denbigh and Flint, and raised a force of 1,200 men.—*Pennant's Tour in Wales.*

and ran away without an attempt to fight. The guns were quitted without an effort to save them. The horse were not of any use, because the fighting was in the streets, and they took advantage of the cross lanes, and made off. In the face of such a disaster, Sir Thomas Aston was powerless. He tried again and again to rally his men; but, as he quaintly puts it, they had "gone past recall." Chagrined and weary, the unfortunate commander rode to Whitchurch for help, but help there was none, for the few dragoons stationed there were in daily fear of a surprise, and the trained bands had been disbanded. The Parliamentary party by this victory obtained a firm footing in Cheshire. Chester, however, remained in the hands of the Royalists, though its position at this juncture must have been one of extreme peril.[1]

The Marquis of Hertford, having as we have already seen had his march to Oxford retarded by the Earl of Stamford, and having moreover suffered a most ignominious defeat, retreated to South Wales to repair his losses and to levy fresh recruits. The dispute between him and Lord Herbert had grown so ugly towards Christmas that the King sent Arthur Trevor down to Monmouthshire to try to make it up between them. Writing to the Marquis of Ormond, Trevor states that on coming to them "he found an old sore but ill-drawn up. I ventured upon a small piece of surgery, and do now hope I have taken away the bone that was between them, or, leastwise, so sealed it that they may

---

[1] Sir William Brereton's account of this battle is given in Cheshire's Successe, *supra*. Sir Thomas Aston's letter is preserved in Harl. MSS., 2135, fol. 93. See vol. ii., Documents xvi. and xvii.

march without much pain on either side."¹ This reference confirms Clarendon's allusion to the quarrel between them. Clarendon attributes it to the insufferable vanity of the Lord Herbert. But I think it was only natural that Lord Herbert should have felt jealous of the intrusion of Hertford into his own immediate neighbourhood. The one objection to Lord Herbert was his religion. He was a Roman Catholic. Charles himself would probably have been glad to grant him a commission. But he and those around him knew too well that if he gave commands and posts to Roman Catholics the Parliament would make use of it as a fearful accusation against him. The Roman Catholics to a man were for the King, because he was known to be liberally disposed towards them, and the Queen professed that faith; while from the Parliament, imbued with the spirit of Puritanism, they had nothing to expect but persecution and extermination. They assisted the King in every possible way. Being as a class wealthy they supplied him with money. And though they could get no position of command in the army, many of their leaders served as volunteers. The Queen, doubtless, did all in her power to prevail upon her husband to grant them commissions; but Charles dared not do so, for many of his Council were as opposed to Roman Catholics as the veriest Puritan in the Kingdom. The case of Lord Herbert was, however, exceptional. He was a personal favourite, his father's wealth was at the service of the King, and his influence had brought thousands to the field to fight for the throne. Who could blame Charles, therefore, for

---

[1] Carte's Collection of Letters, vol. i., p. 14.

appointing the son of the Marquis of Worcester to be Lieutenant-General of South Wales and Monmouthshire? It was probably with the promise of this commission that Arthur Trevor practised his little surgery, so as to enable the rivals "to march without pain on either side." The march of the Marquis of Hertford from Wales took place in the very first week of the new year. Herefordshire now presented no obstruction, so that he might have pushed on to Oxford in that way without any molestation. He, however, marched to Worcester, and thence to Burford, intending to co-operate with the cavaliers in Gloucestershire. Finding that nothing could be done in these parts so long as Cirencester remained garrisoned by the Parliament, he proceeded to Oxford, and laid before the King the desirability of taking that town from the enemy, which he engaged to do if reinforced with an adequate force of dragoons. Rupert and Maurice were ordered to aid him. On the 7th of January they drew up before the town—Rupert and Maurice on the one hand, the dragoons on the other, with some six thousand horse and foot, of whom the majority consisted of Welshmen. The town was summoned, but in vain; and the attack had to be postponed. The Welsh, under the Marquis, went back to Burford, Rupert to Oxford, and Maurice to Farringdon. On the 1st of February they again appeared before Cirencester, and on this occasion they were successful, after a gallant resistance on the part of the little garrison, in winning the town, which, it is said, they most wantonly plundered.[1] "As usual," the Welsh were placed in the front,

[1] Warburton's Prince Rupert, ii., 106.

and had to bear the brunt of the enemy's defence, in which many of them fell, being in that army "a continual sacrifice to the sword."[1]

In the City of Gloucester—the "godly city," as the cavaliers opprobriously, but with great truth, called it,—then garrisoned for the Parliament, and the very Manchester of the South, the news of the loss of Cirencester caused some dismay, which was heightened by the account which they received of the way in which that unfortunate town had been sacked and pillaged: a practice of which Prince Rupert, notwithstanding all the whitewashing of Mr. Warburton, stands too clearly convicted. On the following day the terrible Prince appeared before the City of Gloucester, and summoned it to surrender. Lieut.-Col. Massey, a Cheshire man, was at this time chief in military command in the city —a brave and worthy man, with a strong leaning to Presbyterianism,—who fought valiantly for the Parliament until the conduct of that assembly and those in power drove him to give up that party. And though he was not stedfast in the faith which he at one time professed, his character possesses many traits worthy of admiration. To Prince Rupert's summons, Col. Massey and the Mayor replied that they held the city for the Parliament, and would only deliver it upon an order from that authority. A second summons, in a strain more persuasive, met with no better answer; whereupon the Royalists returned to Cirencester, which they formed into their head-quarters, and whence they were enabled to make many successful sallies,

[1] Somers' Tracts, v. 309.

reducing several places held for the Parliament in the immediate neighbourhood.

Meanwhile, the Lord Herbert, armed with his long-wished-for commission, was assiduously engaged in raising an army of his own. And considering how the country must have been drained by the Marquis of Hertford, it is not without surprise we find that before the middle of February Lord Herbert had collected together a force of about fifteen hundred foot and five hundred horse. These were "well and sufficiently armed," according to Clarendon, and had cost the house of Worcester, it is said, no less than £60,000. About the middle of February Lord Herbert, with this promising army, marched forth, intending to attack Gloucester. The foot he placed under the command of Col. Sir Richard Lawley, and the horse under his brother, the Lord John Somerset, whom Clarendon called a "maiden soldier." At the little village of Coford, in the Forest of Dean, where Col. Burrowes, with a small body of soldiers, aided by the villagers, had a sort of loose garrison for the defence of the Forest, the Welshmen received their "baptism of fire." Against such a force the little garrison played a losing game. They were soon driven from their position and the village taken, but not without serious loss to the victors. Several of their officers were slain, and among them was Sir Richard Lawley, commander of the foot and Major-General for South Wales. The loss of officers was heavy on both sides, while not a single common soldier fell on either side, which the Royalists looked upon as a bad omen. Some forty of the Parliament soldiers were taken prisoners, so that in point

CHAP. IV.
1643.

of numbers the Parliament party had the worst of it. The command of the Royalist foot was next given to Sergeant-Major Sir Jerome, or Jeremiah Brett. In their march through the Forest of Dean they met with no serious opposition after this, and arrived early in March before Gloucester, making their head-quarters at Highnam House, about two miles from the city. Here they made entrenchments and rested, expecting aid from Prince Rupert and Prince Maurice. But the Princes had other matters to attend to just then, so that the Welsh were left pretty much to depend on their own strength, which was in fact very superior to that of the garrison which defended the city. This was practically impotent, comprising scarcely a hundred horse, and not half the number of foot that their besiegers possessed. Consequently, matters were not very promising in the city. However, the timely arrival of Captain John Fiennes with some two hundred horse from Bristol, gave them some encouragement. After this, constant sallies were made, in which the besiegers as a rule came off the worst. While the Welsh were waiting for aid which did not come, swiftly and surely Sir William Waller, a Member of the Commons, who held high military command, was making his way with a large force from London to the West. Having captured Malmesbury, he pretended to march towards Cirencester; but this was only a ruse, for he made instead for the Forest of Dean, and by means of some thirty flat boats, which had been brought all the way from London on carriages for service on the Severn, he managed to cross that river at Frampton Passage unawares to the enemy, and unmolested, though it was done in open day. And thus he was able to transport his whole forces. With a dexterity which cannot but be admired, he advanced through the Forest to Highnam. Before the Welsh were even aware of his approach the whole body under his command appeared in their rear, while the forces in Gloucester, previously warned of Waller's approach, came out of the city and attacked their front. The Welsh, caught as it were in a trap, and surrounded by enemies, were struck with consternation, and without showing any resistance —in all probability, resistance under the circumstances would have been of no avail—they sounded a parley. After a brief negotiation, they surrendered without any conditions whatever, save mere quarter. This was on the 24th day of March. On Lady-Day, the first day of the legal year, near 1,500 men were led captive into Gloucester, and about 500 horses—a number equal to the united strength of Waller and the city. Divers persons of quality were among the prisoners, the most powerful of the gentry of Monmouthshire and Herefordshire being of their number. Even some of the "nine worthies," as those were called who had at the opening of the war sent up from Herefordshire to Parliament a "scandalous remonstrance."[1]

Of this terrible disaster Clarendon writes very bitterly, throwing all the blame upon Lord Herbert. The latter was at Oxford at the time; in truth, he was never with the forces over which he had command, being fonder of intrigues at Court than fighting in the battlefield; while the Lord John Somerset, with three or four troops of horse, kept

[1] Somers' Tracts, v. 310–314. See also Document xix., vol. ii., p. 63.

CHAP. IV.
1643.

all the while at a safe distance from the conflict. Clarendon, being himself at Oxford at the time, doubtless bears true testimony against Lord Herbert; while the fact that Lord John Somerset was not among the prisoners is corroborative of the latter accusation. The noble historian concludes his remarks thus: "This was the end of that mushroom army, which grew up and perished so soon that the loss of it was scarce apprehended at Oxford, because the strength or rather the number was not understood. But if the money which was laid out in the raising, arming, and paying that body of men, which never advanced the King's service in the least degree, had been brought into the King's receipt at Oxford, I am persuaded the war might have been ended the next summer, for I have heard the Lord Herbert say, that these preparations, and the others which by that defeat were rendered useless, had cost above three score thousand pounds." No doubt it did appear to the Royalists a great pity that so much money should have been thrown away; but we may well doubt whether, if the money had been paid into the royal exchequer at Oxford, it would have done any more good to the King's cause than Lord Herbert's venture, which thus terminated in a fiasco before Gloucester.[1]

To the Parliament this was a victory of great consequence. Gloucester was relieved from a most pressing danger, and a fatal blow had been dealt to the finest army which the Principality had yet produced. Gloucester freed, Waller was enabled to set forward to Wales, intending to finally crush the miserable remains of Lord Herbert's army. Before

[1] Clarendon's Rebellion, ii., 522—27.

him the Welsh everywhere fled: quitting their garrisons on his approach. Newnham, Rossbridge, Monmouth and Chepstow, were thus deserted, and Waller triumphantly entered these towns without having occasion to strike a blow. But he was weary of the Welsh ways over the mountains. The natives, accustomed to their rugged hills and ill-conditioned roads, had a great advantage over their pursuers, who were not able to overtake them. Prince Maurice was ordered to pursue Waller, and by hemming him in the rear, while the remainder of Lord Herbert's army stopped his progress in front, to capture him, or at any rate to prevent his return to Gloucester. Waller received timely notice of this; and failing to overtake the Welsh, he determined to make his way back to Gloucester, and, if need be, through the heart of Prince Maurice's army. Having first transported his ordnance and baggage across Awst Passage, he started from Chepstow on the 10th of April, and marched through the Forest. At Newnham he came upon a body of the enemy. These retreated to Little Dean, to which place Waller followed them, and there a hot skirmish ensued: the result being a clear passage for Waller, who thence proceeded to Gloucester, where he arrived in safety, and having sustained but little loss.[1]

Within a fortnight of this, the City of Hereford, which had been for some time a Royalist garrison, under the governorship of Sir William Coningsby, was attacked by Waller. The place was summoned on the 25th of April. The reply was in the

[1] "The victorious and fortunate proceedings of Sir William Waller and his forces in Wales, &c." (K. P. 102—2.) See also Document xx., vol. ii.

usual strain, and an assault was the consequence. The defenders of the city contested stoutly for possession, and made several sallies; but at three o'clock they sounded a parley. Hostages having been exchanged, Col. Herbert Price—Member of Parliament for Brecon, who from the first had drawn his sword for the King,—came forth to negotiate the surrender, and to ask for more honourable terms than mere quarter, which only had been offered them. His mediation, however, did not succeed; though for consolation, he was assured that gentlemen should be treated civilly, ladies honourably, the city and its citizens preserved from plunder. And on these terms the city was surrendered. Many prisoners were made, comprising the leading men of the county. Among these were Lord Scudamore, Sir William Coningsby, five Members of Parliament, and many others of equal distinction: all of whom, except Lord Scudamore, whose parole was accepted, were led captive to Gloucester. Between two and three thousand arms also fell into the hands of the victors; at any rate, so the victors said. But the Royalists do not admit this, and assert that no more than sixty arms were taken: the main body of the soldiers having quitted the city while the treaty was going on.[1]

The extraordinary success which attended Sir William Waller for over two months in these brilliant expeditions, obtained for him the name of "William the Conqueror," and deservedly so, for wherever he came he scattered his enemies before

[1] *Merc. Bellicus*, April 30 (see vol. ii., p. 69), and *Merc. Aulicus* of same date.

him. But his meteor-like appearance, though it dispersed several bands of Royalists, and gave *eclât* to the Parliament's cause, did not produce any lasting effect, for it was not within his power to place garrisons in the towns from which he drove his enemies; so that when he was called away from those parts, nearly all the towns and garrisons of which he had possessed himself fell again into the hands of the Royalists. But the House of Worcester afterwards found greater difficulty to draw men into the King's service. The Welshmen, we hear, would not rise in Monmouthshire, because my Lord Herbert had the command of that county, and professed that they had rather perish than be under the power of a Papist.[1] Ill-success, I think, rather than religious differences, contributed chiefly to destroy the influence of the Raglan family.

While this skirmishing, this marching and counter-marching, was going on in Wales and the Marches, and elsewhere in the provinces, throughout the depth of that winter, the two main armies remained perfectly inactive. Essex near London, and the King at Oxford. Of course, no important result could be expected from provincial warfare, in which only detached bodies of ill-trained men were engaged; still, it afforded good military training to the people, and opportunities to leaders hitherto unknown to show their skill and to win distinction.

About this time, while matters in head-quarters were at a stand still, the Queen returned from Holland, where she had been for the past year negotiating aid, and purchasing arms with the

[1] Secretary Nicholas to Rupert, Oxon, 10th April. Warburton, ii., 161.

CHAP. IV.
1643.

money arising from the crown jewels she had pawned. Barely escaping from the clutches of Admiral Batten, whom the Parliament had deputed to watch her, she landed at Burlington in February, and was escorted to York by Lord Newcastle and a body of troops. Her arrival somewhat awakened both parties from their torpor, while her presence in York soon attracted to that ancient city many of the county gentry, and the Roman Catholics crowded to her court to tender their services. The forces under Newcastle became greatly augmented by volunteers. The Parliament became furious at this open employment of Catholics. Newcastle's army was called "the army of the Papists and of the Queen." But it was of no avail to call names. The aid of the Catholics was too much needed, and was too acceptable to be declined. She attracted many more to her standard. From Scotland came Hamilton and Montrose,—two of the most powerful of the northern nobility,—and from Ireland came the Earl of Antrim, with an offer from the Irish Catholics to form a body to land on the Scottish coast, and then, uniting with the Highlanders which Hamilton and Montrose undertook to raise, to extirpate the Presbyterians. No counsel was too violent for the Queen. She readily accepted every offer of aid, however extreme, and by her untiring energy, she gave to the royal cause in the North a vigour which it had not hitherto possessed, while at the same time she attempted to corrupt some of the Parliament's commanders in those parts. Had it not been for the extraordinary vigilance of the Parliamentary agents, Scarborough and Hull would have been traitorously given up to her: the latter by Sir John Hotham, who at the very outset of the quarrel had refused the King admittance into that town. For this wavering a day of reckoning soon came to pass, and Hotham lost his head for it.

The news of these things naturally created some excitement in London. The friends of peace in Parliament availed themselves of the opportunity, and made one more effort to renew negotiations with the King. The motion was earnestly debated, and rejected by a small majority—of three only. It was only natural that the war party should hesitate to acknowledge their weakness by an act which, if successful, would involve their ruin. Ultimately, however, they gave way; and five Commissioners were sent to Oxford empowered to negotiate with the King for twenty days, first, the question of disbanding both armies, and then the terms of a treaty. One of the five was William Pierpoint, the Member for Much Wenlock, Shropshire—a firm though moderate Parliamentarian. But the King had no desire for peace now; and even if he had, the Queen, whose sway over him was great, had strictly enjoined him not to sanction peace. The negotiations ended fruitlessly—the Commissioners being abruptly recalled to London by an order dated the 15th of April. They quitted Oxford the same day.

The very day the Commissioners returned to Parliament Essex took the field, and opened the real campaign of the year. Hampden and several other officers were anxious he should march at once upon Oxford to besiege the royal head-quarters; but Essex, who was very slow, if not lukewarm, in his employment, hesitated as usual, and sat down instead before Reading — the reduction of which he considered to be of paramount importance. In ten days Reading succumbed. Hampden once more suggested Oxford as the next place to proceed against; but Essex continued obstinate, to the great annoyance of his soldiers, the distrust of the Parliament, and the dissatisfaction of such of the people as had adopted the Parliament's cause. Murmurs were everywhere heard—even to the supplanting of Essex. Several names were mentioned as being better suited to assume the command. The name of Hampden, beloved by the people, was foremost, but he himself had no ambition. The Fairfaxes— father and son—whose vigilance and daring in the presence of weightier forces in the North had won universal admiration, were among the number, as was also the Earl of Manchester, who was energetic in the eastern counties; while blazing with fame from the West came the name of Sir William Waller. But the Earl of Essex could not well be disposed of—any attempt to oust him from command might involve disaster; but what could not be done directly was sought to be effected by indirect means, and by neglect and coldness it was hoped that he would be driven to resign his post. He, however, survived all this—for a time, at least; and before his commission was handed back to the Parliament, as was eventually done, he had at least proved himself an honest man, and had taken part in one brilliant exploit.

The loss of Reading threw Oxford into great alarm—even to such an extent, that it was in contemplation to quit the place at once, and move either westwards to Shrewsbury or Chester, or northwards, for greater security; but the consternation soon subsided, for Essex, as we have seen, did not follow up his success, while the Parliament, torn with many dissensions, discussing trifling matters, and terrified at the discovery of a farce of a plot, did not press him to more active measures.

Coming back from this digression to Wales, we there find Sir William Brereton active in Cheshire, and so far successful that Lord Capel (a worthy man, who had been sent down thither by the King with a commission as Lieutenant-General of Shropshire, Cheshire, and North Wales, to try and repair the messes into which the ill-starred Sir Thomas Aston had brought that county, and whose head-quarters were at Shrewsbury,) tells Prince Rupert, on the 4th of April, that Sir William Brereton is "master of the field in Cheshire," with the exception merely of so much ground as the garrison of Chester commanded; and furthermore, that Brereton was advanced even to Whitchurch: unpleasantly and dangerously near to Lord Capel, wherefore he implores the Prince to come to his aid.[1] But the Prince was then engaged elsewhere—engaged, indeed, presently in an affair which cast gloom all over England, and which deprived the Parliament of one of its most illustrious members, the people of a champion of their rights, and the country of a true patriot. In a skirmish on Chalgrave Common, not far from Oxford, on the 18th of June—a memorable day in English history—John Hampden received his mortal wounds.

[1] Warburton's Prince Rupert, ii., 158.

The Lord Capel, too, was soon destined to see against him in the field other commanders of ability, whose co-operation with Brereton boded ill for his peace. For on the 10th of April, after mature deliberation of the condition of Shropshire, Cheshire, and Warwickshire, the Parliament, by an Ordinance, associated those three counties, nominating the Earl of Denbigh—young Basil Fielding, who in this war had actually taken up arms against his very father, to the great grief and concern of his mother,—to the command of the Warwickshire forces, with headquarters at Coventry; strengthening the arm of Sir William Brereton in Cheshire; and appointing a strong committee for Shropshire, of whom the Earl of Essex was recommended to nominate Sir John Corbet (afterwards member for Shropshire) to be Colonel-General of the forces to be raised in that county.[1] Sir John Corbet is here named as the chief of that committee, but its life and soul was Thomas Mytton—Mytton of Halston. It was through his exertions and the influence of Humphrey Mackworth and Andrew Lloyd that this Ordinance of Parliament was obtained. Mytton, above all others, was instrumental in keeping together the friends of the Parliament in that county, and in neutralizing in a great measure the influence of the Royalists there. And his superlative ability as a military commander, his unswerving fidelity to the Parliament, and his eminent humanity to his enemies, place him in a more favourable light than any man in Wales, or the borders, who took sword in hand during that terrible struggle. But as yet these new allies of Brereton were not in a

---

[1] King's Pamphlets, 118—7. See vol. ii., p. 122 n.

position to take the field, of which the Lord Capel, slow as he was, took advantage. During April, May, and June, continual skirmishes took place between them—each harassing the other as much as possible, but with no important result. Once Lord Capel, at the head of some fifteen hundred men, came before Nantwich, and advanced to the very end of Hospital-street; but the townspeople being forewarned were forearmed, which prevented his lordship from doing anything more important than killing a calf of Mr. Thomas Mainwaring, and stealing some hay from a convenient barn.

> The Lord Capel, with a thousand and a half,
> Came to Barton Cross, and there they killed a calf;
> And staying there until the break of day,
> They took to their heels and fast they ran away.

The other side made many sallies, too: some successful, others fruitless, while one was nearly disastrous. Sir Thomas Hanmer had placed a strong garrison at Hanmer, which, though geographically in the County of Flint, lies in a strip of land which cuts deeply into Cheshire and Shropshire. By some false intelligence, Sir William Brereton had been led to believe that there was a good store of booty at that place easy to be got at. Believing this, Capt. Bulkeley, with a party of horse and some other companies, set out from Nantwich for that place, and ventured even further into the enemies' quarter, where they were met by Sir Richard Willis, Capel's Major-General, at the head of a party of Welshmen, who lay in ambush for them. The result was bad for the Nantwich troops. Many of them were slain. One account puts the killed at a hundred, while the number of prisoners and wounded more

CHAP. IV.
1643.

than decimated the beguiled troops. A Scotch Lieutenant-Colonel named Flagge, and the Reverend Capt. Sankey or Zanchy, Brereton's Chaplain, whom *Aulicus* calls a "little Pope," were among the captives. Burghall, the Puritan minister of Acton Church, near Nantwich, whose diary of the war is a most interesting document, says: "This was said to be the worst day's work the Nantwich soldiers did from the beginning of the war."[1] In the breeches of one of the prisoners was found the surplice of Hanmer Church.[2]

Presently, too, another powerful commander threatened further uneasiness to Lord Capel. On the 11th of June, the Parliament passed an Ordinance appointing Sir Thomas Myddelton, the Member for the County of Denbigh, to be Sergeant-Major-General for the six counties of North Wales.[3] Sir Thomas Myddelton, or Middleton, as his name was spelt in almost all the old Civil War papers, was of Chirk Castle, and a son of Sir Thomas Myddelton, alderman and merchant of London—whose brother was the celebrated Sir Hugh Myddelton, the greatest benefactor of London, who brought the New River to the metropolis, and who also sought to develope the mineral resources of Wales, being the first to work the lead and silver mines of Cardiganshire. Alderman Sir Thomas Myddelton was Lord Mayor of London in 1614. He purchased Chirk Castle, and settled it upon his son—our Sir Thomas—upon his marriage, who thereupon came to dwell there, acquiring from his wealth a leading

[1] Burghall's Providence Improved. See also Certain Informations, No. 24 (K. P. 116, § 1), and *Merc. Aulicus*, 25th week (K. P. 116—8.)
[2] *Aulicus*, 26th week, p. 339.
[3] Husband's Collection; Commons' Journals.

position in the county, and great influence, which he made use of for the benefit of his country, encouraging its industries, and doing all in his power to promote the moral advancement and enlightenment of its inhabitants. In conjunction with Rowland Heylin, alderman of London, whose family I have already incidentally shown to have come from the Principality, he bore the expense of printing the first popular edition of the Bible in the Welsh language. The Bible had been translated into Welsh and printed in the time of Queen Elizabeth, but the copies were exceedingly scarce—if, in fact, not strictly confined to the churches and parochial chapels. The people as yet had not obtained the privilege of purchasing cheap copies, and the credit of promoting a popular edition of the Bible in Welsh is due to Sir Thomas Myddelton and Alderman Heylin,[1] from which I think it can be fairly presumed that he was inclined to Puritanism and opposed to the pretensions which were put forward by the high Episcopalians about this time. He was also a conscientious opponent of the encroachments of the Crown; and at the very outset of the rupture between the King and Parliament—he being then a Member for Denbighshire — he gave his adherence and support to the Parliament, and used all his influence against the King, both in London and in his native county. It was because of this, but more especially on account of a menacing letter which he sent to his countrymen in December, 1642, to submit to and assist the Parliament, that the King sent orders for the Shropshire forces to seize upon Chirk Castle, which was done in January,

[1] Rowland's Welsh Bibliography.

1643, by Colonel Ellis of Gwesnewydd, near Wrexham, and about a hundred soldiers; and Sir John Watts was placed Governor thereof with a garrison. From the possession of his home, though he knocked once or twice violently at its gates, the worthy knight was kept for a long time. Ruthin Castle, also, which belonged to him, was kept from him in the same way.

Sir Thomas's commission from the Parliament was, as I have already stated, dated the 11th of June; but many circumstances, especially the slow progress of his recruiting in London, and the want of money, delayed for a while his setting out for the Principality, and allowed some respite to the Lord Capel: for the same causes also postponed the appearance of the Earl of Denbigh and the active Colonel Mytton.

In Pembrokeshire, and also in Carmarthenshire, the Royalists were busy in the spring of this year. The Earl of Carbery had been some time before appointed the King's chief commander in the western counties of South Wales, and was evidently striving to carry out his commission by promoting the royal cause. In this he appears to have been aided by several others, notably by Sir John Stepney of Prendergast, the Member for Haverfordwest, by Mr. Roger Lort of Stackpole Court, and by the Archdeacon of Carmarthen—Archdeacon Rudd, whose sermons were probably strongly condemnatory of the Parliament. So active were these that we find their conduct the subject of discussion in Parliament on the 19th of April. With much unanimity the House of Commons voted that the Earl of Carbery should be impeached for high treason, "for actual levying war against the King and Parliament," as the Parliament were pleased quaintly to call themselves. The impeachment was ordered to be prepared by Mr. White, the Member who appears to have brought the matter before the assembly. There were two of that name sent to the Long Parliament. One was for Rye—he was a Royalist—the other for Southwark, and this was probably the Mr. White who had the preparation of the impeachment entrusted to him. Whether he was in any way connected with the Whites of Pembrokeshire I have no means of ascertaining. "Baronet Stepney" was voted incapable to sit any longer as a Member of the House in the then Parliament; and Mr. Roger Lort and Archdeacon Rudd were ordered to be forthwith sent for as delinquents—a comprehensive term, including all who were in any way opposed to the Parliament. All deputy-lieutenants and justices of the peace were commanded to be aiding in their apprehension, and even the only Parliament ship in the Haven was to be employed to bring up the delinquents. This single ship was not of sufficient power to maintain due authority over that important Haven, and the chief offence of the accused persons was that they were striving to construct a fort for the King at Milford Haven —a scheme which alarmed the friends of the Parliament at Pembroke, whose letter to Mr. White originated these weighty discussions at Westminster.[1] I do not think the impeachment of the Earl of Carbery was proceeded with—indeed, it would have been absurd to do so seeing that he was beyond their power. All four continued faithful to the

[1] Commons' Journals, under date 19th April.

King for some time after this; but I think all of them by-and-by washed their hands of the royal cause, and abided by what seemed to be the dispensation of Providence, or, what at any rate was the same, the luck of war.

Elsewhere, during the summer of 1643, the affairs of Parliament were in a deplorable state. The Royalists obtained many signal victories, and the Parliamentarians sustained disastrous losses. With the death of Hampden in the only skirmish which the Earl of Essex with his army attempted, commenced the ill-fortune of the Parliament. After this their main army melted away. Fairfax was defeated in the North by the Earl of Newcastle, Hotham was only just prevented from betraying the strong garrison of Hull to the Queen, and the eastern counties, where as yet Royalism had obtained no footing, was threatened by the Earl of Newcastle. But the crowning disasters were those which they suffered in the West. The tide had now turned against Sir William Waller, and his progress was no longer one of conquest. He had set forth to the West early in the summer with all the confidence and the prestige which his success in the spring had given him; but Sir Ralph Hopton, Sir Bevil Grenville, and the Marquis of Hertford were too many for him. At Lansdown, July 5th, and at Roundaway Heath, Wiltshire, July 13th, the energy of the cavaliers, the valour and prowess of the Cornish soldiers, carried everything before them. Demoralization seized the Parliament troops. Garrison after garrison was surrendered to the Royalists without any resistance. Taunton, Bridgwater, Bath, and Bristol had all given in before the end of July.

Bristol, the metropolis of the West, the second city in the kingdom, had hitherto been true to the Parliament; but now, at the mere summons of Rupert, it surrendered itself without an effort, through the weakness or cowardice, if not both, of its Governor, Sir Nathaniel Fiennes. At the siege of Bristol the Royalist ranks contained many Welshmen, some of whom held important commissions, especially in the foot forces. Sir Edward Stradling of St. Donat's, Lieut.-Col. John Stradling, Colonel John Owen of Cleneney, Colonel Herbert, probably of Cardiff, Major Edward Williams, Capt. Lloyd, Lieut.-Colonel Thelwall, of the Denbighshire family of that name, and others, were among them; while of the common soldiers it is said the Welsh counted more than five thousand.[1] The King's prospects were better now than they had been ever since the beginning of the war. Some differences between Prince Rupert and the Marquis of Hertford, and the necessity to settle Bristol, brought the King thither from Oxford early in August. On the critical question, "What next?" the Council of War was divided. The war party were eager for going to London; others, wishing for some rest, and to gain time, were for besieging Gloucester; and in support of this view, it was said that the Welsh forces, considerable in point of numbers, were willing, nay, even eager to attack Gloucester, against which, I have seen it stated, that they had always a grievance,[2] but refused positively to pass beyond the Severn. Besides, Captain William Legge[3] spread abroad a report that Colonel Massey,

CHAP. IV.
1643.

[1] Warburton's Prince Rupert, ii, 237.
[2] Somers' Tracts, v. 310.
[3] A great friend of Prince Rupert, and ancestor of the Earl of Dartmouth.

the Governor of the city, was ready on any pretence to deliver up that city to the King. There was not the slightest foundation for this imputation upon the faithfulness of Massey to his trust, and his conduct throughout the siege which followed is inconsistent with this. The siege was determined upon, and the Welsh, now under the command of Sir William Vavasour,—for the Lord Herbert, conscious of his unpopularity on account of his religion, had resigned,—were ordered to advance upon Gloucester.[1] On the 10th of August the royal forces, commanded by the King in person, occupied the heights overlooking the city, the only defence of which was a small garrison of fifteen hundred men, besides the inhabitants. A summons to surrender was sent, with offers of pardon to all such as should yield. Accompanying the trumpeters were Philpott, Somerset herald, and George Owen, York herald—George Owen of Whitechurch, Pembrokeshire, an eminent Welsh antiquary and genealogist, a member of the Henllys family of that name. From the city came forth two lean-faced men, whose only answer was that the "godly city," as they called it, would not yield. The cavaliers would have scoffed at these sour-faced Puritans had they not been restrained by the more dignified bearing of Charles himself, who merely told them, after hearing their message, "If you expect help you are deceived; for Waller is extinct, and Essex cannot come." The warning was taken back to the city, but the citizens and the small garrison there resolved not to yield, placing their reliance on a Power higher and abler to help the faithful than the arm of flesh.

[1] Warburton's Rupert, ii., 272—274; Clarendon's Rebellion, iv., 181.

Meanwhile London was in consternation, and the Parliament almost in extremity. Commissioners were dispatched to Scotland to pray for help to maintain the Protestant religion, to which, by-and-by, the Scotch assent. And what was of more pressing urgency, the trained bands of the city were brought forth to serve under the Earl of Essex, to go to the relief of Gloucester, which still held out most bravely, frustrating all the attempts of the besiegers. For a certain number of days, while these preparations were being made, all the shops in London were closed. On the 26th of August, Essex set out amid the God-speeds of the entire metropolis, whose fate was now supposed to be linked up with his. For ten days—a long time for so short a journey—his march continued along muddy roads, through continuous rain, and on the 5th of September he reached the top of Prestbury Hill, some five miles from Gloucester, to find the King's quarters deserted and in flames, and the siege of the city raised. Entering the city with ample provisions, the Earl received the heartfelt thanks of those whom he had saved, while he in his turn acknowledged the valour of the soldiers and citizens which had preserved the city, and had been the salvation of the Parliament. Having accomplished his mission, Essex returned towards London, but was met at Newbury by the enemy, who had got thither in advance of him. After a desperate fight he found the road clear and pushed on to London. The loss which the Royalists sustained at Newbury was severe. Lord Falkland, the most upright and honourable adviser Charles had, whose honesty and integrity was unsavoury to the cavaliers, was killed in his clean shirt. Lord

CHAP. IV.
1643.

Carnarvon, beloved by the soldiers, and Lord Sunderland, a young man of great promise, were also among the slain. "This steady march to Gloucester and back again, by Essex, was the chief feat that he did during the war: a considerable feat, and very characteristic of him, the slow-going, inarticulate, indignant, somewhat elephantine man."[1]

While Essex was before Gloucester the negotiations with the Scotch were perfected. Under the name of a "Solemn League and Covenant," a modified form of the original Scotch Covenant, a political and religious treaty welding both countries together in one bond of union for the defence of a common cause, was voted by the Scotch Assembly, and sanctioned by the English Parliament. On the 25th of September, in the Church of St. Margaret's, Westminster, all the Members of the House of Commons then present, standing with heads uncovered and hands uplifted to Heaven, took the Covenant, first verbally, then in writing. "A very solemn Covenant and vow of all the people, of the awfulness of which we, in these days of custom-house oaths and loose regardless talk, cannot form the smallest notion."[2] Two hundred and twenty members signed the Covenant. Of those with whose actions I am chiefly concerned I note the following, viz.:—Sir Thomas Myddelton, Sir John Corbet, Sir William Lewis, and Philip lord Herbert.[3] This Covenant was soon after administered to all the adherents of the Parliament throughout the Kingdom. It was the condition upon which the Scotch promised their assistance.

[1] Carlyle's Letters of Cromwell, pt. ii., Letter xvi.
[2] Ibid. Letter xvii.
[3] Commons' Journals.

Meantime, Lord Capel was having a busy time of it, and a difficult one, in Shropshire, for that much oppressed county, distressed by the heavy exactions which had been suffered by it, was in a state of chronic disaffection. The produce of the surrounding country was exhausted by the soldiers, and the taxation was extremely burdensome. These heavy burdens he levied also over all North Wales, and his "pressing" of Welshmen to the service, hindering them from "their manufactures of cottons and frieze," was naturally distasteful to the country people.[1] And what was more galling, was that they had meekly to bear all this without even the sympathy of anybody. Indeed, the Parliamentary papers taunted them with having brought it all upon themselves, "for both by messages and by letters they invited the cavaliers to come from York unto them, received them with joyful acclamations and ringing of bells, caressed them with feasts and banquets, supplied them with clothes, with money, horses and arms, and formed them into a considerable army of some thousands; whereas, at their first arrival in those parts, the cavaliers were but a few gleanings of despicable and necessitous plebeians in Yorkshire." Moreover, the money raised under colour of paying the soldiers was spent, not in providing the soldiers with necessaries, for free quarter was enforced upon them, but upon himself (Lord Capel) and the cavaliers at Oxford.[2] Coldness in the country and demoralization in the army prevailed at a time when the position of the Royalists in these parts was threatened with no ordinary danger. For on the

[1] Certain Informations, No. 26, 10—17 July. (K. P. 117–17).
[2] Ibid, No. 31, 14—21 August. (K. P. 122—24.)

CHAP. IV.
1643.

night of the 10th of August, Sir Thomas Myddelton with his forces from London, and seven great pieces of ordnance, four cases of drakes, and above forty carriages of ammunition, came to Nantwich, where he was joined by Sir William Brereton, who had just arrived from a successful siege against a strongly-fortified house of Mr. Giffard, a Papist, at Chillington, not far from Stafford. From Nantwich a party went to lay siege to Eccleshall Castle, a garrison of the King. This was deemed of some importance, and the Lord Capel, with Col. Hastings and the Staffordshire Royalists, set out to raise the siege. News of this coming to Nantwich on the 29th of August, Brereton, leaving Sir Thomas Myddelton behind, proceeded to meet them. But he was not in time to prevent the relief of the castle, though in time to frighten away the cavaliers, whose retreat was so hasty that they omitted to take with them the body of the Bishop of Lichfield who had just died there. The place was stormed: a breach was made. A parley followed, and the castle, with all the provisions which had just been brought in, and forty barrels of beer, and much plate and other wealth to the value of £10,000, fell into the hands of Brereton, who returned to Nantwich laden with booty. On Tuesday, the 4th of September, Brereton and Myddelton set out for Drayton, intending for Shropshire. They here summoned a muster of the whole county. The Parliamentarians came in well through the influence of Col. Mytton, and on the following Tuesday, September 11th, they marched to Wem, seized the town, and settled a garrison there under the command of Col. Mytton. This was the first garrison the Parliament established in Shropshire, and this little town continued for some time their head-quarters in that county.[1]

Occasional glimpses of South Wales at this time shows us the Earl of Carbery busy in the western counties, summoning the gentry, calling forth the trained bands, raising volunteers, and, on the whole, getting on as smoothly as possible, for he has but little opposition. He is aided, too, by some men-of-war sent over from Bristol since the seizure of that city by the Royalists. These had arrived in Milford Haven early in August. The sea around was, however, scoured by the Parliament ships, under the command of Capt. Swanley, Admiral of these seas under the Earl of Warwick. Great vigilance was shown by those in command of the vessels appointed for that purpose. About the end of July a Hamburgh vessel, coming from Rochelle in France, and intended, as it was said, for the relief of the rebels in Ireland, was driven on shore near St. David's Head, and there captured; but the voyagers who sailed in it, supposed to be Jesuits, got on shore, and hid themselves in Pembrokeshire. Hearing of this, Capt. William Smith, Swanley's Vice-Admiral, on board the *Swallow* set in for Milford Haven, which he entered on the 7th of August. His object was to secure the apprehension of the fugitives by a "Hue and Cry." On his entry he was informed that two Bristol ships had entered just before him, one of them laden with much treasure, which the merchants of Bristol had placed in it for safety during the siege, but which had been faithlessly made over to the cavaliers. Capt. Smith at once resolved to

[1] Burghall's Providence Improved; Owen and Blakeway's Shrewsbury, i., 488; Ormerod's Cheshire, iii., 225.

give these fight, and all the more resolutely because he ascertained that the officers in command had summoned on board many of the gentry, informing them of the King's great successes in the West, and endeavouring to induce them to give in their adherence to the King, threatening them, moreover, with fearful reprisals if recalcitrant. All these "bravadoes of a proud insulting enemy, grounded neither on judgment or religion," were soon ended by Smith's appearance, for after a parley, in which the Royalists made an insignificant attempt to save themselves, the two vessels were duly taken under his protection by Capt. Smith, who next bestirred himself in causing the "Hue and Cry" to be proclaimed to attack the runaway Rochellers. To this end he addressed himself to Mr. Griffith White of Henllan, Castlemartin, of whose worth and good affection he had been assured by "the character which sounds in the ears of all men that came into these parts." Having gone to acquaint his Admiral of what had occurred, Capt. Smith once more returned to Milford Haven, where his presence became speedily wanted.[1] The possession of the Haven was important. Pembroke, if besieged, would not be able to hold out any time if the Haven was in the hands of the enemy, while no mere siege on the land side would be able to reduce the place if the Haven was still open to them. More Parliament ships were sent, and not a bit too soon, for the Earl of Carbery was advancing into Pembrokeshire. The first place he came to was Tenby. Here he was well received apparently. No sooner, however, had the town declared itself for the King

[1] King's Pamphlets, 89—37. See vol. ii., Document xxiii., p. 76.

than eight ships from Milford appeared before it, and assumed a threatening aspect, but returned without effecting anything. It is said their intention was to set the town on fire; but they were driven thence. There appears also to have been a design to besiege it from land with forces from Pembroke. This was prevented by means of the old system of telegraphy—the firing of beacons—which brought instant aid to the Earl of Carbery.[1] After the "reduction"—such is the word of the old Royalist newspaper, which implies that there must have been some opposition—of Tenby, the Earl proceeded to Haverfordwest. At Haverfordwest, there appears to have been no opposition whatever. Indeed, it would appear that he was rather welcome than otherwise. He appointed it as a rendezvous for the trained bands of the whole county to meet him. From Dewsland and Roos, from Daugleddau and Castlemartin, from Cemmaes and Cilgerran, and from Narberth, the gentry and the trained bands flowed in to him, while the town of Haverfordwest was so extremely pleased with the visit, that the Mayor, Aldermen, and inhabitants presented an address to him expressive of their fidelity to the King, and their readiness to contribute to his cause, to the best of their ability. This important manifesto was passed on the 18th of September, in return for which the Earl of Carbery placed a garrison there, as he had already done in Tenby and other places, whereby Haverfordwest was by-and-by to realise some of the excitement of civil war, and much to its damage, too.[2] The gentry of

---

[1] *Mercurius Aulicus*, 37th week, p. 512. Also vol. ii., Document xxiv. A.
[2] *Ibid*, 39th week, p 589. Document xxiv. B, vol. ii., p. 88.

the county were as eager to testify their attachment to the King as were the townsmen of Haverfordwest. They also signed a declaration of loyalty, and bound themselves to oppose the victualling of the enemy's ships; and furthermore, that they would not contribute in any way for the maintenance of the forces then occupying the town and castle of Pembroke, and that they would do all in their power to reduce them to his Majesty's obedience. This protestation was duly published in the pages of *Aulicus*, and the names appended to it; but among these names we find some who were certainly for the Parliament, which makes me doubt the genuineness of some of the signatures, though believing in the authenticity of the document itself.[1] Among the doubtful names to this document are those of Sir Hugh Owen, Mr. Griffith White, and Mr. John Elliot.

Col. Mytton, with the assistance of Sir Thomas Myddelton and Sir William Brereton, lost no time after the capture of Wem to fortify the place, which was highly necessary, considering the power of the cavaliers in Shropshire. This was deemed of great concernment by both parties: hence the personal attendance of Brereton and Myddelton to superintend the fortifications of the place. While they were there, the Lord Capel, summoning assistance from Staffordshire and all the garrisons around, set out at the head of a large force for Nantwich, which he intended to attack in the absence of Brereton. Thither they pushed as fast as possible. Brereton, however, had speedy notice of their movement, and set out in pursuit. They came

---

[1] *Merc. Aulicus*, 43rd week. See vol. ii., Document xxiv. c., p. 84.

upon a party of them at Prees Heath. Meanwhile the main body of Lord Capel's forces hurried on towards Nantwich, and got to Acton before those at Nantwich were aware of it. But the defenders of Nantwich, handful as they were, were men who had seen a good deal of service. And though the odds were now against them, they did not hesitate to meet the enemy and give him a stout fight in Acton churchyard;—a churchyard which, in my opinion, suffered more from the war than any other churchyard in the Kingdom. Lord Capel's men were driven into the church. Not powerful enough to storm the church, and not caring to spend themselves on a fruitless task, the Nantwich soldiers retreated to the town to prepare for its defence, knowing well enough that an attack was imminent. But they were saved that day, for the attackers, hearing that Brereton was in pursuit, quitted the church and made off, having first of all plundered some houses in the neighbourhood without being over particular as to whether they were the houses of friends or of foes. Brereton, through untrustworthy intelligence, missed them. They went back towards Wem, where Colonel Mytton was now alone with no more than about 300 soldiers. With this small force he actually drove away the enemy, which, in point of numbers, exceeded them by no less than twelve to one—Lord Capel's army being over 4,000 strong. In this conflict Colonel Mytton received most invaluable help from the women of Wem, who fought so well that their valour is perpetuated in the old rhyme—

> The women of Wem, and a few musketeers,
> Beat the Lord Capel, and all his cavaliers.

Retreating to Shrewsbury, the vanquished were pur-

CHAP. IV.
1643.

sued next day by Sir William Brereton, who came upon them at Lee Bridge. A severe conflict ensued, in which considerable execution was done. The Royalists before Wem lost one able commander, and a popular one, Colonel Wynne of Melai,[1] whose death caused dismay in the ranks, in which he evidently was beloved. As an old chronicler has it, "upon the death of Colonel Wynne, the whole business was overthrown."[2] Several other officers of note were wounded, among them being Sir Thomas Scriven, Sir Richard Willis, both colonels, Major Broughton, and others; while of common soldiers, six carriages of dead bodies, with 30 more left on the ground, bore sufficient testimony of the zeal of the struggle. The loss on the Parliament side was small: their greatest loss being the death of Colonel Marrow, an able officer. This occurred on the 17th and 18th of October.[3]

This important victory gave confidence to the Parliamentary soldiers; and they were not men inclined to rest on their swords. So they began in earnest to push into Wales, which had hitherto been entirely in the hands of the Royalists. The Lord Capel, on the other hand, hid himself in Shrewsbury, and was afraid to take the field, lest he should be shut out from the town;—shut out, too, by those within it, for disaffection prevailed extensively there, and the inhabitants had "but a mean, nay, even malignant estimation of his lordship."[4]

---

[1] Lloyd's Memoirs states him to have been of Berthdu, but his monument in St. Chad's, Shrewsbury, places him of Melai.

[2] William Maurice of Llansilin's Pocket Book. See Archæologia Cambrensis, i., p. 35.

[3] King's Pamphlets, 134—4. See vol. ii., Document xxv., p. 86.

[4] Archbishop of York to Ormond, 12th Nov., 1643. Carte's Collection. See also vol. ii., Document xxviii.

Taking advantage of this state of affairs, Brereton and Myddelton quitted Nantwich on the 7th of November, and proceeded towards Holt, resting on the way at Woodhey, Barton, and Stretton. Joined at the last-named place by the Lancashire forces, under Sir George Booth, they set upon Holt, the bridge at which place over the Dee afforded a pass of great importance. The town and castle were garrisoned for the King under "young Robinson, who had lived much at Dublin."[1] Young Robinson hereafter will frequently figure in this Work as the gallant Colonel John Robinson—a Denbighshire man, by the way, residing at Gwersyllt. The garrison at Holt consisted of some 1,000 horse and about 700 foot. The bridge was won, and with it a part of the town. A portion of the Royalists retreated to the castle, which they stoutly defended and kept. The rest took to flight, and in the pursuit many of them were taken prisoners. Among the latter were Captain Price, Captain Jones, and Lieutenant Salesbury. Leaving a considerable force to guard the the bridge, Brereton, Myddelton, and Booth marched to Wrexham, where they quartered that night.[2] Wrexham, notwithstanding that the King himself had whilom addressed his "loving subjects" there, and that Sir Richard Lloyd's influence was great there, seems to have offered no opposition to the Parliamentarians. "Young Booth," writes the old Archbishop of York to the Marquis of Ormond, was left at Wrexham with the Manchester forces to the number of near nine hundred. What had become

---

[1] Archbishop of York to Ormond, 18th Nov. Carte's Life of Ormond, v., 514. See Document xxxi., volume ii.

[2] Burghall's Providence Improved. Ormerod's Cheshire, iii, 225

of Sir Richard Lloyd, the King's Attorney-General, we know not. Vague rumours reached London that he sent in his commission to Myddelton, promising to bring over with him to the service of the Parliament fifteen hundred men, if they would please forgive him.[1] The same newspaper further tells us that Sir Thomas Myddelton took divers knights and gentlemen at Wrexham, and that the Welshmen were extremely glad at his return amongst them, receiving him with great joy and promising to help him to get back Chirk Castle, which had been in the hands of the enemy for near a twelvemonth. Another newspaper states that the town was first taken, but that the castle held out for five or six days, when it fell.[2] From Wrexham the progress of the Parliament soldiers was even and successful. Hawarden Castle fell into their hands without a blow, through the treachery, the Royalists say, of Colonel Ravenscroft, of Bretton, whom the King had placed in command there. Flint Castle could not hold out long, and prudently gave in; and Mostyn — both town and castle — notwithstanding all the loyal efforts of the worthy family who derive their name therefrom, were soon surrendered to Myddelton and Brereton, along with four pieces of ordnance, of which their defensive resources consisted.[3] Mold and Holywell fared no better, and no worse. This even current of success was accomplished by a force of less than two thousand, according to the testimony of the oft-quoted Archbishop of York, who sourly complained, as

---

[1] *Certain Informations*, No. 45. (K. P. 134—6.)
[2] *The Kingdom's Weekly Intelligencer*, No. 28, p. 257. (K. P. 134—10.)
[3] *Ibid.*

indeed was his wont, that "by these contemptible numbers these great and populous counties, for want of a head, arms, and ammunition, are quite routed and scattered up and down these mountainous countries;"[1] and he was extremely fearful that they would soon be harassing him at Conway, the castle of which he had repaired at enormous cost, whither the clergy flocked in great numbers for protection.

In his advance into Wales Sir William Brereton is charged that he "did pull down the organs, defaced the windows in all the churches, and the monuments."[2] In Wrexham they broke in pieces the best pair of organs in the King's dominions, the lead pipes of which were converted into bullets for Sir Thomas Myddelton's use. They were, however, uncommonly honest, pillaging no houses, purloining nothing save from churches, and damaging nothing save what to them appeared superstitious and idolatrous. From Holywell and Northop they took the surplices, and somewhat roughly re-arranged the position of the Communion Table in places where the High Church clergy had placed them in the chancel.[3] For all this they have been much abused and called Goths and Vandals. But, however much we may regret the pulling down of organs, the defacing of windows, and the destruction of works of art, we should never forget that to these men these things were odious, as signs of a faith which they detested, and which to their narrow fanatic minds was damnable.

[1] His letter to Ormond of the 18th November, *supra*.
[2] Harl. MSS., 2125, § 135.
[3] Capt. Byrch's Letter. Carte's Collection, i., p. 29. See vol. ii., Document xxxvi., p. 111.

The effect of this successful invasion of North Wales was soon felt at Chester. That city was now nearly blocked up—the Dee alone remaining open to them. Traffic was hindered, communication with Wales put a stop to. Coals, lime, corn, and victuals, which used to be brought in from Wales, came in no more. "Fire grew scant and dear to the smart of citizens, especially the poor sort."[1] Handbridge, an outlying suburb of the city on the Welsh side, was burnt down by order of the Governor, by Col. Marrow, unknown even to the Mayor, so that the Parliament forces might not shelter there in case of an attack upon the city. The inhabitants of the suburb entered the city and added to the distress of the place.

The western counties of North Wales were in great trepidation at being thus threatened at the very door. Old Archbishop Williams was troubled, and Viscount Bulkeley prepared for the worst, whilst Col. Salesbury of Bachymbyd, Governor of Denbigh Castle, strengthened his lines. To the last-named, Sir Thomas Myddelton sent a summons, couched in terms befitting a soldier, and a gentleman who had been on terms of intimacy with one now opposed to him. This summons is a fair index of the spirit which actuated most of the officers at this time in Wales and elsewhere, when friends and near relatives were ranked in opposite camps: a spirit of a friendlier negotiation than the sterner dictates of war generally call forth, arising from previous honourable intimacy and a desire to avoid the unnecessary shedding of blood. To this friendly

---

[1] Harl. MSS. 2125, f. 135.

summons loyal old Salesbury, "in the name of Jesus," answers—No![1].

This answer from Salesbury was dated the 15th of November—a truly momentous day for all the parties concerned: a day upon which the King reckoned much. For four thousand soldiers, who had been serving in Ireland to avenge the massacre, were sent over from Dublin, under the command of Sir Michael Ernely, Sir Fulke Hunckes, Col. Gibson, and Col. Robert Byron, in vessels ordered to land in Chester. The King, when he learned in August that the Parliament were negotiating an alliance with the Scottish Presbyterians, took advantage of the opportunity which he had long been anxious to do, to effect a peace with the rebels in Ireland. For this purpose instructions were sent to the Marquis of Ormond, an upright honourable man, the King's lieutenant there, to negotiate a treaty with the Council of Kilkenny, the governing power of the rebels; and on the 5th of September a cessation of arms for a year was agreed upon, whereby the soldiers there became available to the King. Charles would have gone much further himself, and would have gladly accepted the aid of the rebels; but he dared not, seeing that it would alienate from him many of his best supporters in England. It was clearly his desire to obtain their aid, and it is beyond a question that he approved of the proposals made by Hamilton and Antrim to the Queen to bring over the Irish Catholics. It was yet premature. As it was, the cessation of arms drove away many who had hitherto been loyal to him. Several officers quitted Newcastle's

[1] *Merc. Aulicus*, Jan. 6, 1644. See vol. ii., Document xxix., p. 95.

army and went over to the Parliament. The King's conduct was violently discussed throughout the Kingdom, and all the more so because some Irish rebels came over with the troops. In the result the act proved disastrous to the King. He had a perfect right to accept their aid, but what disgusted honourable men was the dishonest way in which Charles conducted his secret intrigues. While declaring his fidelity to Protestants he was negotiating with Catholics. Several lords who were in attendance upon him at Oxford made their submission to the Parliament, declaring their conscience did not allow them to co-operate with the Papists who prevailed there.

The first batch of the re-called English-Irish soldiers, as they were called by the Royalists, or Irish, as the Parliament party called them, landed at Mostyn, in Flintshire, on the 18th of November. Another company landed in Anglesey, and were entertained by the Royalists there, more especially Lord Bulkeley and Archbishop Williams. Immediately upon their landing, Brereton and Myddelton withdrew from Mostyn, Flint, and Holywell, to Wrexham. Thence they addressed a coaxing letter to the new-comers, praising them for their exertions to suppress the rebels, regretting they had not been better provided for by the Parliament, hoping they still meant to fight for the Protestant religion, and promising them payment of their arrears if they joined with them. But the answer was a point blank refusal. They had gone to Ireland to suppress the King's enemies. They had come hither to do the same, and to carry this out they now set about in earnestness.[1] The number landed in

---

[1] *Merc. Aulicus*, 48th week, 1644. Vol. ii., p. 101, Document xxxii.

Flintshire amounted to about 2,500. They were all in a sad condition. For a long while they had been neglected in Ireland by both the King and the Parliament. Their pay had been allowed to fall dreadfully in arrear. Their clothing was shamefully bare. They were naturally disaffected. The Marquis of Ormond was very apprehensive of them. He feared that any cajoling on the part of the enemy would carry them over. Had Brereton's letter got into the hands of the men there is reason to believe that a serious defection would have taken place; but the officers were not men to betray their trust.

On the landing of these forces at Mostyn the courage of the Parliamentarians vanished, and it is surprising that with an army of over 2,000 men they did not make any attempt to stem the onward tide. In their hurry to get to Wrexham they omitted to send any reinforcement to Hawarden Castle, where they had a few days before placed a garrison of some 120 men, under Capt. Elliot, and one Ince, a minister. Pushing on from Mostyn, the Irish forces—and I shall call them so, not because they were such in fact, but to distinguish them—set down before Hawarden the very day next after their landing, and laid siege to the castle. Here the little garrison, though a mere handful, showed great courage, and stood out very bravely, trusting probably for aid from Wrexham. But there were no longer any friends at Wrexham, nor even at Holt, for Brereton and Myddelton had quitted Wales and retreated to Nantwich, "so that," as an old chronicler puts it, "the fair hopes of reducing North Wales, Shropshire, and Cheshire, is

CHAP. IV.
1643.

now lost till God give another opportunity."¹ This opportunity, as we shall see, did not come for many a day: many changes had happened, and many scenes were gone through before North Wales was reduced. With this precipitate retreat even their own friends found fault with Brereton and Myddelton. Burghall, the minister at Nantwich, thought "it was a wonder they made such haste as not to relieve Harden Castle," leaving the small garrison "with little provision and in great danger. It was also thought strange that they should leave Wales, which in a manner was quite subdued a little before; and so many good friends who had come to them were left to the mercy of the enemy."² Some of the "friends," however, managed to escape. Simon Thelwall, the member for Denbigh, for one, had to cut for his life, and tramping over snow-covered roads, over mountain and glen, the fugitive sought and found refuge with the "godly garrison at Pembroke."³

The strength of the Irish set down before Hawarden, but they did not stay long; and leaving the management of the siege to a couple of companies under Capt. Sandford, a Cheshire man, Captain of the Firelocks, with about 500 Welshmen, commanded by Captain Mostyn and Captain Davies (of Gwesanau?), and some of Lord Cholmondeley's men, the main body of the newly-landed marched to Chester to rest and repose themselves, being "faint, weary, and out of clothing."⁴

Hawarden Castle held out obstinately for a

¹ *The Kingdom's Weekly Intelligencer*, No. 34. (K. P. 134—29.)
² Burghall's Providence Improved.
³ Thelwall's Letter to Lenthall, vol ii., Document xlvi A., p. 140.
⁴ Harl. MSS. 2125, fol. 135

fortnight. Some of the Irish went over to the besieged. The little garrison was repeatedly summoned to surrender. Even Lord Capel, with a large force from Shrewsbury, came thither to aid the attackers. Being at length assured beyond a doubt that no relief could come to them from Wrexham, the besieged surrendered upon honourable terms.[1] The terms were violated by the Royalists, and some cruelties perpetrated. Captain Sandford, however, is free from blame on this score—the fault being due to the unsoldierly conduct of Lord Cholmondeley's men.[2]

Timely notice of the great want of the Irish forces were sent by the Marquis of Ormond to Oxford, where the Court then was held; to the Archbishop of York at Conway; and to Mr. Orlando Bridgman at Chester.[3] The last-named was at Oxford at the time. He was immediately sent down to Chester to make preparations for their reception. Letters were despatched to the Commissioners in the various counties of North Wales, ordering an instant supply of clothes, victuals, and money. Bridgman arrived in time to be present at the arrival of Sir Michael Ernely's forces. At Chester every possible step was taken to provide clothing for the men. The Mayor sent through all the wards to get apparel for them from the citizens. These gave freely: some whole suits, some doublets, others breeches, shirts, shoes, stockings, and hats, to the apparelling of about 300.[4] Through the

[1] Rushworth, vol. ii., part iii., pp. 298—301.
[2] Capt. Byrch's letter, *supra*.
[3] Carte's Life of Ormond, v., pp. 479, 505. See also vol. ii., Documents xxvi. and xxvii.
[4] Harl. MSS., *supra*.

energy of Bridgman shoes and stockings were provided speedily for about a thousand, and before the 29th of November, by scouring North Wales, he had got together sufficient cloth and frieze to clothe all of them, and this was sent to Chester to be made up. Busy times for the tailors! Before the end of November, Bridgman was at Beaumaris collecting money, and had got together about £1,000.[1]

From Oxford, too, within a few days of Bridgman's departure, another person was sent to Chester —one destined to play a conspicuous part in affairs there afterwards. This was Sir John Byron, whose appointment as Lieutenant of the Tower I have before alluded to. He had just been created a Baron —the first who bore the title which its last possessor has made illustrious. He left Oxford on the 21st November with 1,000 horse and 300 foot. His orders were to assist Lord Capel to open a passage for the Irish to land, and to unite with them.[2] Passing through Eversham and by Shrewsbury he reached Chester about the 6th of December, in the quality of Field-Marshal of Cheshire, Shropshire, and North Wales, under Lord Capel.[3] About this time fresh reinforcements from Ireland landed at Chester. These were under the command of Colonel Robert Byron, a brother of Lord Byron, and Colonel Henry Warren.[4] At this time, too, the Governor of Chester was Sir Nicholas Byron, uncle of the foregoing, so that the Byron family mustered in

[1] Carte's Ormond, v., 525. See vol. ii., Document xxxiii.
[2] Arthur Trevor from Oxon. Carte's Ormond, v., 521.
[3] *Kingdom's Weekly Intelligencer*. No. 35, 5—13 December; Maurice of Llansilin's Pocket Book in Archæologia Cambrensis.
[4] Harl. MSS., 2135, § 15.

great strength in the city on the Dee. The most energetic of them was Lord Byron. At his earnest entreaty Charles placed under him the best part of the Anglo-Irish, so far superseding Lord Capel, whose subordinate he was, and that, too, by means which did not recommend themselves favourably to the sturdy old Archbishop of York.[1]

Under Lord Byron and the Irish the spirit of the war in these parts was entirely changed. He seems to have been devoid of that chivalry which characterised the commanders whose actions we have hitherto been considering. The shedding of blood, instead of being a horror to be avoided, delighted him. Of Lord Byron's cruelty there is sufficient testimony. The many charges brought against him by the Parliamentary Press, if uncorroborated, would not convict him; but when they are confirmed by Royalist statements, and by his own letters, the fact is proved beyond dispute! His barbarity was so great, says Randle Holmes, himself a faithful Royalist, that "he prospered not," while he himself, writing to the Marquis of Newcastle from Sandbach, in Cheshire, on the 26th of December, says, "the rebels had possessed themselves of a church at Barthomley, but we presently beat them forth of it. I put them all to the sword, which I find to be the best way to proceed with these kind of people, for mercy to them is cruelty."[2] How different had been the conduct of Brereton, of Myddelton, and of Salesbury! If hereafter we shall have to consider any charge of cruelty contrary to the usages of war brought against the

[1] Warburton's Rupert, ii., 329.
[2] *Merc. Civicus*, No. 35, p. 374. (K. P. 147—7.)

Parliamentary party, it will be as well for us to bear this in mind. The *lex talionis* can only be justified by conduct such as this.

Whatever forces now remained to the Parliament were quartered at Nantwich, whence they dared not emerge in the face of an enemy counting four if not five times their number. Sir Thomas Myddelton hastened to London, which he reached about the middle of December, to recruit his army,[1] and remained there for a long time, leaving Brereton alone to face the impending difficulties. Before the end of the year all the outlying garrisons of the Parliament were in the hands of their enemies. They fell, too, without any fighting. Crew House, Doddington House, Middlewich, Northwich, Beeston Castle, Macclesfield, Cholmondeley House, Sandbach, and other garrisons, one by one, dropped away from the Parliament. About two thousand prisoners were made, and a great store of arms and ammunition captured. Nantwich alone remained to contend with a force numbering quite seven thousand fighting men.[2]

Amid all his troubles during that gloomy Christmas-time, Brereton—a man of deep religious feeling—must have derived some consolation from the knowledge that in the churches of London bills had been put up asking the prayers of the faithful for his deliverance from the Irish, "it not being doubted but that he will have the prayers of all well-affected persons."[3]

---

[1] *Weekly Account* for December 13. (K. P. 135—14.)
[2] *Merc. Aulicus*, January 6th. (K. P. 139—9.)
[3] *Merc. Civicus*, No. 34. (K. P. 139—12.)

CHAPTER V.
1644

Siege of Nantwich—Raised by Fairfax—Irish forces routed—Fight at Ellesmere—A glimpse of Imperial matters—Oxford Parliament—Rupert appointed to command in North Wales and the Borders—Fresh arrival of Irish—They are sent to Shrewsbury—Rupert arrives there—Goes to Chester—Relieves Newark—Returns to Shrewsbury—State of Pembrokeshire—Major Laugharne and Capt. Poyer, aided by sea forces under Admiral Swanley, defeat Royalists at the Pill—Take Haverfordwest, Tenby, and Carew—Cardiganshire Royalists entreat Rupert to come to their aid—They are summoned by Laugharne—Earl of Carbery resigns—Carmarthen is taken—The Covenant in Pembrokeshire—Swansea summoned—Association of Carmarthen, Cardigan, and Pembroke—Swanley rewarded with a gold chain—Rupert again at Shrewsbury—Arranges affairs in North Wales—The Parliamentarians in straits—Sir Thomas Myddelton appointed Major-General of North Wales—Col. Mytton attacks some Royalists at Duddlestone—Oswestry is taken by him and the Earl of Denbigh—Attempt to regain Oswestry defeated by Myddelton—Marston Moor—Rupert retires to North Wales—Colonel Charles Gerard lands in Monmouthshire—Takes Cardiff, Kidwelly, Carmarthen, Newcastle-Emlyn, Cardigan, Laugharne, Roch, and Haverfordwest—Besieges Pembroke—Help from sea—Gerard's character—Rupert in vain expects aid from Ireland—Goes to Shrewsbury—Thence to Chester—A party of his horse defeated at Welshpool—Tries to strengthen himself in North Wales—Expects powder from Bristol—Lord Herbert of Cherbury—Defeat of Royalists at Tarvin—Rupert goes to Bristol—Army of the North defeated at Malpas by Brereton—Myddelton intercepts the Bristol powder at Newtown—Takes Montgomery Castle—Mytton is besieged there—Relieved by Brereton—Byron routed—Gerard's cruelties in Pembrokeshire—Severities against the Irish—Fight at Beachly—Massey takes Monmouth—Lukewarmness of Welsh Royalists—Puritan gallantry—Powis Castle taken by Myddelton—Shrewsbury threatened—Mytton defeats Sir W. Vaughan—Brereton before Chester—Gerard quits South Wales—Is pursued by Massey—Monmouth retaken by Royalists—Laugharne Castle falls into the hands of Parliament—Cardigan taken by Laugharne—Myddelton appears before Chirk Castle—Brereton before Chester—Résumé of Imperial matters.

LORD BYRON, with the Irish under his command, having driven Brereton back to Nantwich, lost no time in preparing to reduce that place. One attempt only was made to prevent their laying siege to it. In that conflict, which took place at Middlewich,

Brereton lost some 300 men, with nearly as many taken prisoners. The loss of the Royalists was only about fifteen killed and some forty wounded—among the latter being Sir Robert Byron and three captains.[1] This defeat considerably weakened Brereton's strength, who, with the small force which yet remained to him, could hardly expect to maintain Nantwich much longer. Leaving all the available force he had to protect that place, he himself hastened to procure aid: Col. George Booth being left in command. Nantwich was then a small town, hardly better than a village, with its straw-thatched houses; and its fortifications consisted of only rude mud-walls and ditches. Presently the whole Irish forces sat down before it; and in the face of great danger, suffering, and many privations, the little garrison within defended themselves so well that neither expostulation nor menace could move them to surrender. One of the most curious summonses ever received by a beleagured town was a letter which they received from Thomas Sandford, Captain of the Firelocks, and addressed to the "officers, soldiers, and gentlemen in Nantwich." "Your drum," says he, "can inform you Acton Church is no longer a prison, but now free for honest men to do their devotions in; wherefore, be persuaded from your incredulity and resolve! God will not forsake his annointed. Let not your zeal in a bad cause dazzle your eyes any longer, but wipe away your vain conceits that have too long led you into blind errors. Loath I am to undertake the trouble of persuading you into obedience, because your erroneous opinions do most violently oppose reason amongst you; but,

---

[1] Carte's Collection, i., p. 34. See vol. ii., Document xxxvii, p. 117.

however, if you love your town, accept of quarter; and, if you regard your lives, work your safety by yielding your town to Lord Byron for his Majesty's use. You see how my battery is fixed, from whence fire shall eternally visit you, to the terror of the old and females, and consumption of your thatched houses. Believe me, gentlemen, I have laid by my former delays, and am now resolved to batter, burn, storm, and destroy you. Do not wonder that I write unto you, having officers-in-chief above me. It is only to advise you to your good." This summons produced no result, though the little garrison was in extremities. They had scarcely any hope of assistance, for the winter was a most severe one, the snow was deep on the ground, and assistance must come from afar. On the 18th, sometime before daybreak, an assault was made upon the town. Those within defended themselves with singular courage and success. The assault failed, and some three hundred of the Royalists were killed or disabled. Amongst the slain was the writer of the above summons. The siege had now been going on for near a fortnight. Brereton, meanwhile, was busily employed in collecting the fugitives from the fight at Middlewich, and in imploring the Parliament to send some aid. The Scotch had already entered England in fulfilment of the agreement come to when the Covenant was adopted, but they could not come up in time. Young Fairfax, whose genius for commanding was already beginning to claim for him more than ordinary notice, was ordered to go to the relief of Nantwich. Taking with him a raw levy of foot and his own dragoons, they made speedy marches, the snow notwithstanding;

CHAP. V.
1644.

and being joined by Sir William Brereton they came in sight of Nantwich on the 21st of January, and found the place so reduced by famine and sickness that it could hardly continue any longer unsurrendered.

The strength of the united forces under Fairfax numbered 2,500 foot and 28 troops of horse. Lord Byron, on the other hand, was in command of about 3,000 foot and 1,800 horse, so that in point of numbers the advantage was with the latter. The first encounter took place at Delamere Forest. Fairfax there took some thirty prisoners. Acton Church, one of the outlying strongholds of the Royalists, was next attacked. Here the principal body of the besiegers were stationed, having withdrawn themselves to that place after the assault on the 18th. The river Weaver, which runs between the town and the church, was at this time overflowed by the thawing of the snow; and the flat of boats upon it was swept away by the flood, so that the besieging body was disunited, and Lord Byron prevented from rendering timely assistance to those at Acton. Fairfax saw this, and lost no time in preparing to attack the church; but Lord Byron was too quick for him, for he crossed the river higher up—the flood notwithstanding. Fairfax, meanwhile, advanced nearer the town, pushing along narrow lanes and behind hedges; Lord Byron followed and attacked the enemy from the rear, while the remainder of his army engaged the enemy in front. The battle now became hot. The Parliament forces were in some danger, but the excellent tactics of Sir William Fairfax, who commanded the horse, and Sir William Brereton, and other able officers who took part therein, and particularly by the timely sally of the besieged who issued out under the command of Col. Booth, saved them. After two hours' severe fighting, Lord Byron was totally defeated, and had to make his way back to Chester accompanied only by a few stragglers. Lord Byron appears to throw the blame on the Irish forces led by Col. Warren and Sir Michael Ernely, who "retreated without fighting a stroke." Many officers were taken prisoners; in fact, nearly all those who had come over from Ireland. Notably among the prisoners is the name of Col. George Monk—the instrument of Charles the Second's restoration. He had only just arrived at Chester with a commission from Prince Rupert to raise a regiment. He had been in service in Ireland, and was one of those who landed at Bristol after the cessation of arms. About two hundred of the Royalists were slain, while only about fifty of the other side were killed. With the exception of that of Sir Robert Byron's regiment, all the colours were lost, with a large quantity of guns and carriages, and no less than fifteen hundred prisoners. Some six score Irish women who followed the camp were also secured. These had with them long knives, with which they were said to have done mischief.[1]

In this memorable siege the women of Nantwich behaved with great bravery: headed by a heroine named Brett, who defended the works with singular courage when the town was assaulted on the 18th. In commemoration of the raising of the siege, which

---

[1] Fairfax's Letter to Essex. Rushworth, vol. ii., pt. iii., 302; Lord Byron's Account, Carte's Collection, i., 36; and Sir Robert Byron to Ormond. *Ibid*, p. 40. See these Documents in vol. ii., pp. 126—133.

took place on St. Paul's Day, the inhabitants upon every anniversary of it, until of late, wore sprigs of holly in their hats in token of victory, whence the day was called Holly holy-day.[1]

While Nantwich was besieged, Col. Mytton obtained a victory over a large party of the Royalists, sent from Chester to Shrewsbury to fetch arms and ammunition for carrying on the siege. The parties met at Ellesmere on the 12th of January. The Royalists were surprised. Sir Nicholas Byron, Governor of Chester, Sir Richard Willis, Serjeant-Major-General of the Horse, and others, were taken prisoners.[2]

Notwithstanding the cessation of arms in Ireland, which brought a great addition of strength to his army, the position of Charles's affairs towards Christmas was anything but satisfactory. The Scotch were on the eve of entering England, and there was very little money at Oxford. After a great deal of hesitation the King decided upon convoking at Oxford a Parliament, comprising all his adherents who had quitted Westminster. On the 22nd January they assembled at Oxford. Forty-five lords and one hundred and eighteen members of the Commons attended. The same day the roll at Westminster was called. Only twenty-two lords were present, but in the Commons two hundred and eighty members answered to their names. These resolved not to acknowledge the Oxford assembly: Charles, on the other hand, repudiated the Parliament at Westminster, whom he called traitors. The

---

[1] Partridge's Hist. of Nantwich, p. 619.
[2] "A true relation of a notable surprise, &c., at Ellesmere." (K. P. 140—9.) Vol. ii., Document xxxix.

Oxford assembly, as might have been expected, was utterly incapable of doing any service to the King; indeed, it rather injured his cause. It did nothing beyond voting subsidies which could not be collected, and inditing a long letter to the Earl of Essex in favour of peace, asking him to try and persuade " those whose confidence he possessed " —meaning the Parliament at Westminster. The refusal to acknowledge them as the Parliament irritated the latter, and Essex returned the letter without any answer. Below are the names of those with whose actions I am concerned, who signed the letter in question.[1] April the 16th witnessed their last sitting, to the great relief of Charles, who boasted to the Queen that he was at length " rid of this mongrel Parliament, the haunt of cowardly and seditious motions."

When Nantwich fell the aspect of affairs in North Wales was entirely changed, and Lord Byron's plans destroyed. The partisans of the King there, and in Shropshire and Cheshire, who had been elated by the success of the Irish forces at Hawarden and Beeston, and who had thought those parts " were in a manner cleared," were now

---

[1] Orlando Bridgman (for Wigan), Francis Gamul (Chester), William Watkins (Monmouth), Thomas Littleton (Great Wenlock), William Morgan (Breconshire), William Thomas (Carnarvon), John Mostyn (Flintshire), John Salesbury (Flint), William Herbert (Woodstock and Monmouth), William Price (Merionethshire), Sir John Price (Montgomeryshire), Richard Herbert (Montgomery), Charles Price (Radnorshire), Herbert Price (Brecon). The following were disabled by accident to sign, but afterwards concurred: Lord Newport, Francis Newport (Salop), James Scudamore (Hereford), and Sir John Stepney (Haverfordwest). Among those who were employed in his Majesty's service or absent with leave were reckoned—Lord Herbert of Cherbury, Lord Powis, Lord Vaughan, Sir Walter Lloyd (Cardiganshire), Sir Henry Vaughan (Carmarthenshire), Francis Lloyd (Carmarthen), and John Vaughan (Cardigan).

CHAP. V.
1644.

dismayed. They felt the insecurity of their position; and the growing coolness of the yeomanry and peasantry, who had suffered much from the levies of the Royalists, became daily more threatening. Even the Irish who had come over wavered, and many of them had gone over to the Parliament. The loyalists had more difficulty than ever to manage affairs. Contributions they could not levy except by force, and this only increased their unpopularity. Ammunition was scarce, and their means of defence scanty. Moreover, they had not only to contend with forces led by Brereton, but were menaced by men led under the victorious banner of Fairfax whose name even then was sufficient to discourage his enemies. It is no wonder, therefore, to find them, under such depressed circumstances, writing most pressing letters to the King for aid. Prince Rupert alone was thought able and fit to undertake the task of settling the country, and of strengthening and protecting the King's interests in these parts. Accordingly the King determined to despatch the Prince thither, and as matters were pressing, and the disaffection of the Welsh seriously spreading, there was no time to be lost. So on the 25th of January Rupert writes a long letter to Sir Francis Ottley, the Governor of Shrewsbury, in which, after alluding to the fact that he had been entrusted with the care of the army in Shropshire and the counties adjacent, he intimates his intention of making Shrewsbury his head-quarters, and calls upon the Governor to set the castle in order for the reception of stores and ammunition on his arrival. The loyalty of Shrewsbury was not without some suspicion about this time. There was in the town a considerable party of those who did not hold with the King; and though they were not strong enough or sufficiently courageous to declare themselves openly, yet managed to leaven the whole town with a taint of disloyalty, so that the Governor's task of keeping the place for the King had not been of the lightest. Some disquietude had been occasioned by a rumour of a design to betray the town, which, whether true or not, caused divers persons to be put in prison.[1] This having reached Prince Rupert, made him think "with very much apprehension" of the place, "and the safety thereof." The Governor was doubtless pleased at the prospect of help which the Prince's arrival would bring, as it was the only hope he had for the safety of the town. Meanwhile, Sir Thomas Fairfax, Brereton, and Myddelton were not idle, engaging themselves in reducing the smaller garrisons in Cheshire—Lord Byron, with his defeated soldiers having, after the defeat at Nantwich, retreated to Chester. But even Fairfax could not do much in Cheshire when he found "the forces rise but slowly, and a remissness in the gentry that are not active in the work," and being ordered away to assist his father before Hull he quitted Cheshire, having remanded Sir William Brereton and Sir Thomas Myddelton, with their forces, to manage the affairs of that county.[2]

We find that Lord Byron is considerably reduced by the late defeat, and suffers so much from want of money that he can make no provision whatever

---

[1] Owen and Blakeway's Shrewsbury.
[2] Intercepted Letter of Fairfax, 24th Feb., 1644. Warburton's Prince Rupert, ii., 38. Vol. ii., Document xliv.

at Chester for a company of foot, to the number of 1,700, which at this time landed from Ireland under the command of Tyllyer and Broughton; and he is constrained to send them to Shrewsbury, which is not much better off, for they suffered from a terrible want of money there too: so much so that Sir John Mennes writes it "was a thing they heard not of," and nothing but the appearance of the impetuous Prince is deemed capable of repairing the evil.[1] This was now hastened with all speed. On the 5th of February the Prince was appointed by the King "President of Wales," and it was his duty to settle the affairs of that country, to put down the rebels, to incite the people to loyalty, and to recruit there whatever forces he could.

The 6th of February saw Rupert's departure from Oxford, and on the 18th he arrived at Shrewsbury. A few days before this, the Salopians having heard of the Prince's resolution to visit their town, notwithstanding that they had been well-nigh ruined by the many exactions which the necessities of the war had imposed upon them, had by their Corporation agreed to further assess themselves in the large sum of £1,000, to be raised for him at one payment.[2] The Prince's object in coming hither was to try to maintain Shrewsbury in its loyalty to the King. Moreover, it was very necessary that the adjacent counties of North Wales should be settled, and that by some means or other the Parliamentary forces under Brereton and Mytton, and the Earl of Denbigh and Myddelton, should be prevented from having matters carried in their own way. Lathom House,

---

[1] Sir John Mennes to Rupert from Salop, Feb. 10. Vol. ii., Document xliii. a.
[2] Owen and Blakeway's History of Shrewsbury, i., 440.

the seat of the Countess of Derby, was under siege, and it was very expedient that some assistance should be sent to the brave Countess, and that a determined attempt should be made without delay to relieve her. The Prince, therefore, must have found plenty of work—real serious work—to employ himself with while he stayed at this place. And Warburton states that weighty as the work was Prince Rupert did it thoroughly and single-handed. The Prince's historian must have had different data to what I have seen, for I cannot find that he accomplished much.

On the 4th of March he quitted Shrewsbury with about 300 horse and 600 foot, and after making a dash at Market Drayton[1] against some forces under Sir William Fairfax and Col. Mytton, in which he was to some extent successful, he visited some of the King's garrisons in those parts, and on the 11th made a grand entry into the City of Chester. The streets were lined with soldiers, the justices of the peace appeared in scarlet robes, the sheriffs in their best habit, the aldermen in mulberry, and the other civic dignities in the robes of their several offices; while the Prince, accompanied by the Lord Byron and others on horseback, rode up and was met at the Cross by Randle Holmes, the Mayor, who, owing to his lameness (having "been ill of a payne in his legg") came in a coach. The Mayor addressed the Prince in a becoming speech, welcoming him amongst them, and offering him what poor entertainment they could give him, which would not be what he deserved, owing to the reduced state of the city; and prayed him to

[1] Owen and Blakeway's History of Shrewsbury, i., 440.

ease the citizens of the free billeting of soldiers, which had been so very burthensome to them. This speech the Prince "took very kindly," and at its conclusion the people gave a shout for joy. The Prince answered graciously, ungloved his hand for the Mayor to kiss, and so went to Mr. John Aldersey's house in Watergate-street, where he rested, having previously asked the Mayor and his brethren to come to him on the morrow. The outspoken words of the Mayor do not appear to have been approved of by "his brethren" and the justices of the peace, wherefore they refused to call upon Rupert in the morning; and inasmuch as the Mayor's "payne in his legg" had increased during the night, whereby he was incapacitated from going himself, he seems to have amused himself at home by writing an explanation of his speech; and the Prince, with Lord Byron and others, rode about the city and inspected the mud-walls, the castle, and the other works which had been effected for its defence.[1]

In the meantime pressing entreaties for aid from Newark had been sent to the King, and Charles was very anxious that Rupert should proceed without delay to attempt the relief of that place. It was, nevertheless, left entirely to his own discretion. A more pressing message, however, arrived when the Prince was at Chester, which decided him to carry out the desire of the King. This was on Tuesday, the 12th day of March. Accordingly, dispatching Major Legge in advance of him to Shrewsbury to select as many as he deemed fit of the Irish who had come over under Tyllyer and

[1] Randle Holmes' Papers, Harl. MSS. 2125, fol. 320.

Broughton for the expedition, the Prince quitted Chester the same day, and arrived soon after Legge at Shrewsbury. Of the forces at Shrewsbury he took with him about 1,000 musketeers of Col. Broughton and Col. Tyllyer, and about 120 of Col. Sir Fulke Hunckes's. These were sent down the Severn as far as Bridgnorth, where the Prince joined them on the 15th with his own troop and some auxiliaries. On the 21st they made a dashing onslaught upon Sir John Meldrum's forces before Newark, and after a desperately-fought battle, in which a great amount of strategic ability was manifested by the Royalist officers, the Scot had to withdraw his forces a little distance from the town; and by the treachery of Col. King's company, his means of escape having been cut off, he himself was beset and was obliged to parley for terms, which were granted, but not faithfully kept. By this exploit the Prince did considerable service to the King's cause in these parts, in that it kept open for the Royalists a most important pass, while at the same time the enemy was weakened by the loss of a considerable quantity of arms and ammunition. No wonder, therefore, that the Prince caused the Sunday following to be devoted to Thanksgivings for his victory; and that great rejoicings should take place at Oxford, where the Court was, for so signal a victory.[1]

Most of the Prince's forces were taken back to Shrewsbury, and Rupert reported himself at Oxford.

In South Wales also the year opened unfavourably to the royal cause. The western counties of this division of the Principality—Cardigan, Pembroke, and Carmarthen—had in the main been

[1] Rushworth, vol. ii., part iii., 306—308.

exceedingly loyal from the very beginning of the war. The only notable exception was the town of Pembroke. Such of the gentlemen of the county as were favourable to the Parliamentary cause had come into the town very soon after the outbreak, leaving their homes to the chances of the times, and carrying with them all their available goods: so that outside Pembroke there were scarcely any openly opposed to the King's cause; and even those who wavered in their allegiance to the King were soon brought back by the activity of the Earl of Carbery. Garrisons had been placed by him in all the principal towns within his district. The castles were all fortified and garrisoned, and even private houses of a substantial kind, useful as outposts to the towns and more important garrisons, were strengthened and occupied by armed men; and for some time things went on quietly enough. But the heavy exactions which were made upon the inhabitants, and the irregular way in which all contributions for the King were levied,—and in that the Parliament had a great advantage over the King,—had cooled the ardour of many, who were therefore inclined to wish for a change. However, with all the towns so garrisoned the Earl of Carbery paid little heed to the remonstrances which were made, deeming that any inland disaffection could easily be checked; and he therefore devoted himself during the concluding portion of the year 1643 and the beginning of the following year to the consideration of the best course for the reduction of Pembroke to the King's obedience. At an influential meeting held at Carmarthen on the 11th of January, the leading men of the three counties once more protested their loyalty, and sanctioned an assessment to enable the Earl to reduce the Town and Castle of Pembroke.[1]

With a view to this the garrisons at Haverfordwest and Tenby were reinforced, Carew Castle was strongly guarded, and Roch Castle was placed in a posture of defence. Stackpoole Court and Trefloyne, with other strongly-built houses, were also garrisoned; and thus, strong as the position of the Parliamentarians at Pembroke was, they were pretty well hemmed in, and all inland communication put a stop to, so that help from that direction was clearly out of the question, and in all probability they had never calculated upon any. Such a blockade was serious to them only in that it made it difficult for them to obtain any provisions: for the Haven was still open to them and the sea was pretty well in the hands of their friends under the Earl of Warwick. Bristol, however, since its capture by Rupert, threatened them. Some ships were there which might at any time shut them in even by sea, unless the Parliament fleet, by a providential accident, should come soon enough to relieve them. In what caused the deepest apprehension to those within the town of Pembroke, lay the only hopes of the Earl of Carbery for the reduction of that place; for so long as those within had the harbour open to them inland environment would not be attended with any serious danger. Early in the year dispatches were sent by the Earl to Sir John Pennington, the chief in command of the vessels at Bristol, asking that so many ships as could be spared should be sent

[1] King's Pamphlets, 142–17.

CHAP. V.
1644.

at once to Milford for the purpose of constructing some fortification at the entrance to the Haven, which would enable a small force to prevent any vessels in the service of the Parliament, either from Ireland or elsewhere, from entering the Harbour and rendering aid to the beleagured at Pembroke, whether by supplying them with provisions or ammunition, or reinforcing them with men. It had previously been fully determined upon, that immediately on the arrival of such vessels from Bristol the harbour should be blocked and the town of Pembroke besieged. This must have come to the ears of those who were menaced, and a small ship belonging to Major Poyer was dispatched to acquaint the Lord High Admiral of their sore need of help; but the message never reached that authority, for the small craft was soon after brought back to the Haven by the Royalist vessels which had been sent from Bristol.

Upon the arrival of the ships from Bristol the Royalists were in high glee, and made much of the capture of Poyer's vessel. They were full of confidence of the issue of the undertaking; and this the more so, because along with the vessels had come one Captain Richard Steel, "a great talker," who "pretended much to be an ingenier," under whose superintendence they doubted not they would soon render the Haven inaccessible to the enemy.

Col. Laugharne and his party were now fairly pressed, and felt themselves to be in great danger. They saw that no time was to be lost; but the surrounding hosts were legions in comparison with the small force under Laugharne's command. Notwithstanding this, he determined upon a sally. Issuing out at the head of his troop, he proceeded in the direction of Carew, and within two miles of that place came upon a body of the Royalists. Accompanied by seven horse only, he made a bold charge, and successfully. Twenty prisoners, including a captain, were brought back to the town. In other respects this sally was fruitless, and had been of too reckless a nature to be repeated.

The prospects of the Parliamentary force at Pembroke were now gloomy enough. Well nigh hemmed in by land, their only hope lay from the Haven, and even of this chance they would soon be deprived. The Royalists were very hopeful of being shortly able to obtain clear and undisputed command of the harbour, and to reduce the enemy in that part of the country. They had for a long time been attempting to do so, but notwithstanding the coaxings, the cajolings, the threats and rigour of Sir Henry Vaughan (brother of the Earl of Carbery), who was in command of the County of Pembroke, the handful at Pembroke, who had early declared for the Parliament, bravely resisted, and were determined to maintain the Covenant which they had one and all taken. And when these had been brought to the condition above described they were by no means disheartened.

Towards the middle of February, when a siege of the place was actually in contemplation, the weather became rough; and the Haven being the only place of shelter to storm-driven vessels in the Channel, that part of the Parliamentary fleet which guarded the south-east coast of Ireland rode into Milford for shelter. To the garrison at Pembroke this looked like the manifest dispensation of Providence. To the Royalists' vessels at the Pill it did not appear in so favourable a light. Colonel Laugharne lost no time to acquaint Captain Swanley—the Admiral of that portion of the fleet—on board the *Leopard*, of the desperate straits in which they were placed at Pembroke. Assistance was freely promised, and Laugharne returned with a gladsome heart to the town. The aspect of affairs was now entirely changed, and instead of fortifying the Haven the guns of the Bristol ships were called into requisition to defend themselves. For this purpose Sir Henry Vaughan caused a strong position to be made at the Pill, where the Bristol vessels lay, and on the fort which had been erected there to protect the Pill he placed the guns intended originally for the entrance of the Haven. With these he opened fire upon the Parliamentary fleet, which was responded to with great energy, and this was continued for some days. While this was going on, Col. Laugharne, having augmented his forces by about a hundred and fifty men obtained from the ships, marched against Stackpoole, the seat of Mr. John Lort, which was garrisoned by about sixty soldiers for the King. The position of the house was secure, the walls were thick, and the guns of those days not of the best. At any rate, those in the hands of the Pembroke soldiers failed to do any great harm to the building. But what the guns failed in the pluck of the men effected. A breach was made in the walls, and the Royalists, seeing that they had no chance against superior forces, discreetly surrendered. The loss of men was small. Having placed a garrison there, Laugharne next prepared to attack Trefloyne, another fortified house within a mile or so of Tenby. This house was garrisoned with some 150 men and about forty horse. When Laugharne attacked the place a sally was attempted; but the Earl retreated to Tenby, and the house was immediately afterwards surrendered. Forty horses ready saddled, and a considerable quantity of arms and ammunition fell into the hands of the Parliamentarians by this onslaught. Continued success elated them; more help from the fleet was accorded them, and their designs grew in importance. Tenby and Carew, both strongly fortified by the Royalists, were suggested as the places next to be attacked; but on taking counsel it was resolved to proceed against the fort at the Pill, and then to march upon Haverfordwest, inasmuch as it was thought a victory in those places would have the greatest chance of frightening the enemy into submission.

The attack upon the fort at the Pill was commenced from the water by the seamen under the command of Captain Willoughby. These managed to get ashore, and soon planted some guns within a telling distance. To prevent any communications between the Pill and Haverfordwest some twenty musketeers were placed in the steeple of Stainton Church, whence a good command of the surrounding country could be obtained, and a small party of horse was scattered in the neighbourhood to intercept communication. Some messengers were thus captured and placed in safe custody within the church. The Royalists at Haverfordwest were, however, informed of what was going on, and a small party under the command of Sir Francis Lloyd made a descent from Johnston; but, being afraid of the artillery of the Parliamentary forces, retreated. The next morning Colonel Laugharne, by a strategic move, dispersed an ambuscade which had been laid for him, captured the officers, and the men fled to the fort. The Pill village was taken, and an old chapel near there, which was within a short distance, became handy for further movements. An assault was decided upon, but before it could be carried out the beleagured mounted a flag of truce. Quarter of life only was granted—the fort being surrendered, and both men and officers made prisoners. This was a most lucky hit. Mr. John Barlow, master of the ordnance, and five other officers, were among the prisoners made. A great quantity of ammunition, eighteen great guns, with half-a-dozen field carriages, were also taken; and most important of all the Bristol ships, with the barques which had accompanied them, and their guns changed hands. The news of this defeat was quickly conveyed to Haverfordwest. Consternation and terror seems to have struck all the Royalists at that place, among whom were Major-General Sir Henry Vaughan, the Governor of Haverfordwest, Sir John Stepney, Lieutenant-Colonel Butler, the High-Sheriff of the county, and others of note. They were utterly bewildered by the news that the enemy had resolved to appear next before Haverfordwest. And a story is related of them, that their terror was so great that a herd of cattle seen on a hill above the town in the indistinctness of the twilight was taken by them for soldiers, which caused them to depart hastily from the town. Sir Hugh Owen, the Member for Pembroke, was a prisoner in their hands at Haverfordwest. When their unexpected departure was decided upon, he was in the act of preparing for rest; but half-stripped as he was of his clothes, he was hurried from his room and placed on horseback, and even his wife was refused a pillion to ride behind him. Sir Henry Vaughan is accused of having had a personal hand in this ill-treatment of the Member—an action which an old narrator accounts for by remarking "that cowardice had totally and absolutely dispossessed them of their humanity." Haverfordwest, without a shot being fired, fell into the hands of Colonel Laugharne on the very morning after this disorderly retreat of the cavaliers; and within two days Roach Castle also was summoned and surrendered. The Royalists were completely driven away from the district of Roos; the people were easily brought about, and became well-disposed to the cause of the Parliament. In effecting this change in public opinion, credit is given to the influence of John Laugharne, the father of Colonel Laugharne, whose noble carriage and amiability had made him very popular in those parts.

Tenby was next visited by Laugharne and his forces. The town was strongly garrisoned for the King, and some of those who had fled from Haverfordwest had repaired thither. It was first assaulted from the sea—some of the Parliamentary ships, under the command of the Vice-Admiral in the *Swallow*, having gone from Pembroke for the purpose of assisting the land forces in the reduction of the town. They reached the scene somewhat in advance of the land forces, and immediately opened a sharp fire. The land forces soon made their appearance, and placed their ordnance to an advantage on the rising ground above the town. From Thursday to Saturday they continued pouring fire upon the town. It was then surrounded by a wall, upon which but little execution was done, although several houses had been considerably damaged. The great gate, however, was battered in; and the storming of the town was immediately afterwards resolved upon and effected. The Royalists here fought very bravely, and contested every inch of the ground; and long after the gateway had been entered by the Parliamentarians, the fighting was continued in the streets. So desperate was the fighting that the Governor himself (Commissary Gwyn, who is admitted even by his opponents to have shown in his actions "the metal and experience of a soldier,") was wounded. A goodly number were made prisoners, and much arms and ammunition taken. For their obstinacy in defending the town, their houses were plundered according to the usages of war.

Carew Castle was now the only stronghold in the hands of the Royalists in Pembroke, and on Sunday, March 10th, that also was surrendered to Captain Poyer, the Mayor of Pembroke, on terms; and by this the entire county was satisfactorily cleared of all armed Royalists.

And not merely in the County of Pembroke were these actions fruitful of good to the Parliamentary cause, for their influence was felt in the adjoining counties, which were presently summoned by Laugharne. Meanwhile the Royalists of Cardiganshire and Carmarthen were moving heaven and earth for assistance. Prince Rupert, who was in Shropshire and the neighbourhood, was implored to come to the rescue, but he was evidently bent on his northward march, so that they were left to manage their own affairs. The Earl of Carbery was anxious to enter into a treaty with the Parliament party, so as to save the country from the ravages of war; but they being now victorious, felt themselves in a position to decline the proposal of one who, while he had the power, exercised it with an iron hand. All this was performed by the 12th of March, the date of Sir John Vaughan's letter, which, so far as it relates to the capture of Tenby, tallies in every respect with Thelwall's account of it.[1]

After these many successes Laugharne and his party took a little breathing time, and for a short period they could not conclude whither they should next proceed. Both Cardiganshire and Carmarthenshire were in the hands of the Royalists—at any rate, the towns and castles were garrisoned for the King. Laugharne summoned both counties. From Cardiganshire he had an answer which was not deemed satisfactory, and though some of his own party were of opinion that another summons should be given them, Laugharne himself said he would do no such thing except with the sword in hand. His summons to the County of Carmarthen was better received; and Earl Carbery was not able to obtain that general assistance from the county which would enable him to combat successfully with Laugharne, while some of the principal

[1] Archæologia Cambrensis, vol. iv. N. S., p. 66. See vol ii., Document xlvii. Full details of these fights are given in Thelwall's letter to the Speaker (see vol. ii., Document xlvi. A.), and in two other contemporaneous pamphlets, one of which is published in the Appendix to Fenton's "Tour through Pembrokeshire."

men had already made friendly advances to the Parliamentary leaders. In fact, the Earl of Carbery was blamed much for the defeats he had sustained in Pembrokeshire. Charges of a grave nature appear to have been made against him, and these enforced his retirement from the command. He relinquished the command to Prince Rupert. The state of these counties was not such as to give much confidence to the Royalists. The town of Carmarthen, which was the strongest hold, was but meanly garrisoned. At the most they had but between three and four hundred foot, and about a hundred and fifty horse, and these were hardly fit to meet Laugharne's forces, elated with repeated victories; and Cardiganshire was still more incapable of offering any serious resistance. Some hope of aid from Breconshire seems to have encouraged them a little, and the train bands everywhere were put to the drill.

On the 10th or 11th of April Laugharne mustered his forces on Colby Moor, preparatory to his march upon Carmarthen, which place he finally resolved to proceed against first. As we have above stated, this town was not very strongly garrisoned, and the King's cause was somewhat on the wane in the neighbourhood. Nevertheless, the town was fortified with a mud-wall round about it[1] With the aid of Admiral Swanley, and after but a weak resistance, the town was entered by the victorious Parliamentarians, or, as an old Carmarthen chronicler puts it, "the towne of Carmarthen was gotten by the sword by Pembrokeshire men in

---

[1] MSS. roll of Carmarthen events, in the possession of Mr. Alcwyn Evans.

April, 1644."[1] It is said that some Irish attempted to render assistance by sea, but were prevented by the Parliamentary fleet. It was stated in one of the old newspapers that some 1,500 prisoners were taken; but if Sir John Vaughan's letter is correct, that number would appear to have been somewhat exaggerated.

Having succeeded thus beyond all expectations, Col. Laugharne and the Vice-Admiral Swanley assembled the leading men of the adjacent counties, and got them all to take the Covenant. This Covenant was the one "against the horrible plot in London"—the instructions for administering the National solemn Covenant not having then come down. When it did come down that too was administered, and generally taken; and early in April we have it from the pen of a dissentient that "Pembrokeshire urged the traitorous Covenant also in Carmarthen and Glamorganshire."[2]

Cardiganshire was still unsubdued, and so was the County of Glamorgan, in both which counties there were a good many deep malignants, as they were called by their opponents. The reduction of Glamorganshire was what was next aimed at. Swansea, even then a town "of good note," was strongly garrisoned for the King, and into it had removed most of the Royalists resident in the neighbourhood. It was a great eyesore to the Parliamentarians at Pembroke. A summons was therefore sent to the Mayor, and the other gentlemen of influence there, calling upon them to yield

[1] MSS. roll of Carmarthen events, *supra*.
[2] Quotation from a letter of Thos. Lloyd of Ynysymaengwyn to one Thomas Owen. See Warburton's Prince Rupert, i., 521.

the town into the obedience of the "King and Parliament," and promising if they complied they should be received into the "protection of the associated Covenant, and defended against all Irish rebels and Papists, and those that seek to subvert Liberties and destroy Religion," and politely hinting that if they resisted their trade would be despoiled. This summons was signed by Robert Moulton, on board the *Lion* from Milford Haven. To it an answer was sent so sharp in its terms that we are inclined to trace in it the hand of the famous David Jenkins of Hensol, "the Judge of the Mountains," as he was called by the Parliamentarians. The copy I have seen of the answer purports to have been signed by the High-Sheriff and most of the gentlemen of Glamorganshire.[1]

Nothing appears to have been done in pursuance of this summons, and shortly after the Parliament fleet quitted Milford Haven and proceeded to the Downs, much to the dismay of the Roundheads in those parts. During their stay at Milford they had contributed in no small degree to the successes which had been brought to pass; and now that Col. Charles Gerard had been appointed by Prince Rupert to the command of the Royalists in South Wales (of whom more anon), their absence was a serious matter. The gentry, therefore, lost no time in sending up a petition to the Parliament desiring that Capt. Swanley might speedily be sent back. Capt. Swanley and Capt. Smith had gone up to London to deliver in person to the House of Commons an account of their actions, and they were in attendance about the time the petition arrived. It was

[1] *Merc. Aulicus* for May 25th. (K. P. 161—7.) See vol. ii., Document xlviii.

read in the House, whereupon it was ordered that the *Leopard*, the *Swallow*, and the *Providence*, frigates brought to the Downs, should be refitted and revictualled, and should proceed to Wales as was desired. Capt. Swanley himself was called to the Bar of the House to receive the thanks of Parliament for his good services, and as a further mark of esteem it was ordered that a chain of gold of the value of £200 should be given to him, and another of the value of £100 to Capt. Smith, his Vice-Admiral.[1] Their services were required now in South Wales to oppose a more experienced soldier than the Earl of Carbery, in the person of Col. Charles Gerard, of whose doings I shall have occasion in a future page to treat.

Prince Rupert, after his successful march to Newark, returned at the head of his victorious troops to Shrewsbury. Among the faithful there was great rejoicing, both there and at Chester—thanksgiving sermons were preached, bonfires lit, the enemy denounced, and the neutral induced to declare for the King. The Prince's presence amongst them was reassuring. He visited many of the garrisons in North Wales, gave out what instructions he deemed advisable for strengthening the King's cause in those parts, appointed Sir John Owen to be Governor of Conway Castle, then in the hands of the sturdy John Williams, Archbishop of York, much to the annoyance, and notwithstanding the remonstrances, of that extraordinary man —extraordinary both as a Churchman and as a soldier. And unjustly so I think, considering the great outlay of the Archbishop in strengthening the

[1] Rushworth, part iii., vol. ii, p. 76. Commons' Journals.

town and castle. Other places were placed under the command of men in whom the Prince had confidence, and in this his Highness was not always discreet, for in several instances he displaced Welshmen whom Lord Capel had placed in command, and substituted for them creatures of his own. There can be no doubt whatever that the Prince in this respect was ill-advised. He sent English emissaries to various places. These were looked upon with a certain amount of jealousy by the Welsh, and because they were not received in the way they thought they ought to be, as the Prince's representatives, they made constant communications to the Prince, which reflected very unfavourably on the Welsh. Some of these representations will be found in the body of this Work as we progress; many others will have to be omitted. Having made a tour of the chief places in South Wales, Rupert next moved to Chester. On the whole he was successful in his mission. The hesitating were encouraged by his presence, and those who were inclined to be hostile had at any rate for a time to act very cautiously. Sir William Brereton, with his faithful force, and Colonel Mytton, with his steady soldiers, still managed to hold their own. But it was evident that they required considerable reinforcements before they could neutralize the "influence of a prince." The Earl of Denbigh, at the head of the associated counties of Shropshire and Warwickshire, had his hands pretty well occupied in managing the affairs of those counties. Nevertheless, he was constantly informed of the Prince's doings in Wales, and persons from Shrewsbury and from Wales frequently came to him at Coventry to represent the urgent need of aid they stood in. As early as the 14th of March we find him writing to the Committee of Safety of both Kingdoms: "Prince Rupert is said to be gone for Wales to raise great forces, which he is likely to do if not timely prevented, and therefore well hath it become your lordships' wisdom to provide a remedy to his growth and increase, which, by the grace of God, shall be applied with all the convenient speede that may be."[1]

Representations were also made to the Committee of Safety direct from Wales, and these became more and more urgent since Rupert's return from Newark. What with the rejoicings at Chester and Shrewsbury, and the threats which were launched against those who were not for the King, there can be no doubt that the position of the Parliamentarians in those districts was becoming serious. Nothing succeeds like success.

Sir Thomas Myddelton was in London at this time. On hearing of the state of North Wales, and the straits his friends were in, he at once undertook to proceed thither with such forces as he had just raised in London—he having towards the end of February been appointed Major-General of North Wales by a new commission, which gave him almost unlimited power as to levying contributions and sequestrating the estates of such malignants and delinquents as he could lay hold of.

"The valiant and active Colonel Mytton, Governor of Wem," says one of the old papers, "came to town this day (April 5th) the better to inform the Parliament of the affairs in Shropshire, Cheshire,

[1] State Pap. Dom., Chas. I., vol. 315, §§ 243—4.

and the parts adjacent. The faithful Colonel makes a sad relation of the condition of those parts by means of the great concourse of Irish rebels that land there, exercising such horrid and savage cruelties, the like cannot well be paralleled. And as a further aggravation of their misery, we hear also that there be about 6,000 more of these Irish rebels landed in Wales, and 4,000 more expected suddenly to follow, so that without some speedy help by the joining of Sir Thomas Myddelton, Sir William Brereton, and Colonel Mytton, our garrisons in those parts are like to be much straitened, and the whole country wasted by these bloody Irish."[1]

These and other equally pressing representations made to the Committee of Safety determined the latter to lose no time in sending the required assistance. Money was voted to Sir Thomas Myddelton for the use of his troops. A sum of £1,000 had been found by accident in Parpoole Lane, Holborn. The owner could not be discovered. It was therefore given to Sir Thomas Myddelton—not, however, before the Parliament at Westminster had resolved that the money should be repaid with interest out of the Court of Wards and Liveries, when a lawful owner should lay claim to the same. This little incident shews that a thorough sense of honesty governed the assembly in London, the calumny of the cavaliers notwithstanding. A further sum of £2,000 was voted to him out of the sequestered estate of the Lady Shelley, just deceased. Sir Thomas Myddelton was fully armed with power to sequester the estate of the Royalists, and to levy

[1] *Perfect Diurnall*, No. 36 [1—8, April, 1644.]

money for the support of his troops in as full and ample a manner as the chief commanders in other places. Quitting London towards the end of May he marched with considerable celerity to Coventry, where he formed a junction with the Earl of Denbigh. Though it was Sir Thomas Myddelton's original purpose to march without delay into Wales, yet by the time he arrived at Coventry he was compelled, at least for a time, to defer his project, and for this reason: matters everywhere were approaching a crisis.[1]

At this time Col. Mytton, who had returned from London, was at the head of a small body of men in the south of Cheshire and on the borders of Wales. News came to him that preparations were being made for the conveyance of a considerable quantity of ammunition from Oswestry to Prince Rupert, who was much in need of it. A messenger was despatched to the Earl of Denbigh to inform him of this, in order that it should be intercepted by their concerted action, and Mytton approached Chirk for that purpose. Mytton there was told that a party of men had that very morning left Oswestry. The next day two straggling troopers belonging to the garrison at Oswestry were captured, and these on being pressed stated that a small body of musketeers had quitted the town, and were on their way in the direction of Bangor.[2] Mytton then was at St. Martin's. Taking some five and twenty horsemen, and about as many dragoons with him, he went in pursuit, and near Duddleston came upon the enemy, numbering nearly twice as

[1] *Perfect Diurnall.* No. 40 and No. 42.
[2] In Flintshire.

many as he had been told. Coming upon them unexpectedly their capture was easy. About twenty-seven of them were made prisoners, their names clearly indicating their nationality as Welshmen. All their ammunition was also taken.

The Royalists now occupied themselves in strengthening their fortifications at Oswestry. It was Mytton's design, as soon as aid came from the Earl of Denbigh, to attack that town. The Earl made his appearance the following Saturday at Wem, with what force he could spare, which was only his troop of horse and some two hundred foot, the rest of his forces being on their march towards Lancashire. Col. Mytton also had come to Wem to reinforce himself, and he and the Earl of Denbigh advanced the same day near to Oswestry. At this time Oswestry was surrounded by a wall, but the chief strength of the place lay in its church and castle, which were well manned with men belonging to the garrison. On the approach of the Parliamentarians about mid-day these gave them a "hot salute." Fearing assistance might be sent from Shrewsbury, where the main body of the Irish soldiers were, the Earl of Denbigh gave orders to guard the roads leading to the town. Scouts also were sent to the neighbouring hills, and these actually saw some troops advancing towards them, but which from some cause or other never came up. The first attack was made on the church, which was outside the walls.[1] It soon fell: the men within ran to the steeple, but to no purpose, they had soon to

---

[1] "The Church of St. Oswalde," says Leland, who saw it in the time of Henry VIII., "is a very faire leddid church, with a great towrrid steple, but it standith without the new gate." This description is accurate also of the church at the time of the above struggle.

surrender. The gate of the town was next shot in, and after some sharp fighting, in which a woman was killed, the streets were deserted, the Parliamentarians entered, and found that the remainder of the garrison had retired to the castle. From this vantage ground they poured incessant fire upon the enemies. Against the thick walls of the castle the "great sacre" of the Parliamentary party was not of much use. Night setting in the struggle abated. A Council of War was called by the Earl of Denbigh, who throughout the day had braved every danger and evinced great courage. The resolution of the Council was to set fire to the castle gates. A party of troopers was engaged to do this, but being tired out they did not do it in the night. Fresh orders were given at daybreak on Sunday. The women of the town, many of whom had husbands or other near relatives within the castle, hearing of this were alarmed. They came to the victor on their knees, and implored the Earl, before he blew up the castle, to give them leave to speak to their husbands and loved ones. But the poor souls said all this in Welsh. An interpreter had to be obtained, when the Earl was informed of their wish, and consented to it. Quarter of life alone was offered them. This the brave men inside (their wives' prayers notwithstanding) at first would not listen to. They asked for more honourable conditions. Their request was declined, and at last, giving way to the entreaties of the women, they surrendered. Oswestry was thus taken. Many county gentlemen who had assembled in the town were made prisoners, divers officers met with the same fate, and some two hundred common soldiers.

Thanksgivings for this victory were offered up the very same afternoon in the church of the town. And at another Council which was held, Colonel Mytton was made its governor. To avoid plunder the town consented to a composition of £500.[1]

The loss of Oswestry was a great blow to the King's interest in those parts. It formed an important pass into the Principality, and as the Parliamentarians hitherto had not been able to obtain such an advantage in the neighbourhood, it was resolved that Colonel Mytton should remain there awhile, and that a sufficient garrison should be stationed at the place. Having made all the necessary arrangements, the Earl of Denbigh quitted Oswestry and proceeded to Nantwich, where Sir Thomas Myddelton and the Cheshire forces had been quartered for some four days, intending afterwards to march into Lancashire after Prince Rupert. Oswestry, in the eyes of the Royalists, whose head-quarters were at Shrewsbury, was a place of too great a concern to them to be allowed to remain unchallenged in the hands of their enemies. Sir Fulke Hunckes was at this time Governor of Shrewsbury, having succeeded Sir Francis Ottley. He had at his command a considerable body of men, and the many Royalist garrisons around in Cheshire and Shropshire, and the adjacent Welsh counties, were in a position to give help. It was therefore resolved, instantly the Earl of Denbigh had departed, to take advantage of his absence and of the condition of the small body left under Col. Mytton, who could scarcely offer any real resistance

---

[1] "Two Great Victories, &c.," King's Pamphlets, 163—3. *The Kingdom's Weekly Intelligencer*, No. 61. See vol. ii., Document liii., p. 173.

to such overwhelming forces as were at their disposal. All necessary preparations were made—a general rendezvous appointed. Hunckes went out of Shrewsbury at the head of some 2,000 foot and about 600 horse, and these were soon increased by reinforcements from other garrisons. The progress of such a body could not be kept secret. The Parliamentary party throughout the war (at any rate so far as Wales was concerned) never found difficulty in obtaining intelligence of the enemy's movements: so much so, that at an early period in the history of the war such a fact was observed by Clarendon to be very detrimental to the King.[1] Preparatory to his march into Lancashire the Earl of Denbigh appointed a rendezvous of his own forces, and those of Sir William Brereton and Sir Thomas Myddelton, at Knutsford. On his way thither he was informed that the enemy were gathering in a great body from all the neighbouring garrisons, with the intention to attempt the regaining of Oswestry. "Upon mature deliberation," Sir Thomas Myddelton was sent with three of his companies (in another letter this is stated to be his own horse and the Cheshire foot), with as many as could be spared from Wem, to aid Col. Mytton in maintaining Oswestry. These were escorted into that town by the Earl of Denbigh's horse. By this means that garrison was supplied with some 400 musketeers well fitted with all necessaries, and a full troop of horse. Moreover, a "good ingenier" was sent to assist them. Earl Denbigh himself at once proceeded to Manchester to consult with Sir John Meldrum as to the matter of going to the assistance

[1] Rebellion, ii, p. 135.

of York. There it was decided that Sir John Meldrum (to whom the Earl of Denbigh assigned such troops as Nottinghamshire and Derbyshire had sent to him) and Sir William Brereton should proceed to York, and that the Earl of Denbigh should retrace his steps with his own regiment of horse and the Staffordshire horse to Oswestry. In the meantime Oswestry was threatened with a siege by the Royalist forces under Col. Marrow. To his assistance came Sir Fulke Hunckes, and their forces are put down by the Parliamentary party at about 4,000. On Tuesday, the 2nd July, the latter having heard of the approach of Myddelton towards their quarters, ordered Col. Marrow to send out a party of scouts to discover their strength. Marrow, however, took with him the whole body of horse. Hunckes said afterwards that this was against his express command, or at any rate that he expressly forbade Col. Marrow to engage himself in combat with the enemy. Whether Marrow wilfully disobeyed his superior's command, or whether what happened was not his fault but his misfortune, through the better tactics of the enemy, does not appear; but the fact is clear enough, that Sir Thomas Myddelton, sallying out from Oswestry with his horse, completely routed Col. Marrow, and that the defeat of the latter was enhanced by the valour of the Cheshire foot, who pursued the straggling horse of the enemy for a considerable distance, and that all this was done before a word of intelligence of the fight had reached Sir Fulke Hunckes, whose first acquaintance of the fact was the appearance of a messenger from Marrow, and soon afterwards of Marrow himself, bespattered with the dust of the conflict and "all alone." Colonel Hunckes could now do nothing but secure his own way back to Shrewsbury, which was barely done in time to prevent their complete defeat by the Earl of Denbigh's forces, who arrived the next day at Oswestry. The Earl was somewhat chafed by the precipitancy of Sir Thomas Myddelton, whom he had acquainted by messenger of his intention to join him, but who, "finding his opportunity thought itt not fitt to stay for him," whereby the victory was not so complete as it might otherwise have been. It is due, however, to Sir Thomas Myddelton, and the Earl candidly acknowledges it, that the letters announcing the Earl's approach had been concealed.[1] Thus the Earl, though he had detached himself for the purpose of relieving Oswestry from Sir John Meldrum and Sir William Brereton, who were gone on a most important march towards York, found that the work had been well done, and the honour which he sought already won by another. In this movement of his he also lost another chance of winning distinction in a greater victory for the Parliament than the relief of Oswestry. I allude to the great battle of Marston Moor—the most important battle since the beginning of the war. Prince Rupert having been ordered by the King in a letter of the 14th June, dated from Tickenhall, in Worcestershire, to march without an instant delay to the succour of York, which was besieged by the Scots and Fairfax's forces,

[1] Earl of Denbigh's letter of the 11th July. State Pap. Dom., Char. I., Bundle 316. See vol. ii., Document lv. B., p. 183. For a full account of raising the siege of Oswestry see Sir Thomas Myddelton's letter, published in a pamphlet (K. P. 164—16), the foregoing letter of the Earl of Denbigh, and also Sir Fulke Hunckes's letter to Prince Rupert, State Pap. Dom. 316, fol. 132, all of which I give in vol. ii., Documents lv. A. B. and c.

gathered all his forces, leaving only what was absolutely essential to maintain the various garrisons, and evading all those sent in pursuit of him, came before York on the last day but one of the month at the head of a force numbering, it is said, 20,000 men. At his approach the Parliamentary leaders resolved to raise the siege so as to concentrate their power for the purpose of preventing the Prince from throwing succours into the beleagured city; but the Prince was too sharp for them. By skilful manœuvres he entered the city without a conflict. Had he rested satisfied with this success, and awaited reinforcements, which were known to be on the way towards him, the disaster of Marston Moor would probably have been averted; but Rupert was too impetuous, and looking upon the King's letter perhaps as a positive command to fight, he would not follow Newcastle's advice, to defer engaging with the enemy in battle. The conflict was a dreadful one. Both ranks were broken, and unutterable confusion prevailed, the result in the first being decidedly advantageous to the Royalists: the Parliamentary soldiers—Scotch and English—flying in all directions, the Royalists following in pursuit. When they returned from the pursuit, confident of victory, they were surprised to find that the field they thought they had won was already in the hands of a successful enemy—the right wing, though commanded by Rupert himself, completely routed by Cromwell and his army of invincible Ironsides: men who fought not for the mere sake of fighting, but with the faith and purpose that they were fighting for a cause dearer to them than their lives— for Religion and Liberty. These men could not easily be defeated. They had already been christened Ironsides, and under the command of such an able general as Cromwell they never flinched in their duty and never sustained a defeat. Notwithstanding the defeat of Prince Rupert's wing, those who returned from the pursuit of the Scotch resumed the struggle with Cromwell and Manchester; but when night set in not a Royalist remained on the field, save three thousand slain and about 1,600 prisoners. Cromwell had before given good proofs of his commanding qualities, but his merits shone pre-eminently here, and it was mainly due to him that the result was what it was. The Earl of Manchester, his superior officer, no doubt can claim some of the credit, but Cromwell was so dissatisfied with his conduct that he wrote to the Parliament, and afterwards declared personally in the House, his grave accusations against the Earl of Manchester, which, as we shall see later on, brought about a great change in military matters.

The Prince and Newcastle late in the night entered York, but not together. The rupture between them was too great to be healed. Rupert decided to leave the city with his horse and whatever foot remained, and Newcastle resolved to depart for the continent forthwith. These messages they exchanged, and each kept his word. Prince Rupert marched towards Chester with the wreck of his army. Newcastle embarked for the continent, and York soon afterwards capitulated.

Leaving Rupert on his march from York, we shall now take a look at matters in the southern division of the Principality. The Earl of Carbery having failed in his attempt to subdue the Parliament party in Pembrokeshire, and having everywhere sustained serious defeats, resigned his sword to Prince Rupert. The Royalists in these parts were very pressing upon the Prince to appear in person in the west, to interrupt the victorious course of Laugharne and Swanley; but matters of graver import required his presence elsewhere, and Col. Charles Gerard, at the head of a troop of horse, was dispatched to attempt the task. When summoned to this Gerard was somewhere in the west, for we find that he landed at the Black Rock, near Chepstow, in Monmouthshire. I have in vain endeavoured to ascertain the date of his advance into Wales. I have searched almost every newspaper of the time, and they were many, but without success. Most of these papers were advocates of the Parliamentary cause, and though on the whole I have reason to credit them with a fair amount of truthfulness, yet they manifest a provoking reticence on matters which did not benefit that cause. On the other hand, the Royalist papers, though bristling with some sparkling wit, do not appear to pay so much regard to the truth as those of their opponents—they were not merely reticent when defeat had attended their armies, but often flatly denied the truth, and even claimed victory when overwhelming disaster had been the fate of the party; while small skirmishes, in which their soldiers had had the best, were magnified into victories of immense importance. Both sides at times were given to exaggeration, but the palm in this respect certainly belongs to the Court papers. With regard to Gerard's movements in Wales, scarcely a word for some time appears in the Parliamentary papers, and probably for a while his movements were not of such decision as to justify even his own side in making much ado about them. Even *Mercurius Aulicus* maintained a degree of reserve which fully justifies this inference. But this silence on their part was not long required, for it is evident that by some dashing exploits Gerard soon drove back the tide of "Pembrokeshire men," who, having passed out of their own county, had penetrated even into the distant east of Glamorganshire, and had planted at Cardiff a "strong garrison," much to the annoyance of such as were loyal in that county. How the Parliament party had become possessed of Cardiff, whether by the onward march of the land forces, or whether by an attack from the sea by Swanley or Moulton, does not appear. But that they had done so is evidenced by the testimony which will be presently adduced to show Gerard's accomplishments in these parts. Cardiff seems to be the only place of importance which had fallen into the hands of the Parliament in Glamorganshire, whence it may fairly be inferred—and this inference is supported by the fact that Swansea was summoned, as we have already seen, from the sea—that Cardiff had been entered into by sea forces under Swanley or Moulton. From Glamorganshire Gerard made his way into Carmarthenshire. Kidwelly had in the meantime fallen into the hands of his enemies. Against that place he directed his power, and it appears with the same success as he had experienced at Cardiff. And now for the first time we come upon anything like a date by which to gauge Gerard's movements. That he had entered into Carmarthenshire early in June is evident from a summons dated the 12th day of June, under the hand of Hugh Carrow, one of the high constables for the County of Pembroke.[1] The copy preserved is one addressed to the petty constables of Walton, in Pembrokeshire, calling upon them, in obedience to the Commissioners appointed for the management of that county, by the ordinance for the association of the three counties of Pembroke, Cardigan, and Carmarthen, which had been sanctioned by the Parliament but some few days before, to collect all the fighting power of their parish between the ages of sixteen and sixty, and to conduct them to a place of rendezvous to meet the said committee. This summons is interesting in many respects. It shows that on the 12th of June Gerard's advance into Carmarthenshire was spoken of as having occurred "lately." And from its general tone we may infer that the pleas likely to tell on the Pembrokeshire people were those which called upon them to fight for their Religion and Liberty. Speaking of this, *Mercurius Aulicus* says that the Committee of Pembrokeshire had "forged slanders" in warrants to abuse the people.

Having taken Kidwelly and placed a garrison there, Gerard marched to Carmarthen. What resistance was offered to him I have not been able to discover, but that some contest ensued is apparent from their own account of it, where it is stated that Gerard "fell on the town of Carmarthen, which he presently mastered, and there placed a strong garrison under Colonel Lovelace, and left a garrison also at Abermarlais."[2] All this had been done before the

---

[1] *Merc. Aulicus*, 29th week, 1644. See vol. ii., Document lvi. B.
[2] *Ibid.*

18th of June, under which date, in a contemporary paper, it is stated that a messenger out of the County of Pembroke had informed the Committee of Examinations (in London) that "Col. Charles Garret [Gerard], with a party of horse, is in the town of Carmarthen, and is fortifying it for the King."[1] By Sunday, the 23rd June, the whole of the County of Carmarthen was in the hands of the Royalists, much to the joy of *Mercurius Aulicus*, which boasts that there is a likelihood "now that bloody mariner [Swanley] begins to fear he may ere long be brought to reckon for it. For Swanley not satisfied with piracy and sea villanies, did practice by land also, both in Pembrokeshire, Carmarthenshire, and Glamorganshire, till that gallant gentleman, Col. Charles Gerard, made him face about, driving the barbarous felon to the place from whence he came [Milford Haven I presume]. Two of the three counties are perfectly cleared, and the third so chastised that the rebels are already at the water-side. The Welsh gentry and commons were so much startled at the horror of the fact that they now rise as one man to punish the malefactors."[2] The "fact" here alluded to has reference to Swanley's throwing overboard several Irishmen captured by him, upon their refusing to take the Covenant.

Before following the enemy to the water-side, Gerard made a detour to Newcastle-Emlyn and Cardigan, in which he experienced the same uninterrupted success which had attended all his movements since his landing at the Black Rock. It is

---
[1] *The Weekly Account*, No. 42.
[2] *Merc. Aulicus*, 26th week. June 29, 1644.

said that the County of Cardigan had been at this time much distressed by the Pembrokeshire men. Cardigan seems to have been the first object of attack. Here, according to their own account, the Royalists slew and made prisoners more than two hundred, and cleared the whole country of the Parliament party. Falling next upon Newcastle-Emlyn, he took that place also; and having left garrisons at both places began his march into Pembrokeshire, which county from the beginning of the war had been "infested with the rebels and was considered the most seditious of all." Laugharne Castle soon fell into his hands, and early in July Roch Castle also. Haverfordwest, Pembroke, and Tenby, were now the only places left in the whole of South Wales which had not been brought to the obedience of the King.[1] The preceding number of the same journal, under the date of July 13, states that Haverfordwest had been taken by Gerard, and that the enemy had "left them no hold in all South Wales, but only Tenby and Pembroke Castles," which is confirmed by other papers. So that out of the seven hundreds into which the County of Pembroke was divided, two only remained in the hands of the Parliament party—Castlemartin and Roos. Having carried everything before him in this triumphant progress, Gerard sat down before Pembroke, thinking of inducing the enemy to make their appearance, but day after day passed and they made no stir. Nor was there any present necessity for their doing so, for hard pressed as they appeared to be, and driven fairly back to their last place of refuge, they felt there

---

[1] *Merc. Aulicus,* 29th week, *ante.*

no fear of the enemy. The town was well fortified and strong, and what was of the greatest consequence, the Haven was still theirs, where was a strong body of shipping at their service, under experienced and daring commanders. The Parliament papers of this date are vague and lack preciseness. Some sort of an attempt to intercept the onward course of Gerard appears to have been made, but at what point it is difficult to say. It must have been before the final approach to Pembroke—probably between Roch Castle and Haverfordwest. *The True Informer*, issued on the 27th of July, states that out of Gloucestershire "it is advertised that Col. Lohun [Laugharne], Governor of Pembrokeshire, and Capt. Moulton, with his sailors, have routed Col. Gerard, a commander under the Earl of Carbery, in his advance towards Pembroke, slew and took 500 of his men, and divers arms, besides several carriages and most of their baggage, and forced him and the rest of the Welsh runts to fly into the mountains for shelter." In its next number, issued on the 3rd of August, it reiterates the above account, which goes far to establish it as a fact, and boasts of it because it "stopped their intended progress into Pembrokeshire, which they would have plundered and spoiled, as they had done before in Monmouthshire, Glamorganshire, Carmarthenshire, and Cardiganshire, in all which places they had done much mischief, and had taken many forts and castles, viz., Cardigan, Emlyn, and Laugharne Castles, since the landing of Colonel Gerard and his Irish and Popish forces at the Black Rock in Monmouthshire." This account so far corroborates *Aulicus*. But while giving all credit to the victory claimed by the Parliamentary party, it must be admitted that it appears to have been but of little use, for it is clear that they were at last fairly driven back to the "water-side." But though the landsmen were thus brought to bay, the sailors had still a free field. They scoured the coast and captured whatever came in their way. Captain Moulton was especially on the alert, and his watchfulness was soon rewarded by the capture of "nine ships near Milford Haven, which were laden with wine and tobacco, going from the west, and had in them above 100 pieces of ordnance, all which will be now employed for the use of the Parliament soldiers," who doubtless derived much comfort from such good things. While Moulton was making such excellent use of his time, and Gerard was keeping his eye on the garrisons at Pembroke and Tenby, Swanley taking advantage of the absence of the latter appears to have advanced by sea to the coast of Glamorgan, and landed there. It is said that he regained "many of the forts and towns which the enemy had lately taken there," and moreover, that he had managed to capture some 1,500 head of cattle from the enemy, which he took with him back to Pembroke "with very little loss." What with nine ships laden with wine and tobacco, and 1,500 cattle taken on a single expedition, the position of those within the walls of Pembroke could not have been distressing, and a siege under such circumstances would not entail those serious inconveniences which generally attends sieges, and which the town of Pembroke itself had a taste of within a few years of this date.

Gerard had succeeded beyond expectation. He had entirely cleared three counties of the enemy, and in the fourth had driven them back to their only place of refuge. A finer opportunity to develope the affectionate loyalty of the people could not have presented itself, but Gerard was not the man to avail himself of it. He was a mere soldier, daring, audacious, and cruel. Courage he did not lack, nor soldierly ability and tact; but he was wanting in that discretion, forbearance, and judiciousness which are essential to a successful diplomatist; and as we shall presently see, instead of encouraging those who were loyal in Wales, he treated them off-handedly, and even contemptuously; distrusted those who would have aided him, and bestowed all his favours on creatures of his own. The leaders of the people, men of repute in their respective neighbourhoods, who were looked up to and had a following, he never attempted to conciliate. Such as had been appointed governors of towns and commanders of garrisons by the Earl of Carbery he displaced, appointing in their stead men known only to himself and like himself. And even if the Royalist journals speak the truth, when they state that upon his first appearance in Wales he was well supported by the local gentry, and that the people rose as one man to fight for the King,—which probably is slightly exaggerated,—his after-conduct caused a manifest change. High-spirited as these men were, they would not submit willingly to be ridden over rough-shod by a man who, though he had the King's commission, failed to treat them as they deserved, and this unconciliatory conduct of Gerard's ultimately neutralised his power and

CHAP. V.
1644.

influence, and caused him to be removed from command. He was rapacious and unprincipled—cold-blooded and cruel; and Wales by-and-by rejoiced in its deliverance from the control of such a man.

We shall leave him for the present and return to North Wales. After the disastrous defeat on Marston Moor, Prince Rupert quitted York, and his movements for a little time were uncertain. It was unknown whether he would attempt to move southward towards the King, proceed to the north, or go into Lancaster, but this suspense was not long maintained, and his presence in Lancashire was soon discovered. It is difficult to understand why he and his wrecked force was not pursued immediately upon his quitting York. It was not done. Those of the Parliament forces who were engaged at Marston Moor did not show much activity to follow their victory. Rupert was allowed to go whither he list, and a fortnight elapsed before even York was entered. After the capitulation of York, Sir John Meldrum and Sir William Brereton were ordered to pursue Rupert, who was then recruiting in North Wales and Lancashire, and expecting reinforcements from Ireland, which, however, did not come. Meldrum and Brereton lacked no energy once they were dispatched in quest of him, and soon came upon a portion of his forces in Lancashire, with whom they had a successful skirmish. Finding himself pressed, and having been disappointed at the non-appearance of the Irish whom he had expected, he quitted Lancashire and entered Cheshire. He was still hopeful of assistance from Ireland, and *Mercurius Civicus* states that "Prince Rupert, *alias* the Duke of Plunderland, is come to Chester with 3,000 horse, where he waits for some more of his Majesty's Irish Catholick subjects, to *advance the Protestant Religion.*"[1] Here again our newspaper authorities become conflicting, and often unintelligible. Instead of Cheshire it is said that he had made for Shropshire, " that there Sir Thomas Myddelton and Sir William Brereton fell upon his rear and took some prisoners, and that the Prince with 3,000 or 4,000 men had fled to Shrewsbury to try what success of strength he may get from Wales."[2] Of his chances to recruit in Wales the Roundheads were not much afraid, and boasted that "the Welsh have been over and over pricked and pulled (alluding, I presume, to balloting or conscription); there is not a man left but is cousin to one Array man or other, and can get off without bribes."[3] His plans some thought were to join with the King, and to prevent this he was carefully watched by the Earl of Denbigh and Sir Thomas Myddelton on one side, and Sir John Meldrum and Sir William Brereton on the other.[4] Warburton, who had the advantage of having before him the Prince's diary, states that Rupert having skilfully evaded the forces under the Earl of Denbigh, which was on the watch to cut off his retreat, brought at length his remaining followers in good order to Shrewsbury, which place was reached on the 20th of July, whence it appears that the old newspapers were inexact in saying he had reached Chester. That he did not long remain at Shrewsbury is clear, for there is the best evidence

---

[1] No. 61, for the week ending 25th July.
[2] *London Post*, No. 1, Aug. 6.
[3] *Parliament Scout*, No. 59, Aug. 3
[4] *Mere Civicus*, No. 63, Aug. 8.

that he was at Chester on the 3rd, whence he indited a letter to Sir John Mennes, Governor of North Wales, Dudley Wyatt, Lieut.-Governor of North Wales, John Morgan, Esq., the High-Sheriff of Merionethshire, and others, calling upon them to cause inquiry to be made as to what had been collected, and how much remained unpaid of the impositions and taxes imposed upon the counties in North Wales for his Majesty's use, and to collect with as little delay as possible what was due. The several counties of North Wales had been heavily taxed by the King's party, the necessities of which became much greater when the Irish forces landed there; and there can be no doubt whatever that such exactions, and, what was far worse, the raids constantly made upon their cattle, caused the Welsh yeomen to pray for a riddance of the King's men, and alienated their affections from his side. The Prince was in sore need of money and ammunition. No aid had come from Ireland, where his only hopes lay, and consequently he sent pressing messages to the King for powder. He did not take with him to Chester all his forces. Some he left at Shrewsbury, and a small body of horse he forwarded to quarter at Welshpool, in Montgomeryshire. Col. Mytton, who was about this time in the neighbourhood of Shrewsbury, had a slight skirmish with the party at that place under Hunckes, and hearing of the enemy's horse quartering at Welshpool he marched that way. At this time, which was the beginning of August, Sir Thomas Myddelton was quartered at Nantwich. He also heard of the horse at Welshpool, and instantly set out for that place. On Saturday, the 3rd of

August, Mytton joined Myddelton, and their united forces numbered some 550 horse and foot, and with these on the Sunday they pounced unexpectedly upon the party at Welshpool, which consisted of Rupert's own regiment of horse, under the command of Sir Thomas Dallison, and, surprising them, took some 300 horse, with much arms, some 40 common soldiers, and several officers. Prince Rupert's own cornet was killed, and Sir Thomas Dallison fled. The latter was surprised, and being at the time in bed he escaped in his shirt, leaving his breeches behind him, in which was a letter written by him, but not sent, to Prince Rupert, complaining of their weak state at Welshpool, and stating that "my Lord Powis" had given him some 113 caps and some cloth for his Highness. Returning from this successful exploit they drove away some 200 head of cattle, the property of the Lord Powis, from the very walls of Red Castle. Myddelton returned to Nantwich, and Mytton to Oswestry, into which places it is said many of Rupert's horse disaffected came in daily.[1]

It was now Rupert's duty to try by every possible means to strengthen his footing in North Wales, and it is said that his object was to make Chester his winter quarters. For this purpose letters were written to the principal men of the several counties reminding them of their allegiance, and inciting their loyalty by every possible means. Those who were wavering or faltering in their loyalty, and such as were doubtful, he thought a personal interview would be the best means of securing

---

[1] *Kingdom's Weekly Intelligencer*, No 67, Aug. 14; No. 64 *Merc. Civicus*, and No. 43 *True Informer*. See also vol ii, Document lvii.. 194.

CHAP. V.
1644.

their co-operation; and to these he wrote asking them to meet him either at Chester or Shrewsbury. Among others he wrote to the celebrated Lord Herbert of Cherbury. This able but eccentric nobleman, by some means or other, had created in the minds of those at the head of the King's affairs in those parts doubts as to his loyalty, and hence he was asked to meet the Prince, but he excused himself in these terms, in a letter dated from Montgomery Castle, August 23, 1644:—
"I shall humbly crave to tell your Highness that though I have the ambition to kiss your most valorous and princely hands, yet, because I am newly entered into a course of physic, I do humbly desire to be excused for the present. Beseeching your Highness nevertheless to hold me in your former good opinion and favor, since I am your Highness's most humble and obedient servant."[1] Whether this was a feigned or a real excuse it is now impossible to say. From what happened soon afterwards, and which in due order we shall refer to, the Royalists would naturally infer deception. His answer was by no means of an encouraging nature; but before it was written Rupert had met with a serious repulse.

As is before stated, he was in sore need of ammunition, and Irish supplies failing, messages had been sent for aid to the King's quarters in the West of England. Lord Digby, the Principal Secretary of State, writing to the Prince from Boconock, in Cornwall, under the date of 15th August, states that the great care of the King was

[1] Warburton's Rupert, iii., 22.

for his Highness, how to supply his "wants of ammunition," for which he said all that could be, was done, and that "there are a hundred barrels of powder sent from Bristol through Wales, and commanded to Charles Gerard to have them conveyed so fast as shall be necessary." They did not, however, come fast enough to be of service to Rupert, and some of it became useful to the enemy.

The Prince was still at Chester with some of his horse, while a portion of his forces remained under Colonel Ogleby in Lancashire. Sir John Meldrum looked after the latter, and Sir Thomas Myddelton and Brereton were vigilant in Cheshire. Some days before the 21st of August, Colonel Marrow (of whose actions at Oswestry I have before written) went out of Chester with a small body of horse, and quartered at Tarvin, a small village some four miles eastward of that city. Hearing of this, Brereton and Myddelton, who were then at Northwich, marched thence to Frodsham, a small town on the banks of the Weaver, a little above its exit into the sea, where they expected to find the enemy, thinking that their design was for Lancashire. Finding them not, they crossed Delamere Forest, which was not then so contracted as it is now, and came to Ashton, where they received definite intelligence that the Cavaliers were at Tarvin. Thither they at once proceeded, and on their way they came upon some of Marrow's men, who had been sent out as scouts. These they pursued to Tarvin, where they fell upon the body of the enemy and worsted them. Some of the latter fled into the church, and others betook themselves to Chester.

The latter were followed with good effect by Colonel Sankey, and the attack upon the church was left to Colonel Jones.[1] Many prisoners were made, some were slain, and a number of horse captured. Colonel Marrow himself was mortally wounded, and died as soon as he was taken back to Chester.[2] This officer, even by those who were opposed to him, is spoken of in high terms as a gallant soldier. He had come from Ireland in the previous December, and what made his death at this time especially sad was the fact that he had "married a wife with a good fortune" but three weeks before.[3]

Chester was frightened at this ill-luck, and the military authorities there saw that they would be placed in great danger if they did not stem the enemy's progress. Two regiments of horse,[4] or according to another account,[5] about 800 horse and foot, went out next morning to avenge Marrow's death. Brereton and Myddelton, expecting that they would be attacked, were in readiness to receive their opponents. A desperate fight ensued, and in the end the Royalists gave way and fled, having sustained a loss of about 400 men, of whom 300 were slain, the rest being made prisoners. In all the Parliamentary newspapers Prince Rupert is stated to have been engaged in this fight. But it is toler-

---

[1] There were three eminent men of the name of Jones colonels of the Parliament army, viz., Colonel Michael Jones (the one above alluded to), afterwards Lieut.-General of Ireland, Colonel John Jones, the Regicide, and Colonel Philip Jones, of Swansea, afterwards Comptroller of the Household to Cromwell, and one of the members of his House of Lords.

[2] "A true relation of two great victories obtained over the enemy, &c.," (K. P. 171—25). Vol. ii., Document lviii.

[3] *Parliament Scout*, No. 62.

[4] *Merc. Civicus*, No. 66.

[5] *Scottish Dove*, No. 46.

ably certain that the Prince was not in Chester at this time, for Colonel William Legge, the Governor of Chester, writing on the 22nd August—the very day upon which the second battle was fought—to "his most dear Prince," states that "the night your Highness lay at Ruthin, Marrow's horse were beaten." The Lord Byron also gives an account of that action, which, he says, took place "on the spot where your Highness killed the buck as the horse were drawing out."[1] Had the Prince taken part in the fight there would have been no occasion for these letters. According to Legge he was at Ruthin at the time, and this is confirmed by a pamphlet published on the 27th August, which states that Rupert had gone to Ruthin for fear of the Earl of Manchester, rumours of whose advance towards Chester had been prevalent for several days.[2]

This defeat was so serious that Prince Rupert gave up all idea of going back to Chester. Of his movements for some time afterwards his antagonists were entirely ignorant. All sorts of rumours were abroad. Some thought he had gone to South Wales to join with Gerard.[3] Others thought he had sought refuge in the innermost recesses of North Wales. His destination, however, was nowhere else than Bristol. Accompanied by a small retinue of horse, numbering between a hundred and two hundred, consisting of portions of his own, and Colonel Vaughan's and Colonel Trevor's regiments, he crossed the mountains to Ludlow, and thence proceeded to

[1] Warburton's Rupert, iii., 22.
[2] "Three victories obtained against Lord Ogleby and others of Rupert's forces, &c."
[3] *Weekly Account*, No. 52.

Bristol, where he gave out that more were coming, and that regiments of Welsh soldiers out of Monmouthshire and Glamorganshire would soon cross the Severn and come to their aid.[1] In all probability the Prince did expect reinforcements from South Wales. Gerard had by this time subdued nearly the whole of South Wales—Haverfordwest having been taken by him on the 22nd of August; and Tenby was in imminent danger, its Governor, a brother of Major-General Laugharne, having been captured when attempting to send assistance to Haverfordwest.[2] And the Prince had desired him to proceed to Bristol. But other matters, to which I shall presently refer, occupied Gerard and prevented this juncture. The Prince also expected help from the North. A general movement for the West appears to have been decided upon. Sir Marmaduke Langdale, with some 3,000 horse, quitting Cumberland, passed through Lancashire, where he was much harassed. When he entered Cheshire his strength scarcely exceeded a third of the number he originally started with. Brereton now prepared to cut off his passage. On the 26th of August the two forces met at Malpas, in Cheshire—the Parliament army comprising only about 800 men, under the command of Col. Jones. Notwithstanding the disparity in number, Col. Jones did considerable execution; but he would doubtless have been worsted were it not for the timely appearance of Sir William Brereton. Even with this reinforcement they numbered less than the Royalists. The

---

[1] *London Post*, No. 2, September 3; and *Kingdom's Weekly Intelligencer*, No. 70.
[2] *Merc. Aulicus*, Aug. 31, 1644.

latter, however, lost several of their officers, which disheartened the soldiers. So they beat a retreat to Chester instead of pursuing the road to Shrewsbury as they intended. Sir Marmaduke was himself wounded. Two colonels and three majors were slain, and several other officers made prisoners.[1]

Sir Thomas Myddelton was at this time at Oswestry with Col. Mytton, where he received orders from London to march into Montgomeryshire for the double purpose of dispersing the Royalists there and of intercepting the powder which had been sent from Bristol to Gerard, with instructions from Lord Digby to forward it without delay to North Wales, where it was much wanted for the supply of Chester and Liverpool. The latter place was besieged by Sir John Meldrum, and the want of ammunition was very great there. Powder also was running short at Chester. In obedience to the order Sir Thomas Myddelton quitted Oswestry on the 3rd of September, and marching all night got to Newtown early in the morning, where was a small temporary garrison of Royalists under the command of Sir Thomas Gardiner. These were surprised, Gardiner himself, with his cornet, and about forty soldiers, were made prisoners, and some thirty-six barrels of the Bristol powder, with a large quantity of match, and twelve barrels of brimstone, were captured. Myddelton thence advanced the same day to Montgomery. The castle here was a fortress of great strength. Sir John Meldrum, who appeared before it some time after this, characterized it as "one of the goodliest and strongest places that he ever looked

[1] "The Successes of our Cheshire Forces, &c." (K. P. 172—8.) Vol. ii., Document lix.

upon." In it lived the Lord Herbert of Cherbury, the well-known author of "The Life and Times of Henry VIII.," and other works, a nobleman of great literary abilities, but exceedingly vain and of eccentric habits. Hitherto he had taken no active part in the war. It is true he at first favoured the Royal cause, and was one of those who attended the Assembly at Oxford which Charles called a Parliament. He had, however, contented himself with a sort of neutrality, pleasing nobody and being respected by both parties. It was this which occasioned Rupert to ask him to come to Shrewsbury, which he declined on account, as we have seen before, of the "course of physic he had entered upon." No sooner had Sir Thomas Myddelton entered the town than he summoned the castle, which was instantly surrendered. Myddelton entered it with his men, and placed there in safety their newly-acquired store of ammunition. Lord Herbert continued to reside in it, and, for aught we know, was right glad to welcome the Parliament forces. Knowing well enough that an attempt would be made to gain this important fortress, Myddelton's first concern was to bring in a stock of provisions for the garrison, so that they might be prepared, if necessary, to undergo a prolonged siege. But while he was about this, and before he had accomplished it, Sir Michael Ernely, with all the available forces of horse and foot out of Shrewsbury and the adjacent Royalist garrisons, came upon him suddenly and put him to route. The foot under Colonel Mytton sought shelter within the castle, and Sir Thomas Myddelton withdrew with his horse to Oswestry, being pursued a part of the way, in which pursuit he sustained the loss of a few stragglers. A close siege was now laid to the town —earthworks were thrown up, trenches dug, and every preparation made to reduce the place. The position of those within was a desperate one; but disappointed as Myddelton must have been, he saw there was no time to be lost. Sir John Meldrum had considerable forces in Lancashire, and to him Sir Thomas at once proceeded, where he received every encouragement. Liverpool could not be stormed, and Meldrum could well afford to withdraw a large body to go to the relief of Montgomery. This he accordingly did. Sir William Fairfax also came with some forces from Yorkshire, and Sir William Brereton brought with him all the Cheshire foot. These joined to Sir Thomas's horse formed a goodly army of some 3,000. They came in sight of Montgomery on the 17th of the month, and found that Ernely's Shrewsbury forces had been strengthened by the whole power of Lord Byron out of Chester, and by Colonel Wodehouse out of Ludlow. In fact, the whole strength of the Royalists in North Wales and the borders had been brought together. They were under the command of Lord Byron, and numbered between four and five thousand. The importance of the issue was well understood on both sides. On the approach of the Parliament party Lord Byron withdrew from his position before the town, leaving, however, a sufficient complement of men in the trenches to guard their works, and ascended the hill above the town, a position of some advantage. The Parliamentary army occupied the ground which he deserted. In this position they remained during the night. At a Council of the Parliamentary leaders it was decided not to give the offensive, but to try first of all to re-victual the town. For this purpose nearly a third part of the horse was dispatched to bring in provisions and to secure forage. The absence of this foraging party gave the Royalists an opportunity to assume the offensive, and descending the heights they dashed on most bravely, intending to cut off their enemy's retreat by taking possession of a bridge across the Severn, which had fallen into the hands of the Roundheads the night before. In the first onslaught fortune favoured the Royalists—Sir John Meldrum's horse were forced back again and again, but each time rallied, and for some time the issue was doubtful. Even when it came to the "push of the pike"—our fixed bayonets—the advantage was on Lord Byron's side. The battle grew desperate. Officers and men on each side conducted themselves with great bravery: the Cheshire foot especially, who, having to contend with perhaps the finest foot in England, "carried themselves more like lions than men." Sir William Fairfax so far engaged himself that he was taken prisoner, but was rescued by some of his own party. The brave soldier had, however, received a wound which proved mortal—his death happening the next day. The Royalists ultimately were completely routed. They fled in all directions and were pursued. In their retreat their loss was immense—many were slain and numbers made prisoners. The latter were brought back to Montgomery. During the fight the besieged soldiers under Mytton issued forth, and dealt furiously with such of the enemy as had been left in the trenches. The loss of the Parliament army was less than the severity of the fight would lead one to suppose. Their greatest loss was Sir William Fairfax and Major Fitz Simons. Of common soldiers they admit a loss of about sixty, while all accounts place that of the Cavaliers at 500 slain, including several officers, and between 1,200 and 1,500 prisoners. Among the prisoners, too, were officers of distinction: Colonel Broughton, who had landed in the winter from Ireland, Sir Thomas Tilsley, who had been sent down by the King from Oxford, and others. Nearly all the enemy's horse managed to escape—those under Byron flying to Chester, those under Hunckes betaking themselves to Shrewsbury.[1] Arthur Trevor's account of this battle is highly to the discredit of his party. "Our men," says he, "ran shamefully when they had no cause of fear, so that we are ordained to be the mocking-stock of war." He further says that "not a hundred foot came off."[2]

The importance of this victory could not be over-rated. The power of the Royalists in North Wales was destroyed; Chester, Shrewsbury, and Ludlow greatly endangered, and that portion of the army of the north under Langdale, which was on its way to the King, weakened and dispersed; while the demoralization which generally attends a defeat would soon begin to pervade the wreck which yet held together. Saddened by the loss of so brave a

---

[1] "Letters from Sir William Brereton, &c., of the great Victory, by God's Providence, given them in raising the Siege before Montgomery Castle, &c." (K. P. 174—4.) See vol. ii., Document lx. A. B. C. and D.

[2] Carte's Collection of Letters, i., p. 64. Vol. ii., Document lx. F.

general as Sir William Fairfax, the exultation of the victors, though deep, was not boisterous, and the victory was not so much attributed to the skill of man as it was to the Providence of God, whose agency the Puritans discovered in every occurrence of life, whether on the battle-field or in the closet.

Having settled matters at Montgomery the Parliamentary Generals discussed their future movements. Some of the Salopians had held out inducements for them to proceed to Shrewsbury, on the ground that inside the town there was a large party who only wanted an opportunity to show their affection for the Parliament, and that most of the inhabitants were sick of the Irish who had eaten up the place. Sir John Meldrum fully intended to act upon this information, and only gave it up when he learnt that Colonel Hunckes had reached the town with his horse in safety. A sufficient garrison having been left at Montgomery, under the command of Sir Thomas Myddelton, Meldrum and Brereton quitted the place—the former to attend personally to the siege of Liverpool, the latter to further the interest of the Parliament in Cheshire, and, if possible, to lay siege to the City of Chester. Colonel Mytton also quitted the castle, and returned to Oswestry, of which he had been appointed Governor. Leaving each engaged in his own design we will now take a look at matters in South Wales.

In August we left Gerard in Pembrokeshire, where he kept strict watch over Laugharne and his party, who were confined to Pembroke and Tenby. Baulked in his attempt to reduce these two strongholds, Gerard practised his cruelties to his heart's content in the surrounding neighbourhood, and distressed the inhabitants very much. Nothing was safe from him. Life had no sacredness in his eyes, and property no rights. It mattered little to him on whom he practised his villanies. The offensive and offenceless were alike ill-treated and plundered, and in the Irish who had come over to him, and who were eager to avenge Swanley's "water-rats," he had as heartless a set of savage blood-hounds as he could have wished. The wail of the suffering occasionally reached London, but the Parliament at this time was powerless to assist them. No succour could be sent to Laugharne beyond such help as the fleet could give. Captain Moulton was assiduous to do all he could, but he was unable to put a stop to Gerard's ravages. From a letter of the 21st September, from a person of credit in Pembrokeshire to a friend in London, is extracted the following picture, painful to a degree. It might be a little over-coloured, but there is sufficient evidence to prove Gerard a man who, possessing the brutal courage, lacked the honour of the soldier and gentleman, and was devoid of anything approaching humane feelings.

"The barbarous and cruel enemy drive away our cattle, rifle our houses to the bare walls. All provisions of victuals, where they come, carried away or destroyed. Divers villages and country towns, being neither garrisons nor any annoyance to the enemy, burnt down to the ground. The standing-corn they burn and destroy. All sexes and degrees [are] stripped naked by the enemy—aged and unarmed. Persons inhumanly murdered in cold blood, and others half-hanged, and afterwards stigmatized, and their flesh burnt off their bodies to the bare bones, and yet suffered in great torture to live."[1] Well might that newspaper exclaim, "If this be not cruelty I appeal to the malignants who read it." Of its truth hundreds, it says, could depose. It is a serious indictment to bring against a soldier, and if it stood on the bare testimony of a letter, could hardly be credited; but it receives sufficient confirmation at the hands of our indignant countrymen, who had seen their country bleeding long enough, and who accused Gerard of inhumanity in the presence of the King, when in a voice not to be misunderstood they demanded that he should be removed from the command.[2] I very much regret to find that one Welshman—a man of learning and position—is said to have backed Gerard in his heartless conduct, and surpassed him, as it is alleged, in cunning and craftiness. Says an old newspaper[3]—"There is a lawyer in Wales whom they write is the patron of this villany, and what the barbarous soldier cannot act, he endeavours by attainder to take away their lives, indicting Major-General Laugharne and the rest of the gentry, of high treason. The man's name is David Jenkins . . . . . who . . . in times of peace lived like a heathen and swore like a devil." Of David Jenkins we shall say no more here than that he was judge for the three counties of Carmarthen, Pembroke, and Cardigan, who lived at Hensoll, in Glamorganshire. But by-and-by he will engage our attention. To the Welsh generally it is due to

---

[1] The *Kingdom's Weekly Intelligencer*, No. 77, 15-23 October.

[2] This will be noticed when Charles's visit to Cardiff in 1645 will be discussed.

[3] *Weekly Intelligencer, supra.*

state that in Gerard's forces there does not appear to have been any great number of Welshmen. It was chiefly composed of English soldiers and those who had come over from Ireland. A few Welshmen, however, held commission under Gerard —Henry Stradling being one of them. The hatred to the Irish now became daily more violent. The press in London constantly upbraided them, and they are credited with having had the chief hand in the cruelties practised in Pembrokeshire. And the anger of the Parliament against them became intensified by such reports. Their influx into North Wales had undoubtedly protracted the war there, and now a large body of them had landed in Scotland, and had chosen Montrose as their chief, and under him were perpetrating unheard of ravages in the North. These were the men who had massacred the Protestants in Ireland. They were fighting for the King. The King, therefore, could not have been sincere in his attempt to put them down after the Irish massacre, and was now doubtless in league with them to exterminate Protestantism in England. Thus the Roundheads reasoned, and if to us their reasoning appears foolish, it should be remembered that we can hardly realize the feelings which the exciting events of that period engendered. No wonder that a spirit of determinate enmity towards the King, whose army swarmed with Irish, should pervade the mass of the people. "The sword in England," threatened the *Kingdom's Weekly Intelligencer*,[1] "will never be sheathed till his Majesty repent of the favor to, and continuance of the bloody Irish, whom

[1] No. 77. 15-22 October.

his Majesty calls his loving subjects"; and the popular clamour culminated in the Parliament passing an ordinance of a most severe character, commanding that no officer or soldier, by sea or land, should give any quarter to any Irishman, or Papist born in Ireland, who should be taken in arms against the Parliament in England. This ordinance, which militates against all the rules of civilized warfare, and which certainly cannot under any circumstances be defended, was afterwards in some instances carried into effect, and made the war far more bloody and desperate than it had hitherto been, giving rise to a spirit of cruel retaliation, which utterly demoralized many of those engaged in the war. But setting aside the execution of this terrible ordinance, the conduct of the Parliamentary officers in Wales and in England had been humane, and almost totally free from reproach, against whom, as Hallam truly says (except in carrying out the above ordinance), there can "certainly no imputation of this nature be laid."[1]

We have already seen that Prince Rupert upon his arrival gave out that he expected forces from South Wales. The Parliament newspapers rather ridiculed the idea of Rupert being reinforced by Gerard, who they thought had sufficient work on his hands in Pembrokeshire; but they were mistaken. The Prince had already sent word to Gerard of his necessitous condition, and commanding him to move eastward with the least possible delay; and Gerard had succeeded so well in his enterprise in South Wales, having driven his enemies fairly to their last retreat, that he felt himself in a position,

[1] Const. Hist., ii., 178.

without as he thought endangering the King's interests in those parts, to comply with the Prince's command; and prepared to move eastwards accordingly. Sir Marmaduke Langdale, whose course had been seriously interrupted, and whose loss had been considerable, was also on the march, and had brought the wreck of his army into Herefordshire and Monmouthshire with the intent to push onwards to Bristol. To avoid a too long and circuitous march preparations were made at the command of the Prince to secure the passage of the Severn at Aust, near Portskewet. Sir John Winter, whose knowledge of the country was of great service, was placed in command of a party of horse and foot transported from Bristol to Beachley, for the purpose of erecting such fortifications at the latter place as should be deemed necessary to secure the passage from molestation.

Intelligence of this movement had reached the Committee of Safety in London. To prevent the junction of Langdale, Gerard, and Rupert was of importance, and the more especially because the position of the Parliamentary army in the West was in danger enough without the King receiving any additional forces. Colonel Massey was at once instructed to use every diligence in frustrating the enemy's plan, which he immediately prepared to do. But he was forestalled by the Royalists, for already Sir John Winter had crossed the passage and had been busy with his men—about 500 in number—in fortifying Beachley. They had been four days at work when Massey arrived. His march had not been unmolested, for the enemy out of Chepstow, some 600 strong, attempted to

CHAP. V.
1644.

interrupt his progress; but in this they failed. Early in the morning after his arrival Massey successfully assaulted the works, captured many prisoners, and such as were not made prisoners only escaped by means of boats.

Finding his object realized so easily, Massey was loath to withdraw from that part of the country without doing some service of a more signal character. The County of Monmouth, mainly through the influence of Raglan Castle, had hitherto been eminently loyal, and had contributed men and money in aid of the King in a greater degree perhaps than any other single county. All the castles were garrisoned by the Royalists, as were also many private houses. Waller early in the war had made a dashing incursion into the county, and before his superior ability the less skilful commanders which the county produced had been forced to give way, and the gates of the towns had been thrown open to him; but as he was called away, and was not able to leave any garrisons behind, no permanent benefit to the cause of the Parliament had resulted from his raid. Massey had but a few men with him: his whole force, horse and foot, did not exceed 600 men, but they were all thorough veterans in war, and like Massey himself they fought in defence of a cause which they considered just; but against overwhelming numbers, for the entire forces of the county could be concentrated and brought to bear against him within a day, he must have felt it almost hopeless for him to combat, and would have gone back probably, however reluctant he would have felt, to Gloucester, had not an unexpected circumstance changed his chances.

In the town of Monmouth at this time was a Lieut.-Colonel Kyrle. He had taken arms originally for the Parliament, whose commission he held. Upon the loss of Bristol he deserted his cause, and joined the Royalists, and, with an inconstancy which is to say the least discreditable, he now determined to go back to his old friends, and to offer as a peace-offering the betrayal of Monmouth. So it was arranged between him and Massey that the latter should pretend to go back to England, and Kyrle would follow him as if to fall upon his rear, and that Kyrle would then go back to Monmouth with a body of Massey's men ostensibly as prisoners, who on their entry would seize the sentinels. In furtherance of this plan Massey gave orders for retreat, and marched eastwards, but stopped some three miles on the forest side of Monmouth. Intelligence having come to Monmouth, Kyrle drew out at the head of a small number of soldiers, and under cover of night approached Massey's ambuscade. They were surprised, and marched back towards the town. But the plan was nearly frustrated. Kyrle's cornet, not privy to the plot, escaped back into Monmouth and gave the alarm. The town was immediately on the alert, and the drawbridge drawn in. But when Kyrle appeared as victor, with a number of pretended prisoners, the bridge, after some debate, for some suspicion seems to have prevailed, was let down, and Kyrle and his party, with a few of Massey's men, were let in. The bridge was again drawn up. The men who had come in with Kyrle now began to doubt him, but it seems unjustly, for at his instigation they fell upon the guard at the

CHAP. V.
1644.

CHAP. V.
1644.

bridge, overpowered them, and so let in the main body. After some struggle the town was mastered—the Governor, Colonel Holtby, and most of the garrison, favoured by the night, which was dark and wet, made their escape. This was on the 26th of September.

The news of the loss of Monmouth spread rapidly throughout the county, and caused no little commotion. This was a place, in the opinion of many, which formed the very key to South Wales. It certainly was of great consequence to the surrounding parts, and its occupation by the rebels could not but prove ruinous to the royal cause thereabouts. The very sense of insecurity made the county gentry to coalesce, and to forget for the nonce their petty jealousies. But the mass of the people, in face of the continued successes of the Parliamentary party, and the uncertainty of the issue, were growing tired of war. They had already suffered enough. Their possessions had been drained, and scarcely a cot in the county but had tasted of the bitterness of so bloody a conflict, so that the influence of the gentry was much on the wane. I believe most of them still were thoroughly loyal, but between them and the unprincipled and unscrupulous Cavalier there was nothing in common. The Cavaliers could no more understand the rational constancy and loyalty of the Welsh than they could forego their roystering proclivities. Hence I find that whenever the English Cavalier spoke of the Welsh loyalist he invariably did so with disrespect and contumely. Thus Samuel Tuke, writing to Prince Rupert from Llantarnam, in the County of Monmouth, on the 30th September, four days after the loss of Monmouth, says "that there could be no trust in the country gentry—greater part nigling traitors."[1] Doubtless Tuke's conduct was not reciprocated by the Welsh gentry, and hence the vituperation; but it is hardly fair to the loyalists of Monmouthshire, who spared neither kith nor kin to aid the royal cause, to be thus maligned, simply because they were probably sick and weary of a struggle that had cost them so much, and not so enthusiastic as a soldier of fortune, whose very existence depended on the continuance of bloodshed. But when he added that "their tenants rise, disarm, and wound their men for coming to quarters consigned to them," he wrote what was probably the bare truth. And who can blame them. Already ruined by the levies made upon them, their houses no longer their homes, with unscrupulous soldiers free-billeted upon them, and exasperated by the conduct of the Cavaliers, they were heartily sick, as the peasantry generally are, of the ravages of war, and they yearned for peace. Is it surprising to find that they now made a stand against the further billeting of soldiers, seeing that their goods had been plundered, their means wasted, their daughters ruined, and they themselves abused and often cruelly ill-treated? The Marquis of Worcester however, still possessed great influence in the county, and his loyalty never waned. So he called to his assistance the loyalists in the county. Some of Langdale's men from the North had reached this part of the country, and their appearance was hailed with joy. Forming together a body of some 500 horse and about 1,000 foot, they proceeded towards

[1] Warburton's Rupert, i., 525.

CHAP.
V.
1644.

Monmouth, and were met by Massey, whom fortune once more befriended. The Cavaliers were beaten, many of the Welshmen taken prisoners, some officers slain, and Sir William Blaxton himself was wounded. Massey was anxious to propitiate the Welsh, and he took steps to explain to them the object of the Parliament, "which was not to destroy or enslave their persons, or take away their goods, but to preserve their lives and fortunes, to open the course of justice and free them of their heavy burdens." He treated them with kindness, and afterwards sent them home, everyone with a little letter to his master of a like effect. The Welsh after this "began to entertain better thoughts of the Parliament party."[1]

The Royalists, though taken aback, were by no means disheartened at the repulse they had received. From day to day they harassed the outposts, and gave much annoyance, and it became necessary for Massey to extend his outposts and to strengthen them. Many of the neighbouring houses were therefore stocked with soldiers. In one of these— Wonastow House, then the seat of Mr. Milburn,— some ten foot soldiers and about sixty horse were stationed. The enemy suddenly came against them and stormed the house. Those within were very short of ammunition, and would have fallen into the hands of the enemy had it not been for the alertness of a servant maid, who supplied them with two six-pound bags of powder. This, with lead out of the windows and the pewter pots which they melted, enabled them to keep back their attackers until timely aid came from Monmouth to

[1] Rushworth's Hist. Collections.

relieve them. The Royalists were again worsted: three officers, Major Somerset, Capt. Bacon, and another Major were slain, and Capt. Lewis and some forty soldiers made prisoners. Those who fled were pursued over Winster Bridge. In this conflict a large quantity of arms fell into the victor's hands, "so that muskets were sold at sixpence a piece." The Royalists were commanded by Sir Trevor Williams of Llangiby, whom we shall presently see for the Parliament, and ultimately suspected even by the latter—whom Cromwell characterised as a "blustering blade." The horse engaged were some of Rupert's own, and the foot "poor forced Welshmen, whom the horse pricked forward with their sword points." In the house Capt. Bailey, a Stroud man, and Lieutenant Page, a Scotchman, were the officers. The maid was rewarded for her valuable service. The Governor of Monmouth not only gave her two pieces of money, and took her into his service, but even kissed her for the good service she did! Fancy the stern old Puritan so relaxing his austerity and kissing the buxom wench! The whole war, I trow, produces no picture like it. It is the only act of gallantry which in my whole reading, and that has been extensive, I find a Puritan to have been guilty of. And it is the more refreshing on that account. The Cavaliers romped and flirted and dallied with the women. Such conduct was levity in the eyes of the Roundheads. It is a noteworthy fact, this kissing of the maid by such a stern sullen warrior.[1]

Massey's victories were much thought of in London. All the newspapers spoke in the highest terms of his successes. His defeat of Lord Herbert, with

[1] *The Country Messenger*, No. 2, October 11. (K. P. 176—14.)

some 1,500 men, was a matter of great exultation. Massey wrote most hopefully. To conquer the whole of South Wales all he asked was a reinforcement of about a thousand horse and some five hundred foot. The press advocated his cause; but it was difficult at this time to send him succour, and I am not aware that he ever received the aid he sought.

Red Castle, the seat of Lord Powis, a strong fortress overlooking Welshpool, attracted the attention of the Parliamentarians after the capture of Montgomery. Into it had been poured for safe keeping the valuables and wealth of the surrounding country. Many of the gentry had also quitted their own houses to seek shelter within its walls. Meldrum, on departing from Montgomery, summoned Lord Powis to give in his adherence to the Parliament. The summons was, however, treated with contempt, and Meldrum passed on his way to Liverpool. The Lord Powis was by no means content with a passive loyalty. He had not done much heretofore, but now he began to harass the scouts from Montgomery, sent out to bring in provisions. The position of the castle was important. It obstructed the free passage from Oswestry to Montgomery, and interrupted communications between those places. There were sufficient reasons, therefore, for an attempt to reduce it. Late in September Sir Thomas Myddelton summoned to his assistance the surrounding country, who showed a readiness beyond expectation. On Monday, the last day of the month, he advanced with about 300 horse and 100 foot from Montgomery to Welshpool, where he quartered Monday night and the whole of Tuesday. Wednesday night the moon shone forth, and by its light they drew near to the castle; but waited until about two o'clock for the moon's going down before they commenced the attack. They then approached the precincts. It was a formidable fortress. The gates were all down. But the rich booty within made the party anxious and impatient for an assault. The master-gunner (one John Arundel) was ordered to place a petarre against the gate. This was fired, and the gate burst open. A sharp struggle followed. Those who were within offered every possible resistance, but to no purpose. The interior of the castle was soon reached, the valuable stores rummaged, and the Lord Powis, with his brother, two sons, and a large number of officers and men, were made prisoners. The castle was found to be well stored with sufficient provision to maintain a prolonged siege.[1]

By this Sir Thomas Myddelton had pretty well quieted affairs in that part of the country. The gentry came round to him in great numbers, and the people generally were only too glad at the chance of security. Sir Thomas wrote exultantly to London, where his services were duly appreciated. Having placed a garrison at Powis Castle, he returned to Montgomery, of which place he appointed Sir John Price of Newtown the Governor, and leaving with the latter such a garrison as he could spare, Sir Thomas departed for Oswestry.

Sir John Price was assiduous in his new office. Originally a staunch Royalist, he was keen enough to see which way the tide was turning, and he took it

[1] *True Informer*, No. 49, Oct. 6—12. *Kingdom's Weekly Intelligencer*, No. 76. (K. P. 176—17 and 23.)

CHAP. V.
1644.

at the flood and found himself in a responsible position. Soon after I find him writing to London that the people thereabouts were all giving in their adherence to the Parliament, and that he was hopeful soon to be in a position to do "something for the assistance of his neighbours of Pembrokeshire."[1] This account is confirmed by Sir Michael Ernley, who, writing to Prince Rupert from Shrewsbury on the 21st of September, states that "since the disaster at Montgomery the edge of the gentry is very much blunted—the country's loyalty strangely abated. They begin to warp to the enemy's party."[2]

Shrewsbury was next looked after by Sir Thomas Myddelton. This town from the very outbreak of the war had been loyal to the King. Charles at a very early period in the struggle made it his temporary head-quarters. And it was there that Prince Rupert, while in command of Wales, made his head-quarters. Nevertheless, there was a considerable party in the town who were firm believers in the justice of the Parliament's cause. Many of them had suffered much in consequence. The gaol was filled with them. Their property had been confiscated and themselves subjected to great indignities. From time to time these had found means to communicate with the Parliamentary leaders in the neighbourhood. The Earl of Denbigh early in the summer had been implored to assault the place, and assured that the friends within would render what aid they could. Sir John Meldrum, when he came before Montgomery, had the same request and assurance repeated to him,

[1] *London Post*, No. 9, October 16. (K. P. 177—4.)
[2] Warburton's Rupert, i., 519.

and so had Sir Thomas Myddelton. But the place in itself was strong. It was also well garrisoned. There the flower of the Irish army, which had come over in the preceding winter, had made their head-quarters, to the no little discomfort of the inhabitants. These, it is true, had been thinned and weakened very much of late. Still the force within was strong, and an assault upon the town would probably end in disaster. So Sir Thomas did not essay it. Around the town several of the more important county houses had been garrisoned. Most of these outposts Myddelton now captured, and by the end of October his success had been such that all the passages to Shrewsbury, save along the Severn from Bridgnorth, were blocked up,[1] and even this passage was all but blocked up by Colonel Mytton, by his taking a few days afterwards High Ercall, the seat of the Lord Newport, which is situated somewhat to the south-east of Shrewsbury, and between that place and Bridgnorth, "by which means they have blocked up the river Severn, and driven them into that extremity that neither barge nor boat can pass down to Worcester; and by the taking of Red Castle the Severn is blocked up on that side also, so that now no relief can come from Wales to Shrewsbury by water."[2] About this time also Colonel Mytton heard that Sir William Vaughan had issued out of Shrawardine. For what purpose does not appear. This Sir W. Vaughan was one of the staunchest loyalists in the country. He had been unflinching in his adherence to the King, and had been appointed the governor

---

[1] *Mercurius Civicus*, No. 73. (K.P. 176—6.)
[2] *The London Post*, No. 10, October 23. (K. P. 177—18.)

of that castle. He had for a long time harassed the Parliamentarians in those parts, and is said to have not been over-scrupulous as to his mode of putting down his opponents and confiscating their property. Mytton, who was always vigilant, hearing that he had come out of his castle at once proceeded in the direction. Coming suddenly upon them, they were surprised and taken prisoners—Sir William himself being of the number, along with twelve other officers. Mytton was very anxious to effect the capture of the castle, and thought if he brought the Governor a prisoner before it, the men within would surrender. A parley ensued. Sir William Vaughan was allowed to go in to treat, but I am sorry to say he broke his parole, caused the bridge to be drawn up, and refused to come forth. If this is true, it was not a creditable act. And in all the war, I am happy to say, but a very few officers sacrificed their honour in that way. Mytton was not powerful enough to attack the place, so he withdrew, taking with him the other officers whom he had made prisoners.[1]

Meanwhile Sir William Brereton was watchful around Chester. By the great defeat at Montgomery Lord Byron had lost the bulk of his soldiers, and the position of the city was not enviable. The citizens who had already suffered much from the war were now pressed to the service. On the 8th of October a slight skirmish took place at Tarvin, at which Brereton was the victor. Of the Royalist forces it is said some sixty were made prisoners, "many of them being citizens, for they

[1] No. 61, *True Informer, supra.*

have few soldiers there besides the inhabitants."[1] Brereton now had it pretty well his own way. Passage after passage he blocked up. Means of communication between the city and the outlying posts were cut off. Even the foraging parties sent out were constantly harassed. The unfortunate city was nearly surrounded by the enemy, and the miseries of a siege were even now beginning to be felt within the walls.

There were many reasons why Col. Gerard should at this time quit Pembrokeshire. He had the direct command of Prince Rupert to lose no time to come to him at Bristol, or to join the King's forces. This order was sent early in September, but could not then be obeyed. Some preparations were necessary, and it was requisite he should in a measure settle affairs there before he took his departure. But when he heard of Massey's victorious march into Monmouthshire he saw that if he did not exercise great diligence his passage to the King would be prevented. He also knew too well that his own tyrannical conduct in South Wales had embittered most of the inhabitants against him: so that if Massey moved westwards he could count upon little help from the Welsh. He therefore decided upon quitting Pembrokeshire. Leaving such garrisons as he could afford, he passed through Carmarthenshire and Glamorganshire, and entered Monmouthshire. His object was not to fight with Massey, but rather to avoid him and so proceed to the King, who had by this time returned from Cornwall, and was hovering between Worcester and Oxford. Gerard's presence in the

CHAP.
V.
1644.

[1] *London Post*, No. 10. (K. P. 177—18.)

county, at the head of a considerable force—by some stated to be somewhere between three and four thousand men—was inspiriting to the Royalists. Sir John Winter came over from Bristol with over 500 men to attempt again the work in which he had, as we have seen, been rudely interrupted. The passage across the Severn at Beachley was by him and Prince Rupert deemed to be worthy of a more serious struggle than the last. Their object was to have a place at which they could securely land a force from Bristol and the West, so as to interrupt communication between Gloucester and Monmouth. Beachley is a long strip of land which pushes into the Severn estuary a considerable distance, and situated between the mouth of the Wye and the Severn channel. A deep trench across would join the two rivers, and as ships could ride there with comparative safety, once the place was properly strengthened, it would by no means be difficult to keep. And if Gerard and Winter had arranged to be assisting each other there can be no doubt whatever that the fortifying of the place would have been effected. But there appears to have been no concerted action between them at all. Massey, however, in the absence of any action of Gerard, was allowed to send out a party of some 100 musketeers and about eight troops of horses by night to Clurewell, where they expected reinforcement from Newnham. The next evening, the 14th of October, they approached Beachley. Here they found the works in a state of considerable progress. Every precaution against a surprisal from land had been made. Ships rode in both rivers with ordnance ready pointed inland. The line was guarded by "hammer-guns and murtherers," placed on the flanks on both sides. To attack the place at high water, when the ships were in position to guard the works effectually, would be madness. Nothing was done that night, but low water in the morning gave an opportunity. Massey himself at the head of a small party at dawn forced some pallisadoes, which enabled some foot and the Forlorn Hope to enter. The quickset fence, however, was lined with musketeers, who at once began to pour their volleys upon them. But Massey, notwithstanding the desperate position he was in, and the rough usage he sustained, his "head-piece" or helmet being knocked off by the butt-end of a musket, fought stoutly, and his horse coming to his rescue, the victory was theirs. Some 200 soldiers were made prisoners, and several officers. Sir John Winter escaped, but with great difficulty. Throwing himself over a ledge of rock, he dropped into a boat which was in readiness for him, and made off.

Gerard evading Massey passed by Usk to Abergavenny, and thence made his way towards Worcester, whence it was supposed he intended to join the King, who had but a few days before, after a disastrous defeat at Newbury, retreated to Oxford for his winter quarters. Instantly the Committee in London heard of Gerard's movement they ordered Massey to thwart his design, and to hold himself in readiness to join with the main body of the Parliament forces. This was on the 10th of November. Massey lost no time in obeying superior orders. Quitting Monmouth with only his own regiment of horse, he proceeded to Evesham, but Gerard was there before him, and, moreover, too powerful to be attacked. And what was worse than all, he had the mortification there to learn that Monmouth, which, during his absence, he had entrusted to the care of Major Throgmorton, had been retaken by the Royalists.[1] The Major, anxious perhaps to win laurels for himself, and blind to the prospect of there being any danger for Monmouth, marched with some 300 men towards Chepstow on Sunday, the 17th of November, with the intention of attacking the castle. In the town of Monmouth were many Royalists, some of whom were tenants of the Raglan family. These sent information of the defenceless state of the town to the Lord Herbert. The latter instantly sent for help to Col. Progers, the Governor of Abergavenny, and to Sir Trevor Williams of Llangiby, whose name we have seen before and shall see again in the course of this history. Lord Charles Somerset, with 150 men, set out from Raglan, and the other forces met not far from the town. Early on the morning of the 19th they got to the higher side of the town that looks towards Hereford. Surmounting a bank, they approached the gate—Dixton's Gate—which, by the aid of a crow-bar, they forced open. The affrighted sentinel bolted. The body of horse entered, and riding through the town they surprised the main guard, the garrison for the most part being at that unearthly hour in bed. The town was won. Many prisoners were made—among the number were Col. Broughton, Col. Stephens, Mr. Catchling of Trelech, and Mr. Jones of Usk, members of the Committee for South Wales.

[1] Rushworth's Hist. Collection, vol. i., pt. iv., p. 29.

A quantity of ammunition and a fair store of arms were also captured. Massey hastened back from Burford, where these bad tidings reached him, to the relief of the party that had gone over to Chepstow. He met them in the Forest of Dean. Thence they marched to Ross to relieve Pembridge, but came too late to be of any service, and all was once more lost to the Parliament in Monmouthshire. It was a great victory for the Royalists, and an event which could well have been averted. It was all very well for the defeated Roundhead to say he "was never in so base a place" in his days. It was entirely their own foolishness. Indeed, the very same Roundhead acknowledges "I fear presumption is and was our fault." This writer does not appear to have been discouraged. "We are not daunted as yet," he says, "but by God's good blessing hope to recover all again, but the waters are up there and here too [wherever that was], so that there is no marching to do good."[1] And in this slough we will leave them for a while.

As early as the 8th of October intelligence from Milford Haven was received in London to the effect that Gerard had retreated from Pembrokeshire. "The inhabitants of the county do now begin to live in some quiet," said the informant, and Capt. Moulton was at the Haven with his ship on behalf of the Parliament.[2] Strict Puritan this old sea captain must have been, and a stout hater of "Popish innovations." Even amid the din of war he had one eye to watch these. He visited St. David's Cathedral, and in this shrine, in which Laud

---

[1] Letter signed J. C. in K. P., 185–6, dated 25th November.
[2] *London Post*, No. 8, under date October 8.

himself whilom officiated, he found something which he deemed worth a journey to London to exhibit. No less than a cope, two crosses, and "other relics of Rome." These he put by with great care, and afterwards in person appeared in London with them. No wonder the Puritan journals praised his "exemplary service." He, moreover, brought with him news as to the condition of Pembrokeshire: that on the defeat by Myddelton and Brereton of Prince Rupert's forces in North Wales, many of them had come to the South and joined with Gerard; that the "insulting enemy made great spoil and havoc . . . killing, burning, and destroying all that came before him." Many of them he said were Irish rebels. Gerard, however, at last was gone, and Laugharne was again in the field and very hopeful.[1]

About the middle of November one Capt. Beal had been dispatched from London by sea with certain foot forces to help Sir Thomas Myddelton. It was intended they should land in Anglesey. But stress of weather drove them into Milford, much to the joy of the Parliamentarians at Pembroke, whose strength was thus unexpectedly recruited.

The forces under Laugharne at this time were said to be five hundred horse and five *thousand* foot, which clearly is a mistake. Reinforced by Beal's contingency he set out from Pembroke, and proceeded against the town of Laugharne. There both the town and the castle were garrisoned for the King. In reply to summons the garrison refused to surrender. Force was then resorted to. Preparations were made to undermine

[1] *Weekly Account*, No. 62, Nov. 6. (K. P. 180—8.)

the works, and they were partially executed when the besieged sounded a parley and surrendered on fair terms. The town was secured from plunder. Some officers were made prisoners, and a quantity of arms and ammunition changed hands. This was a good beginning for Captain Beal, who immediately afterwards set out on his march through Wales to join Sir Thomas Myddelton.[1]

Beal, on quitting Laugharne, marched north. At Lampeter, in Cardiganshire, he was met on the 2nd of November by a party of Myddelton's men, and they found ample work in repressing the Royalists in Merionethshire, Montgomeryshire, and Radnorshire, who had for a long time been carrying on a high-handed game. Until the fall of Montgomery and the capture of Red Castle these counties had been entirely in the hands of the Royalists, and those who were inclined for the Parliament had to swallow their convictions. Now, however, matters were changed, and the Parliament was decidedly in the ascendancy in these parts. Sir Thomas Myddelton had found a powerful ally in Sir John Price, of Newtown, who at one time had been for the King, but who had come over recently. His influence was considerable, and he was wisely appointed Governor of Montgomery Castle. It was the fate of many an old mansion to suffer destruction at this time. Mathavarn, the seat of Mr. Pugh, was burnt to the ground. Abbey Cwm Hir, occupied by Richard Fowler, had been garrisoned for the King. Early in December Sir Thomas Myddelton appeared

[1] *Perfect Passages*, No. 7, December 4. (K. P. 184—5.) See also *Cambrian Quarterly Magazine*, vol. i., p. 70.

CHAP. V.
1644.

before that place and summoned it. The answer was a flat denial, whereupon it was taken by storm, and in it were taken prisoners Colonel Barnard, the Governor, Mr. Hugh Lloyd, the High-Sheriff, several officers, some seventy soldiers, and some arms and ammunition.[1]

Myddelton's next concern was to attack Chirk Castle, his own property, which the Royalists had secured at the outbreak of the war, and had retained ever since. Ruthin Castle, also his property, was in a similar position. Of the garrison at Chirk Castle, Colonel John Watts was the Governor. A few days before Christmas Myddelton appeared before the castle, and sent in a summons to Watts calling upon him to surrender, it being probably, as *Aulicus* states, Sir Thomas's intention to keep Christmas in one of his own houses. The Governor, however, had counted upon spending his Christmas there himself; and the consequence was a siege. For three days it lasted. Crafty engineers from Oswestry were brought over to effect with "crowes and pickers" an entry into the castle, but it was all in vain. "My stones beat them off," Watts writes to Prince Rupert on Christmas Day, and "their prime engineer was slain by the castle side," much to the grief of Myddelton and the delight of *Aulicus*, which goes into raptures of blasphemy in commenting on the event.[2]

In the meantime Major-General Laugharne was doing what he could "to draw the hearts of the inhabitants of Cardiganshire." In that county,

[1] *Perfect Occurrences*, No. 20. (K. P. 15—6, large 4to.) See also vol ii., Document lxv., p 219.
[2] Memoirs of Chirk Castle. See also vol ii., Document lxvii, p 224.

though the majority of the gentry were Royalists, there were many persons of influence well-affected to the Parliament. James Phillips of the Priory, James Lewes of Coedmore, and others, were well known to be so. These were anxious to have Laugharne amongst them, for they had been much harassed by the Cavaliers, in whose hands were all the castles, such as Aberystwith, Cardigan, and Newcastle-Emlyn. The heavy rains which fell—the season was a wet one—kept Laugharne back awhile, and it was not until within a few days of Christmas that he came in sight of the town of Cardigan. The castle there was then strong and well-garrisoned, under the command of Major Slaughter, one of Gerard's appointees. The town also was in their hands. They had been, recently, fortunate enough to secure the ordnance of the frigate *Convert*, which had been wrecked in the Bay, and they had made ample precautions against a siege. They relied chiefly on the castle, which they had considerably strengthened by the erection of a half-moon within the castle yard. The town surrendered " willingly" to Laugharne, but not so the castle, which sent forth its defiance. Against the castle the Parliament soldiers had no sufficient ordnance to proceed, so they had to wait patiently before it until some of the guns of the *Leopard* were brought thither from Milford. A weary fortnight, according to a Royalist paper, was spent in this delay, almost even to the despair of the besiegers, who heard rumours that Gerard was on his way back from England to relieve it. But when the ordnance from the *Leopard* had been mounted, the half-moon was attacked and a breach effected in it, through which the attackers stormed an entry, and "the enemy, as men bereft of all sense, having not the power to give fire to their guns, although the linstocks were in their hands ready lighted, cast down their arms and cried for quarter, the which was granted." In the castle, which fell on the third day of the siege, were taken Major William Slaughter, the Governor, and his wife, Captain Vaughan,[1] Captain Nicholas Butler,[2] Captain Richard Pryse,[3] "one Dr. Taylor, a divine," Lieutenant Thomas Barrow, or Barlow, and others, with between a hundred and a hundred and fifty common soldiers. About 200 of the Royalists were killed during the siege, and a large quantity of arms and ammunition was taken. The most interesting circumstance connected with this siege was the capture of the "one Doctor Taylor," who was no other than the celebrated Dr. Jeremy Taylor, the well-known author of several of the most beautifully-written devotional books in the English language. He was at the outbreak of the war a chaplain-in-ordinary to the King, whom he accompanied for a short time in his campaigns. The turmoil of the battle-field, however, was not congenial to him, wherefore he retired into Wales and lived for some time under the hospitable roof of the Earl Carbery, at Golden Grove. There he employed his time in keeping a school, and in composing some of his best known works. It was at Golden Grove he penned his "Holy Living and Dying," and his "Golden Grove," or Manual of Daily Prayers. What brought him to Cardigan

[1] Probably of Golden Grove.
[2] A member of the Pembrokeshire family of that name.
[3] I should think this Capt. Pryse must have been the eldest son of the first baronet of Gogerddan, which house at this period was Royalist.

it is now impossible to discover; but if the Capt. Vaughan whose name appears amongst the list of officers taken at the castle was a member of the Golden Grove family, it is very probable that the worthy Doctor accompanied him thither. A Royalist account of the capture of Cardigan Castle attributes it to treachery—that a sergeant was bribed to betray a sally port, by which access was obtained and the place surprised. But as this story of *Aulicus* is contradicted, and the Parliamentary account is vouched by two witnesses in distinct communications, I am inclined to disbelieve the story of treachery. Very exaggerated accounts of the victory, however, seem to have reached London. In one of the newspapers it was said that 900 were killed and 1,500 made prisoners.[1] Another said that Laugharne had completely routed the remainder of Gerard's army in Wales, which was also untrue.[2] General Laugharne having arranged matters at Cardigan, and having placed there a small garrison under the command of Lieut.-Col. Powell,[3] took his departure to recruit his forces, and intending next to proceed against Newcastle-Emlyn. Col. Powell spent his Christmas at Cardigan. His holidays, however, were soon disturbed; but as this takes us to the beginning of another year, I take leave of him and of the year 1644, which, so far as Wales was concerned, opened gloriously for the Parliament; but has ended darkly

---

[1] *Parliament Scout*, No. 83. (K. P. 189—18).

[2] *London Post*, No. 20.

[3] *The Scottish Dove* says it was a Col. Jones who was left in command: probably Col. Jones of Nanteos; but the majority of my authorities state that it was Lieut.-Col. Rice Powell.

280   Civil War in Wales

CHAP. V.
1644.

enough for the King,[1] though unsatisfactorily for the Parliament, which was split up into two hostile camps—the Presbyterians and the Independents.

[1] These details of the siege of Cardigan I have extracted from a letter of Admiral Swanley to Earl Warwick, of the 1st Jan. (K. P. 189—1); a letter of Capt. Smith to the same (K. P. 195—22); No. 65 *True Informer*, and *Merc. Aulicus* for Feb. 2—9. See these in vol. ii., Documents lxvi. and lxix. A and B.

CHAPTER VI.

1645.

State of Imperial affairs at beginning of the year—Treaty of Uxbridge—Reorganisation of the Parliament's army—Siege of Beeston Castle and Chester—Shrewsbury lost to the Royalists—Rupert and Maurice relieve Beeston—Rupert recalled to suppress club-men in Herefordshire—Chester in straits—Hawarden besieged—Attempt to regain Cardigan Castle—Great defeat of the Roundheads at Newcastle-Emlyn—Cardigan deserted—Haverfordwest and Picton Castle taken by Gerard—Beginning of the real campaign—Self-denying ordinance and its effects—Victories of Cromwell at Brampton Bush, &c.—King raises siege of Chester—Is defeated at Naseby—Retires to Wales—Entertainments at Raglan—Charles resolves to go to Bristol, but is prevailed upon to remain—Siege of Hereford—The King attempts to recruit his army in Wales and fails—His difficulties in Glamorganshire—Gerard removed from command—Victory of Parliamentarians in Pembrokeshire—Charles quits Cardiff—Marches through Brecknock and Radnorshire, and thence to Oxford—Uprising of the Welsh for the Parliament—The King relieves Hereford—Once more visits Raglan—Loss of Bristol—Charles marches northwards—Is defeated on Rowton Heath, near Chester—Leaves North Wales for Newark—Account of the King's journeyings in Wales—Carew, Manorbier, and Picton Castles taken by Laugharne—Carmarthen is also captured—Chepstow and Monmouth taken for the Parliament—Design to betray Monmouth foiled—Col. Mytton defeats Sir William Vaughan near Denbigh—Glamorganshire declares for the Parliament—As also does Brecknockshire—Surprisal of Hereford by the Roundheads—Siege of Chester.

AFTER the defeat which the royal cause had sustained at the battle of Newbury, the intention of marching upon London being frustrated, the King retired about the beginning of November into Oxford, and in that city once more established his winter quarters. The inactivity of the Parliamentary generals in not following up their victory caused a serious split in that camp, and occasioned much dissatisfaction in London; which, however, was only the outcome of far more serious differences in the Parliament itself, where Presbyterian was waging mortal war with Independent, each anxious to gain the ascendancy. Oliver Cromwell, as the leader of the Independents, charged the Duke of Manchester with neglecting opportunities, to the great danger of the Parliament and the protraction of the war. In Oliver Cromwell the Presbyterians had a most stout enemy—a favourer of sectaries—one who had openly declared himself as the defender of liberty of conscience. So much alarmed were they at his growing influence that they even schemed his impeachment. Failing to do this they endeavoured to bring about peace. After a warm discussion in Parliament, negotiations with the King were opened. On the 20th of November the Earl of Denbigh, with eight other commissioners, one of whom was William Pierpoint, member for Shropshire, left for Oxford with proposals for peace. The King, deluded for a time with the reports of certain successes of Montrose in Scotland, was very dilatory in replying to the proposal, and treated the commissioners rather rudely, at the same time refusing to give the assembly at Westminster the name of Parliament. However, ultimately it was decided that forty commissioners, twenty-three from the Parliament and seventeen from the King, should meet at Uxbridge to discuss the conditions of a treaty. They met on the 29th of January. Preliminaries were disposed of smoothly enough; but on the real conditions for a peace insurmountable difficulties presented themselves, and the King was obstinate. The failure of the negotiation was what was really expected by all who had studied the character of the King by the light of his own letters discovered on the field of battle at Naseby, which "made a sad impression against Majesty—gave in fact a most melancholy view of the veracity of his Majesty 'on the word of a King.'"[1] Christopher Love, a fanatic preacher, and a native of Cardiff, addressed a large congregation at the church at Uxbridge on a market day, against the treaty, in language of great violence. "No good can come of it," said he, "these people are here from Oxford with hearts full of blood; they only want to amuse the people till they can do them some notable injury: this treaty is as far from peace as heaven from hell." This was evidently the view taken of it by the Independents at large, and more especially by Cromwell and others in the House of Commons, who had now become the war party; for even while the preliminary negotiations were being carried on about Christmas, these were preparing for war. In their eyes it had become necessary to remove certain officers from high command. They dared not do so directly, and the "Self-denying Ordinance" was invented to remedy the difficulty. By that ordinance, which met with tremendous opposition both in the House of Commons and in the Lords, being thrown out, in fact, by the latter, but ultimately carried, all members of Parliament, peers and commoners, were disqualified from holding command. The Lords threw it out as it was principally levelled against members of their own

CHAP. VI.
1645.

[1] Carlyle's Letters of Cromwell. Letter xxix.

House; but these sending in their resignations, it was passed. The Earls of Essex, Manchester, and Denbigh were thus disposed of. The army was next reorganized, and the supreme command given to Sir Thomas Fairfax, whose valour, uprightness, and success had for a long time made him very prominent. Leaving Fairfax at Windsor, where he made his head-quarters, carrying out the remodelling of the army, we shall now take a view of matters as they were in Wales at the beginning of this year.

Long before Christmas Beeston Castle, one of the most important outposts of Chester, was under close siege. It still continued so, much to the discomfort of Captain Valet, the Governor, whose greatest suffering was from the want of firing. Chester, too, was in straits, for not only was it besieged on the eastern side, but also on the Welsh side, whither the Parliamentarians under Brereton had once more penetrated, which made the fires of those within the walls less bright, and their tables less heavy, for they depended principally on North Wales for provisions and fuel. The importance of Chester to the Royalists could not be overestimated. Without it their power in North Wales would soon go. Lancashire was already sufficiently alienated from them. As a landing place from Ireland it was simply invaluable. At Oxford, therefore, the relief of Chester must have been most seriously considered. Prince Maurice was at length deputed to undertake its relief. The command of all North Wales was given to him, with full powers to grant honours and rewards, to make levies, and otherwise carry out his commission.[1] Making his way through Worcester he reached Shrewsbury about the middle of February. He remained there only for a few days, and taking thence with him as many as could be spared of the Irish forces which had come over from Ireland, with the officers, he set forward to Chester, keeping along the Welsh side of the Severn; and leaving Shrewsbury considerably denuded of its strength, weaker, perhaps, than it had been at any period since the beginning of the war: in so weak a state, in fact, that the Parliamentary faction within the town took heart, engaged in counsel, and conveyed intelligence to the Committee of Shropshire, whose headquarters were at Wem. An eminently active committee was this, comprising Colonel Mytton, Samuel Moore, Andrew Lloyd, Hugh Mackworth, and Thomas Hunt, and quick to move in any matter which promised success. One Huson, a minister, who had acted as a spy for them in the town for some time, was their chief adviser as to the internal state of the town. The committee, to whom Shrewsbury had all along been an object of deep solicitude, saw that their opportunity had arrived, and they resolved to attempt to gain the place. Communications were opened with Sir William Brereton, who approved of the resolution, and who, notwithstanding he was menaced by a powerful enemy, consented to aid the committee. For this purpose he despatched Colonel Bowyer, an able soldier, on the 20th of February, to Wem, with between six and seven hundred horse and foot. Mytton at this time was absent at Oswestry,

[1] *Parliament Scout*, No. 83. (K. P. 189 –18.)

of which place he was now the Governor. He was also communicated with, and approved of the scheme, and at once prepared to help. Colonel Reinking, the chief military officer at Wem, joined by Bowyer, left Wem on the night of the 21st of February, and on the road was joined by Mytton with his horse, numbering in all between eleven and twelve hundred. They came before the town about three o'clock that morning. Between them lay the Severn, whose banks on the town side were strongly palisadoed. Carpenters were sent across to saw down the palisades, and the foot under Colonel Reinking followed, who, putting easily to flight a few surprised sentinels, soon mastered the town, and let in the horse under Colonel Mytton. Surprised at so unearthly an hour, when most of the inhabitants, civil and military, were in their beds, very little blood was spilt—all accounts agree in this—probably not more than half-a-dozen lives were lost altogether, which made glad the heart of pious Richard Baxter, himself a Shrewsbury boy, and was a matter of rejoicing to many others. In the town dwelt Sir Michael Ernely, the Governor, a great many officers and Commissioners of Array, and many of the gentry of the neighbourhood, who had fled thither long ago for refuge. Most of these were made prisoners, being prevented by the soldiers from seeking safety in the castle. That fortress held out until noon the next day, as also did a strong position at Frankwell, in the west part of the town. At twelve o'clock they were surrendered on very fair conditions—those within being allowed to march out with their personal arms, leaving behind them the magazine and ammunition Those who were taken in the town were kept prisoners —some of them being sent to Stafford[1] and some ultimately to London, where they were placed in the Tower. Owing to the large number of sympathisers with the Parliament who had continued to dwell there, the town was saved from plunder. The loss of Shrewsbury was a great blow to the Royalists. It had been one of their strongholds from the beginning. The Parliament rejoiced exceedingly, thanksgiving services were ordered, and until the Restoration the Salopians, inured to the change, commemorated the event by a general holiday on the anniversary of its capture.[2]

An unhappy wrangle took place between Col. Mytton and Lieut.-Colonel Reinking—each of them claiming the honour attached to the capture of so important a place, and each evidently anxious to secure the governorship of the town. The first printed account of the event, though written without the connivance or knowledge of Mytton, did not satisfy Col. Reinking, who afterwards published "a more exact relation of the taking of Shrewsbury,"[3] which in its turn occasioned the appearance of "Colonel Mytton's reply to Reinking's relation of the taking of Shrewsbury."[4] Upon the merits of this dispute I do not propose to dwell. Both officers did their duty, and neither got the governorship of the town,

---

[1] In the State Paper Office is an interesting appeal to the Earl of Pembroke by one James Palmer for the release of one Herbert Vaughan, taken prisoner there, and also on behalf of the Earl Powis. Dom. Charles I., vol. 319, f. 249. See also vol. ii., Document lxxi., p. 239.

[2] Several accounts of the taking of Shrewsbury were printed at the time, and are preserved amongst the King's Pamphlets of the British Museum. See vol. ii., Document lxx., p. 237.

[3] King's Pamphlets, vol. 206, § 15.

[4] *Ibid*, 208, § 10.

CHAP. VI.
1645.

which was kept in abeyance by the Parliament, the management being vested in a committee.

Prince Maurice got into Chester on the Welsh side. He was not in quite a position to attempt the relief of Beeston, but ordered Col. Robinson, the Governor of Holt Castle, to make an attempt, which was done accordingly, but without success, Brereton defeating them and killing Col. Owen, one of their officers.[1] Under Maurice the Welsh were very slow to recruit, and after the loss of Shrewsbury nearly all the neighbouring garrisons were quitted, among them being Sea Hall, Tong Castle, Morton Corbet Castle, which they burnt down.[2] Seeing that Prince Maurice alone would not be able to beat Brereton out of his strongholds around Chester, orders were soon sent to Prince Rupert, General Gerard, and Sir Marmaduke Langdale to go to his assistance, which caused Brereton considerable uneasiness. The Scotch sometime ago had entered England in pursuance of the agreement come to when the Covenant was adopted in England; but up to this they had remained perfectly inactive. Pressing representations were now made to them of the danger with which Brereton was threatened, the answer to which was a movement southward on the part of the Scotch. Col. Rossiter was also ordered to go to the aid of Brereton. If united their forces would number some 6,000, as against some 5,500, which was computed to be the strength of Maurice, Rupert, Gerard, and Langdale.[3] By the middle of March the Royalists had

[1] *Kingdom's Weekly Intelligencer*, No. 90. (K. P. 197—2).
[2] *Scottish Dove*, No. 13.
[3] *Merc. Civicus*, No. 95, p. 861. (K. P. 198—8.)

concentrated their forces and had relieved Beeston Castle, which had been besieged for a long time. In their progress through the country they burned and destroyed all the small outposts of the enemy, and caused great devastation of property.[1] Beyond Beeston Rupert did not go. He would not fight, nor did he attempt the relief of Chester, which one would fancy had been the sole object of his march. It is very difficult to understand why he should have come so far to do so little. Was it fear of the Scotch who were now advanced into Lancashire? The reason assigned was some difficulties which had arisen around the City of Hereford. That city had been for some time a powerful stronghold of the Royalists, under the Governorship of Sir R. Scudamore. To maintain the garrison there constant levies had been made on the surrounding country people, who became so exasperated at length that they clubbed together for self-protection, and mustering a strong body of armed men they appeared before Hereford and demanded in a threatening attitude a redress of their grievances. To quell these Rupert quitted Cheshire. He did quell them, but only for a time. Chester was thus left in a position worse than ever. Rupert promised Lord Byron he would not quit the neighbourhood until the city had been victualled and ammunition had been sent in; but he was not so good as his word. And worse than all, Prince Maurice also left and carried away with him all that remained of the old Irish regiments—1,200 at least, according to Lord Byron, who complained bitterly to Lord Digby of having been left alone with "only a garrison of

[1] *Perfect Passages*, No. 24. See vol. ii., Document lxxii., p. 240.

citizens and his own and Col. Mostyn's regiment, which both together made not up above 600 men." And even of this the number was soon reduced to one-half, for "one-half being Mostyn's men," he says, "I was forced soon after to send out of town, finding them, by reason of their officers, who were ignorant Welsh gentlemen and unwilling to undergo any strict duty, far more prejudicial to us than useful."[1] Byron's greatest want was the want of ammunition. At the time of his writing he had not more than 18 barrels of powder, and no money to buy more, even if there had been any to buy. A few days before, it is true, a quantity of ammunition purchased in Ireland had been landed in Anglesey, whence it was conveyed along the coast and intended for Chester. But Brereton being informed of it by his excellent scouts, blocked up the road, which caused the Royalists to place it for safety in Hawarden Castle.[2] A regiment of Brereton's forces was at once sent to besiege the castle, which had already experienced some rough vicissitudes during the war. These on their way captured Sir John Hanmer's house at Northop; and finding when they arrived at the castle that those within refused to yield, they began without delay to undermine the structure itself.[3] But did not carry it out.

After Beeston had been relieved, Col Gerard, pursuant to express orders, set out for South Wales, where, as we have seen, Major-General Laugharne had shown some activity during his absence. The

---

[1] Lord Byron to Lord Digby, from Chester, 26th April. State Pap. Dom., Charles I., 319, § 289. See vol. ii., Document lxxv.
[2] *Kingdom's Weekly Intelligencer*, No. 95. (K. P. 202–3.)
[3] *A Diary or Exact Journal*, No. 51. (K. P. 206–6.)

town and castle of Cardigan had been taken by him about Christmas, and Newcastle also had been summoned. Some attempt was made to recapture Cardigan Castle very soon after by some forces which Gerard had left in the counties. Most of the accounts state that Gerard was present in person, but this could not be, as he was away between Worcester and Cirencester at the time. Lieut.-Col. Powell had been left in charge of the garrison which Laugharne placed there; but he had not been long in his office before some of the enemy appeared, and by some means got possession of the town, whence they laid siege to the castle. There was very little provision within. Of this the enemy seem to have been aware, which emboldened them to send a very peremptory summons, to which an obstinate denial to yield was the reply. It was not without some difficulty that Col. Powell was able to send word to Laugharne of the straits he was in. The latter lost no time in marching to the rescue; but when he came to the Tivy he found that the bridge had been broken down to prevent his passage. Nothing daunted, he shot an arrow across to the castle with a letter to inform them of his arrival. By means of rafts he crossed the river with his foot soldiers, and fell upon the rear of the enemy, while those within made a sally, the result being once more a victory for the Parliamentarians, the Royalists sustaining a heavy loss.[1] Since that time Laugharne had not been much molested, and he was in a fair way of clearing the country of those who had been left there in small

[1] See Capt. Smith's and Admiral Swanley's letters, *ante* p. 280. Also various other extracts in vol ii., Documents lxix. A. and B.

garrisons by Gerard. Of Laugharne's successes Parliament was in due course informed, and that his next movement would be towards Carmarthen. Five hundred pounds were voted him,[1] which sum was afterwards followed by a further vote of three thousand pounds.[2] But before Laugharne could proceed to Carmarthen, Gerard was pushing his way triumphantly through North Wales, routing Sir John Price at Llanidloes, and sending a detachment from Newtown, under Sir Edmund Cary, to attack Sir Thomas Myddelton, and to scour the country as far as Shrewsbury. Between Shrewsbury and Oswestry, at a place called Knocking, the two last-named met, and Myddelton had the worst of it.[3] About Tregaron and Lampeter, in Cardiganshire, Gerard plundered much, and swept away the provisions of the county;[4] and thence, on the 23rd of April, he came quite suddenly upon Laugharne's forces before Newcastle-Emlyn, and completely routed them, killing, according to the Royalist account, 150 on the spot. The vanquished took to flight, and were pursued through Cledey and Kilrhedyn in the direction of Haverfordwest. The same account states that in the pursuit nearly 500 prisoners were taken, with over 100 horse and a large quantity of arms. The very next morning Gerard pursued his march to Haverfordwest, which the Parliamentarians evacuated on his approach. Cardigan Castle was also deserted by its garrison, who having set fire to the fortress put to sea and made for Milford. Losing no time, Gerard crossed

---

[1] *An Exact Journal*, No. 43 (6th March).
[2] No. 79 *Mercurius Britannicus*.
[3] *Mercurius Aulicus* for 30th March, p. 1520. (K. P. 202—21).
[4] *Perfect Passages*, No. 29.

the water to Picton Castle, the seat of Sir Richard Phillipps, which was then garrisoned for the Parliament—Sir Richard Phillipps being one of the few in the county who were inclined to favour the authorities at Westminster. This was a great stronghold, and those who were at this time within it had added to its strength. They declined to yield it up and defended it bravely; but it was before midnight stormed and taken by the Royalists, who lost in the assault nine common soldiers, with one officer wounded—a Col. Butler. In the castle were taken three barrels of powder, some one hundred and fifty arms, twelve trunks of plate, and a large sum of money. The baronet's son and two daughters were made prisoners. Carew Castle also was taken. Once more, therefore, the tide was in favour of the Royalists, and the Parliament party had been driven back to the water-side, Pembroke and Tenby alone affording them refuge from their enemy.[1] Once again was Milford Haven all important to them, and its dangerous condition was made known to Parliament. On the 20th of May "many serious discourses" passed at Westminster "about the relief of Pembroke and Tenby, and the recovery of Milford Haven, and to enable, if possible, their party to take the field again." The task was felt to be a difficult one—the difficulty lying in recovering what was lost more than in keeping what they had.[2] But the commanders there had determined to stand by their trust, and resolved rather honourably to lose their lives together with

---

[1] *Merc. Aulicus*, 11th May, 1645. See vol. ii., Document lxxvi. Extract B.
[2] *Moderate Intelligencer*, No. 12. (K. P. 209—7). See vol. ii., Document lxxvi. Extract c.

CHAP. VI.
1645.

their said towns and garrisons than basely, by yielding, betray them with their religion and their liberties.[1]

The campaign had now, however, commenced in real earnest. Cromwell having been ordered to lead a party of horse to the road between Oxford and Worcester, to intercept communications between Rupert and the King, started without any delay, and was the first to lead a corps of the new army against the Royalists. He defeated the latter in three encounters—at Islip Bridge, April 24, at Whitney on the 26, and on the 27th at Bampton Bush. The King was dismayed, while London rejoiced that Cromwell's resignation had not been accepted by the Parliament. Thus opened the campaign of 1645—a campaign destined to prove fatal to the King's cause, and ultimately to the King himself.

On the 7th of May the King quitted Oxford, and having been joined by Rupert, proceeded through Worcestershire and Staffordshire, designing either to raise the siege of Chester, or to give battle to the Scottish army, which had already entered England, and which had been by no means as active as the Parliament wished. On hearing of the King's marching towards them they withdrew to the border, a movement which caused much annoyance in London. The siege of Chester was raised on the mere approach of the King. His Majesty reached Newport in Shropshire on the 17th, where he was met by Sir William Vaughan,

[1] "An exact and humble remonstrance touching the late conflict of arms in and near the County of Pembroke." (K. P. 209—16.) Vol. ii., Document lxxvi. A.

Governor of Shrawardine Castle, who, on the way, had worsted some Shrewsbury horse near Wenlock. From thence the King proceeded to Drayton in Cheshire, where Lord Byron met him with some troops of horse from Chester, and acquainted him with the news that the siege of that city had been raised, and that Sir William Brereton had retreated into Lancashire.

Having secured by this an easy passage to Ireland, should such a course become necessary, the King and his army next bent their steps eastwards, with the design to march towards the eastern counties, where hitherto he had not been able to have any hold whatever. This menacing of the very bulwark of the Parliamentary party at once decided them upon calling Cromwell back from before Oxford, which was at this time under siege. Coming before Leicester, which was garrisoned by a small force of Parliamentarians, at Rupert's suggestion the place was stormed, and successfully. This loss, which occurred on the 1st of June, was deeply felt in London, and Fairfax was recalled from Oxford, and received urgent instructions to march at once after Cromwell, and to intercept the King's progress. Lord Loughborough, with a small force, was left at Leicester, and the King and the body of his army pursued their course. In the neighbourhood of Northampton he heard that the enemy had raised the blockade of Oxford, and were close upon them in considerable force under the leadership of Fairfax and Cromwell. On the 9th the King had written to the Queen, "Never since the beginning of the Rebellion have my affairs been in so good a position." And this spirit prevailed when the approach of the enemy was announced. This was late in the evening of the 13th of June. A Council of War was instantly assembled. Some counselled delay. Reinforcements were expected: among others Gerard with his forces from Wales. Others were for an instant conflict, and the impetuous Rupert caused it to be so decided upon. At dawn the next morning the forces met in combat. This was the battle of Naseby—a battle so decisive and so important as to require no detailed account here. The Parliamentary army was completely victorious. The King and his forces were utterly routed. The King himself showed considerable bravery, but his horse all ran away, and never stopped until they had reached Ashby de la Zouch. Cromwell's tactics are considered to have decided the victory, and after this no more need he fear the self-denying ordinance. His commission was safe enough now. But the victory itself, disastrous as it was, was not half so fatal to the King's cause, and indeed to the King's character, as the capture of the King's letters proved. These were eagerly perused by Fairfax, Cromwell, and Ireton, and soon afterwards sent up to London, and publicly read on the 3rd of July at the Guildhall, in the presence of a vast concourse of the citizens. These letters convinced the people that Charles had been playing them false, that it was manifest he had never desired peace, and that all his protestations were insincere.

Peace now became impossible, and the endeavours of the Lords and the Scottish Commissioners to get up another negotiation were utterly silenced by this exposure of the King's duplicity and dishonesty. The letters were published. Disgust, distrust, and anger became general. The war party took advantage of this revulsion of the public feeling. They found no difficulty in making new levies of troops, and in obtaining money for carrying on the war. Fairfax proceeded westwards, and the Scots advanced into the interior.

Utterly prostrated as was the Royalist party at this blow, and threatened with imminent ruin, the sagest of the King's counsel advised him to march without delay, with what forces remained to him after the discomfiture at Naseby, to the western counties, where Goring and Greenville were still at the head of a considerable force, harassed only by the untrained and ill-armed "clubmen," so that by effecting a junction with the army under Goring some preparations might be made for an attempt to stop the course of Fairfax, who had received the orders of Parliament to proceed to the West, and who, having captured Leicester, was then actually on his way thither at the head of an army elated with success and fired by a deep religious enthusiasm. Charles, however, never did listen to the advice of those who had his interest really at heart, but was ever unfortunate in his choice of counsellors. The worthless Digby and Ashburnham at this time led the King as they pleased. And instead of trying the only chance he had he determined to go to Hereford, and from thence to Wales, where he thought the people were still true to him, and where he was in hopes of being able to recruit his forces. Flying from town to town, Hereford was reached by the King on the 19th June. The presence of the King even under such momentous reverses was reassuring to some extent, and some degree of loyalty was evoked. Many of the gentry of the surrounding counties came in to pay their homage. The levies upon the counties were put in some method; but before anything like final order was arrived at there was some misunderstanding between Rupert and the King's most intimate advisers, which ended in the former betaking himself to Bristol, which he was most anxious to preserve, and so the management of the affair commenced at Hereford was left in confusion and disorder.[1] General Gerard (who had come out of Wales with the intention to join himself with the King before the latter went to the eastern counties, but had not been able to reach in time,) with above 2,000 horse and foot, joined the stricken forces of the King at Hereford. A fortnight was there spent with very little success, for the greatest difficulty was experienced in recruiting soldiers. On the 1st of July his Majesty left Hereford, and at the head of a small body proceeded to Abergavenny, attended a part of the way by the Governor of Hereford and some of the county gentlemen. The object in going to Abergavenny was to meet the Commissioners of Array of Monmouth and the various counties of South Wales. "Mountains" were promised by these Commissioners; but nothing came of their promises.[2] Presently we shall find out the reason why they did not prove so good as their word. In the meantime many of the Welsh soldiers that had come under Gerard had gone over with Rupert to the assistance of Bristol.

[1] Sir Edward Walker's Historical Discourses, p. 132.
[2] *Ibid.*

Finding that the meeting at Abergavenny proved of little advantage to his cause, the King proceeded on the 3rd to Raglan Castle, the seat of the Marquis of Worcester, where at any rate he was certain of a hearty welcome and a princely entertainment. His troops were scattered to the surrounding outposts of Treargaer, Brongwin, Bettws, &c. Even now it was not too late for the King to proceed to the assistance of Goring, and to try the fortune of a second issue, of which, as Sir Edward Walker tritely remarks, "even had it been lost it could not have proved worse than their being afterwards both in the West, and in other places destroyed by pieces without either conduct or honour." But false counsel again prevailed, and the unstable Charles was lulled to sleep by the charms of Raglan, as if the genius of the place had conspired with his fate. Sport and entertainments were enjoyed with as much zest as if no crown had been at stake. The King, surrounded by the Duke of Richmond, the Earls of Lindsey, Lichfield, and Carnewarth, and the Lords Digby and Bellasis, felt himself, as it were, restored to his natural position, and the presence of ladies only was wanted to turn the secluded walls of Raglan into a brilliant and thoughtless Court. Nearly a fortnight was thus spent in almost utter indifference and inactivity, and all this while the Parliamentary forces were beclouding the lovely roads of England with the dust of their heavy and determined tramp to the West; and the Scots were advancing into the very heart of the country, and were already within a short distance from Hereford, carrying everything before them unopposed. One can hardly conceive the possibility of such a state of things, but the King no longer had around him honourable men. Many of his best advisers had gone away disgusted, and others had been slain in the field, and now he was left alone with a parcel of as unprincipled and unscrupulous a set of advisers as ever a Prince had, who cared little for their country, and whose sole object was to gain influence over the King for their own aggrandisement.

News, however, soon came of the defeat of Goring by Fairfax at Lamport, and this aroused them from their apathy. An attempt was made to raise forces in South Wales. The Commissioners were met by the King at Cardiff on the 16th, who having visited Sir Wm. Morgan at Tredegar, again returned to Raglan on the 18th. More disasters from the West were reported. Prince Rupert from Bristol was pressing for aid. Gerard's foot, as already stated, had erewhile gone over the Severn, and the Scots were approaching Hereford. Even Charles saw it was useless to sleep any longer. Fresh counsel was invoked, and it was resolved at last that the King should speedily go over to Bristol, and that all the disposable forces which he had should follow him as soon as possible. This was communicated to Prince Rupert, who at once came over and met the King and his council at the house of Mr. Moore, called the Creek, near Chepstow, and it was here finally arranged that the King should cross the Severn. That night the King returned to Raglan, the next day was spent in preparing for removing to Bristol, and on the 24th Charles set out for the Black Rock, where boats were in waiting to carry him across. The design, however, was abandoned at the last moment, and we are left in a mist to discover the causes of this sudden change. Digby, as every one knows, had an all-powerful influence with the King, and he well knew that the clear-sighted Rupert had long ago seen through him, whence their hatred was tolerably mutual, and there can be no doubt that that nobleman had a great deal to do with this action of the King. Symonds, in his diary, states that the gentlemen of Wales persuaded his stay, and raised a hubbub. But be the cause what it may, the King instead of crossing the channel, went to Cardiff, to which place he had scarcely come when he received tidings of the loss of Bridgwater—one of his chief strongholds in the West, and a place by him thought to be almost impregnable. A severer blow could scarcely be given to his hopes. There was now no place to bar the enemy from swarming with his triumphant forces before Bristol; but the King still had hopes that the last-named place was sufficiently strong to hold out for a while, so that the siege of Hereford, which the Scottish army, under David Lesley, Earl of Leven, had now commenced, was permitted for a while to engage the King's attention. There was no time to be lost to effect its relief. Orders were therefore sent to the sheriffs of the several counties of South Wales to summon their *posse comitatus*, and to bring them armed to the King with as little delay as possible. And thus the King fondly hoped he would be able to raise a sufficient force to attempt the relief of Hereford.

But everything was changed in these counties now. Wales had been ever prominent in aiding the King: had been most forward in supplying him with men, arms, and money; but its ardour was now gone. The men in whom the people trusted had been removed from command, and a set of adventurers had been placed in their stead, who, instead of serving the King, had more in view their own enrichment, and who had for a long time devastated the country, making scarcely any distinction in their plundering raids between friends and foes, until they had changed the former into enemies, or had driven them from the King's service with disgust; while those who were originally for the Parliament found greater cause than ever for their opposition to the King. Lord Capel in the North, Earl Carbery in the South, while they were at the head of the King's forces in their respective parts, had acted as honourable men, and though they were not so successful in the field as the King could have wished, they aided his cause more by neutralizing those inclined for the Parliament than any of their more unscrupulous successors in command ever effected by conquest in the field. Lord Byron in the North, Sir Charles Gerard in South Wales, had by this time pretty well alienated the affections of almost all men from the King. The latter especially had made himself most obnoxious. He was a passionate, reckless, and unscrupulous man, who, by some means or other, had ingratiated himself into Prince Rupert's favour, through which he was advanced, as we have before stated, into the position of Major-General of the King's forces for South Wales. At the head of a body of rapacious Cavaliers he had committed great ravages, had levied contributions in a most heartless manner, and had behaved to everybody with a perfectly unwarranted rigour, treating great and small with the greatest discourtesy and harshness.[1] And thus the people would serve the King no longer, but would gladly be rid of him, and of the swarms of locusts which he had inconsiderately poured over the country.

It is no wonder, therefore, that the King's attempt to raise a force in Wales did not meet with a ready or a hearty response. The *posse comitatus* of Glamorganshire truly was brought together, to the number of 4,000; but it was not to march to relieve Hereford. It was rather to state their grievances and to complain of their ill-usage; and in their complaints the people were well backed by some of the leading men of the County of Glamorgan, such as Sir John Awbrey of Llantrithyd, Mr. Carne of Ewenny, Col. Prichard of Llancayach, and Mr. Button, who, it is stated, at this time were in correspondence with the rebels in Pembrokeshire.[2] Whether this was so or not I cannot say, but that disaffection considerably prevailed even among those who had hitherto been most loyal to the King there can be no doubt. So that Charles's attempt to raise a force in South Wales was not successful. Alluding to the raising of the *posse comitatus*, Sir Edward Walker says, "like unskilful magicians we by this means raised such devils as we could never lay again," and Clarendon in more classical terms states the same thing.

[1] Clarendon's Rebellion, iv., 76.
[2] Walker's Hist. Discourses, p. 134.

CHAP. VI.
1645.

The King was at Ruperra, a guest of Sir Philip Morgan, from the 25th to the 29th of July. In the meantime a meeting had been arranged between the assembled countrymen and the King, and on Tuesday, the 29th, Charles, accompanied by the Duke of Richmond and others, and a regiment of his guards, proceeded to Cardiff, where he dined at the charge of Sir T. Tyrrell, the Governor at the Castle, and in the afternoon proceeded to the rendezvous of the countrymen, which was at St. Fagans. The gentry of the county were there in a body on horseback, and the people were drawn up in battle array, winged with horse and a reserve.[1] The King was aware that there was a hitch in matters, but he was by no means prepared for such a hostile demonstration, and he must have been dismayed at the sight of it. He, moreover, approached them and ascertained for himself the true state of affairs. The Welsh were by no means daunted by the presence of the King, but stoutly proclaimed their grievances, and submitted certain propositions to him for his acceptance, the which if he granted would induce them to give him certain aid. They demanded to have the Governor at Cardiff removed, and a Welshman put in his place; to have the choice of their own officers; to have the Papists removed out of the county, and to have the arrears demanded by Col. Gerard remitted. The King's answer was gracious enough. He promised that he would grant them all reasonable demands. But they would not accept a mere promise: they desired to see the changes they sought actually effected. One man, more daring

[1] Symonds' Diary, Harl. MSS., 991.

than his fellows, stepped forth, and boldly declared their distrust of his promises, and cited proofs to show that he was not always bound by his promises, amongst others, the fact that they had a warrant under the Great Seal, calling upon them to contribute £800 a month towards the defence of the county, and that in less than a week after, Gerard produced another warrant, signed by the King himself, which subjected them to a contribution of twice that amount. Other grievances they stated. Gerard's cruelties and injustice were complained of in strong terms. Gerard himself was present at these debates, and in his turn he upbraided the gentry in no measured terms, which conduct, as it did not invoke from the King any marked reproof, only incensed them all the more, and increased their clamour for his removal.

The King returned that night to Cardiff, and the assembled countrymen bivouaced out in the open air. Our account below[1] states that the next

---

[1] The following account, though extracted from a party paper, so agrees in general with the Royalist account of the proceedings at Cardiff, while it supplies some information not elsewhere given, that I transcribe it here:—

"Since my last there is come to my hands a particular and exact relation of the proceedings in Wales at and since his Majesty's late being there, which, although it be not very recent, yet, having been formerly imperfectly related, as I could only give you a hint of it the last week, I shall here communicate it briefly.

"The King sent to Monmouthshire and Glamorganshire to meet at five or six several rendezvous, then to meet at the general rendezvous at Newport, and to bring as many men as they could.

"Glamorganshire met five hundred foot in all, and the horse about a hundred. The gentry endeavoured to draw them along to the general rendezvous. This was last Monday fortnight. As they were drawing them out one Smith made a speech to them to this effect: 'Let us consider whither we are going, and whom we leave behind,' which was an English governor at Cardiff who had threatened to fetch in what they had; and mentioned

CHAP. VI.
1645.

day the King demanded security to come and treat with them, or to send to him men to treat, whereupon they sent ten gentlemen and ten countrymen, "minding the gentry as they were going out not in any way to engage them without their consent," and they in a body drew nearer to Cardiff, making their rendezvous at a place called Kevenon, or Cefnon, within four miles of the town, and here they lay in the field until Saturday. Cefnon is the name of a hill which runs between the Taff and the Rhymney. It is of some interest in this history, not because it was a rendezvous on this occasion, but because at the foot of this hill was born the Welsh ancestor of Oliver Cromwell. Exact old Leland, in his *Itinerary*, refers to it in these words: "A two miles from this hill by the south, and a two miles from Cardiff, be vestigia of a Pile

---

other abuses the country had sustained, and therefore [he] thought it was best [for them] to stay for their own safety. To whom all agreed not to stir.

"The gentry hereupon and some horse repair to the Lord Digby with the tidings. Whereupon a hubbub is raised, and five thousand [assemble] together the next morning.

"The day following the King comes to them and desires to know the cause of their meeting. They answered for the preservation of their country. The King said he was for that, too, and desired to know what they would ask further. They demanded 1st to have the Papists removed out of the country. 2ndly, to have the English garrison removed out of Cardiff, and a governor and garrison of their own put in. 3rdly, seven thousand pounds arrears demanded by Gerard remitted. The King answered fair, and said they should have all reasonable contentment. One stepped forth and said they had not all promises performed that came from his Majesty, for they had a warrant under the Broad Seal for £800 a month, and within a week Gerard showed them the King's own hand for £1,600 a month. The King seeing them talk so peremptorily desired to talk with the gentry. They minded the gentry as they were going not in any way to engage them without their consent. The King departs to Cardiff, and they continue at their rendezvous till Saturday.

"The King demands security to come and treat, or to send to him men to

or Maner Place decayed at Egglisnewith, in the parish of Llandaff. On the south side of this hill was born Richard Williams, *alias* Cromwell, in the parish of Llanilsen." This Richard Cromwell, or Williams, who signed himself nephew of the Lord Cromwell, the great counsellor of Henry VIII., was the great-great-grandfather of the greater Oliver Cromwell. To return: On Friday the King assented to all their propositions, whereupon they agreed to furnish him in a month with 1,000 men and the sum of £800 to arm them. But the King's manner of acceding to their requests clearly betrayed the fact that it was extorted from him, which took away from his assent much of its value. Gerard and his officers were removed from command in those parts, and Sir Jacob Astley put in his place. Sir Timothy

---

treat. They send ten gentlemen and ten countrymen to treat, and their articles agreed on were—

"1st. That Sir Tim. Tirrell and all the garrrison do march the forth.

"2ndly. They agreed to furnish the King with 1,000 men and £800 to arm them.

"According to this agreement the King and the whole garrison marched forth to Brecknock, one Sir Richard Basset made governor, and a garrison of countrymen put into Cardiff Castle. The King only left about four or five officers to receive and conduct the 1,000 men thence. No sooner were the countrymen in the town but they searched for these commanders; but they were hid and shifted out of the town, only Sir Jacob Astley remained behind. Endymion Porter and others shipped at Swansea for Ireland. Then news came to the King that about 700 men were killed and taken at Brecknock, and those that escaped got to Carmarthen.

"The King went Wednesday last to Hay, and Thursday to Bridgnorth.

"The King went out of Cardiff this day sevennight. Gerard made a lord there in recompense for being put out of command in Wales, &c., it being the country's demand. Sir Jacob Astley in his place.

"The first rendezvous of the countrymen was at Munrow Vaughan, the second at Richard's Hill, and other times at other places.

"This relation was taken the 11th August, from one who was an eye-witness thereof."—*Mercurius Civicus*, No. 118 (pp. 1042-44) of August 28th, 1645.

CHAP. VI.
1645.

Tyrrel was removed from the governorship of the town, and the English garrison therein removed, and Sir Richard Basset of Beaupre had the place conferred upon him, having been nominated by the people. Such other officers were also appointed as they nominated. Charles, nevertheless, created Gerard a baron, which "unreasonable preferment" only galled the Welshmen. A more foolish act cannot well be conceived. Even the friends of the King blamed it. Clarendon and Walker speak of it in terms of dissatisfaction, and the more so, because in the first place of the bad effect it would have upon the populace, and in the next place because it was conferred upon an unworthy person,[1] who thus obtained a higher reward "than but for that accusation he could never probably have arrived to."

These negotiations had hardly been completed,—in fact, the people were not dispersed,—when news came from Pembrokeshire of the defeat of that part of Gerard's forces which had been left at Haverfordwest to maintain the King's cause in the western counties: by which the King's last chance in those parts was frustrated and his power nearly annihilated. Gerard, when he quitted South Wales, had left a considerable body of soldiers at Haverfordwest—according to one account to the number of 1,100 foot and about 450 horse—under the command of "two young" Major-Generals, viz., Major-General Stradling and Major-General Egerton. Pembroke and Tenby at this time were in the hands of the Parliament, and garrisoned by a small body under the command of Major-General Laugharne. Tidings

[1] Clarendon's Rebellion, iv., p. 81.

of the defeat of the Royalists at Naseby had undoubtedly reached them, and of the King's sojourn in Glamorganshire, and being doubtless informed of the state of affairs at Cardiff, a state of affairs which must have proved as damping to the ardour of the force at Haverfordwest as it was encouraging to them, such circumstances doubtless induced Laugharne to try once more the issue of battle with them. Accordingly, on the 28th July, he drew out his forces, to the number of about 550 foot and 200 horse, out of Tenby and Pembroke—more they could not spare—and proceeded in the direction of Haverfordwest, reaching Caneston Wood, where they came upon seven scouts, one of whom was killed and the others made prisoners. Here they lay until Friday, the 1st of August, receiving however a reinforcement of about 150 seamen just arrived at Milford. On Friday, Stradling and Egerton drew their forces out into Colby Moor.[1] The fight commenced about six o'clock in the afternoon, and was hotly contested for about an hour, ending however in the utter routing of the Royalists, who attempted to fly in the greatest confusion and disorder to Haverfordwest. About 150 of these were slain, and about seven hundred prisoners made, including several officers of note, and a considerable quantity of arms, carriages, and ammunition, was also captured. Night came on, and the darkness saved the town from an attack. During the night the town was deserted—a small garrison only being

[1] Some seventy years ago many relics of this fight were unearthed by the plough on the Moor. Fenton mentions this in his history of Pembrokeshire, and states that there was a tradition of a battle having occurred there in Charles the First's time; but he curiously enough doubts it on the ground that he had seen no account of it in any newspaper of the time.

placed in the castle. So early on Saturday the victors entered the town, and began on Monday their assault on the old fortress, which was successfully stormed and scaled on Tuesday, and all within made prisoners.[1]

From the West of England, also, news of a disheartening character reached the King. These reverses coming within so short a time of his writing so hopefully to the Queen must have sorely tried Charles.

The country, tired both of King and Parliament, and sick with the ravages of war, loudly cried for peace. The King's prospects were never sadder. Even Prince Rupert, who at any rate cannot be looked upon as a kid-glove courtier, counselled Charles to seek peace. From Bristol he wrote a letter to the Duke of Richmond on the subject. This was shown, as it was intended to be, to the King. But Charles, whose evil genius even in the darkest moment raised illusory hopes in his breast, would not listen to any advice so sensible, but regarded far more his own high notions of kingly dignity than he did the sufferings of his people. He therefore treated Rupert's advice with contempt, and wrote to him the most spirited letter, if the most blind, which ever emanated from his pen. Below will be found an extract from it:—

"Now, as for your opinion of my business and your counsel thereupon, if I had any other quarrel but the defence of my religion, crown, and friends, you had full reason for your advice, for I confess

---

[1] "A true relation of the late success of the Parliament's Forces in Pembrokeshire, &c." Printed for Ed. Husbands, Aug. 25, 1645. See vol. ii., Document lxxix., p. 266.

that, speaking as a mere soldier or statesman, I must say there is no probability but of my ruin; yet as a Christian I must tell you that God will not suffer rebels and traitors to prosper, nor this cause to be overthrown; and whatever personal punishment it shall please Him to inflict upon me, must not make me repine much less give over this quarrel, and there is as little question that a composition with them at this time is nothing else but a submission, which, by the Grace of God, I am resolved against whatever it cost me, for I know my obligation to be, both in conscience and honor, neither to abandon God's cause, injure my successors, nor forsake my friends. Indeed, I cannot flatter myself with expectation of good success more than this, to end my days with honor and a good conscience; which obliges me to continue my endeavours in not despairing that God may yet in due time avenge his own cause, though I must aver to all my friends that he that will stay with me at this time must expect and resolve either to die for a good cause, or, which is worse, to live as miserable in maintaining it as the violence of insulting rebels can make it.

"Having thus truly and impartially stated my case unto you, and plainly told you my resolutions, which, by the Grace of God, I will not alter, they being neither lightly nor suddenly grounded, I earnestly desire you not in any wise to hearken now after treaties, assuring you that as low as I am I will do no more than was offered in my name at Uxbridge: confessing that it were as great a miracle that they should agree to so much reason as that I should be within a month in the same condition that I was immediately before the battle of Naseby. Therefore, for God's sake, let us not flatter ourselves with these conceits, and believe me the very imagination that you are desirous of a treaty will but lose me so much the sooner. Wherefore, as you love me, whatsoever you have already done, apply your discourse hereafter to my resolution and judgment. As for the first, I assure you they shall not cheat me, but it is possible they may cozen themselves, for be assured what I have refused to the English I will not grant to the Irish rebels, never trusting to that kind of people (of what nation soever) more than I see by their actions, and I am sending to Ormond such a dispatch as I am sure you and all honest men, a copy whereof by the next opportunity you shall have. Lastly, be confident. I would not have put you nor myself to the trouble of this long letter had I not a great estimation of you, and a full confidence in your friendship to

"C. R.

"Cardiff, August 3, 1645."[1]

Charles's object in coming to Cardiff had utterly failed. All hopes of raising in Glamorganshire any force for the relief of Hereford was found altogether impossible. Even the counties of Monmouth and Brecon, which, from their geographical position, would form the basis of any operations in that direction, were equally unwilling to risk any more for the royal cause.[2] It was therefore considered

---

[1] In Halliwell's Letters of the Kings of England this is given as July 31, quoting the Harl. MSS., 4231, as his authority. That, however, is a mere copy; but it gives the same date for the King's letter to Ormond referred to in his letter to the Prince.

[2] Walker's Hist. Disc., p. 136.

high time for the King to study his own safety. He was in the midst of danger. The Scots were at Hereford; and Laugharne, victorious in Pembrokeshire, was rumoured to be on his way eastwards. Moreover it was clear he was not safe in the hands or power of even those whom he had just been negotiating with, who were "whispering among themselves as if they intended to seize his person and deliver him to the Parliament to make their peace."[1] He had only two courses to chose from, either to pass over the Severn and join Rupert or Goring, or else to make his way to the North. Goring was not in a very flourishing condition. Fairfax had driven him very hard, and Bristol was threatened. To cross the Severn therefore would be probably attended with considerable risk. Some news of Montrose's successes in the North had been brought to Cardiff, and it was therefore finally resolved to quit that place, and by stealthy marches over the mountains to make for the North —a course which was "embraced as having a greater probability of success" than the other.[2]

Accordingly, having entrusted the management of his affairs in Glamorganshire to Sir Jacob Astley, the King, on the night of the 4th of August, set forth from Cardiff at the head of a small force, which consisted of Col. Gerard's horse, the King's own Life Guards, Sir Marmaduke Langdale's and Sir William Vaughan's regiments. These had a few days previously been recruited by about 200 foot, under Sir Thomas Glenham, who had marched thither from Carlisle upon the surrender of that

[1] Ludlow's Memoirs (Ed. 1721), vol. i., p. 159.
[2] Walker, *supra*.

place to the Scots, under the command of Leven. They marched over the mountains to Brecknock. On the way the King dined at Glancayach, the house of Mr. Prichard,[1] and at Brecknock he rested for the night at the Priory, the house of Col. Herbert Price, who was then the governor of the town.

In all these dark and despairing days the safety of his son had been an object of deep concern to the King. While at Raglan the King had sent for Lord Colepepper, who had accompanied Prince Charles in the West; but, owing to the dangers of the road, Colepepper had not been able to arrive until Charles was ready to depart from Cardiff. He accompanied him to Brecknock, and there in the quiet seclusion of the Priory the subject was discussed between them. Even Charles was now convinced that his chances were but very precarious, and that he himself was menaced with considerable danger, so much so that he felt it necessary to provide for the safety of his son, so that whatever should befal him personally, the succession of his house might be secured. Consequently he dispatched Colepepper to the Prince with the following letter, dated Brecknock, 5th August, 1645:—

"CHARLES,—It is very fit for me now to prepare for the worst, in order to which I spoke with Colepepper this morning concerning you, judging fit to give it you under my hand, that you may

---

[1] *Inter Carolinum*, sub. dat. In Symonds' list of the gentry of Glamorganshire Mr. Edward Prichard of Llancayach is put down as worth £800 a year. Prichard soon after declared himself for the Parliament, and in due course of time was appointed governor of Cardiff Castle.

give the readiest obedience to it. Wherefore know that my pleasure is, whensoever you find yourself in apparent danger of falling into the rebels' hands, that you convey yourself into France, and there to be under your mother's care, who is to have the absolute full power of your education in all things except religion, and in that not to meddle at all, but leave it entirely to the care of your tutor, the Bishop of Salisbury, or to whom he shall appoint to supply his place in time of his necessitated absence. And for the performance of this I command you to require the assistance and obedience of all your council; and by their advice the service of every one whom you and they shall think fit to be employed in this business, which I expect should be performed, if need require, with all obedience and without grumbling. This is all at this time from

"Your loving Father,
"CHARLES. R."[1]

The next day (being Wednesday the 6th) the King and his forces passed out of Brecknockshire into Radnorshire. His Majesty dined on the way at Sir Henry Williams's seat at Gwernyfed, and reached old Radnor in the evening, where he partook of supper at a yeoman's house.[2] There being no accommodation for his retinue, the Court here dispersed. What they did for lodgings Heaven knows; and on Thursday, having travelled all day without any dinner,[3] Ludlow Castle (of which Col. Wodehouse was Governor) was reached. Hence

[1] Clarendon, iv., 83.
[2] *Iter Carolinum.*
[3] *Ibid.*

CHAP. VI.
1645.

they passed through Shropshire, Staffordshire, Derbyshire, Nottinghamshire, and into Yorkshire, the King on the way calling upon all his faithful adherents to go with him to join Montrose, who had recently obtained some victories in Scotland. News, however, came that David Lesley had quitted the siege of Hereford, and was in pursuit of the King with the Scottish Cavalry. Courage the Royalists at this time possessed not, nor had they any confidence in themselves. At these tidings many of them left the ranks, and recruits could not be had. The King, therefore, was obliged to give up his project for the North, and to betake himself to Oxford, which place he reached on the 28th.

No sooner had Charles left Cardiff than the party disaffected to him there began to show their power. Though the King had made to them all the concessions they required, and had removed from command all such as were obnoxious to them, nay, had even entrusted the garrison to a countryman of their own, they do not appear to have been satisfied. A few English officers, along with Sir Jacob Astley, had been left behind; and inasmuch as these were entrusted by the King to bring to him the 1,000 men which had been promised,—a promise which, I am afraid, was made with a great deal of mental reservation,—they made it a point, as soon as they got fairly into the town, to search for these and drive them away. The poor fellows hid themselves—or were kindly hidden—from the infuriate mob, and when an opportunity presented itself they "shifted" out of the town, Astley alone being left behind. Sir Richard Basset, in all probability, was anxious to maintain order, and, perhaps, even to keep inviolate the compact made with the King, which caused the townspeople and the others who had come in there to resolve to put him out of the governorship unless he submitted to them, and threatened in case of resistance to set the town on fire.[1] And in this their resolution they doubtless were much aided by Laugharne's continued successes in Pembrokeshire, where most of the King's garrisons were now in the hands of the Parliamentarians, and where the people were already beginning to see the advantages of freedom from the ruinous raids with which Gerard and his creatures had overran and almost laid waste the country. In fact, the Royalists were fast giving in, and the common people openly declaring for the Parliament everywhere in South Wales. "Even the County of Glamorgan, where the Parliament was never wont to be named but in detestation, begins to clear up, and the greater part of the gentry declare for the Parliament."[2]

Sir Jacob Astley, single-handed almost as he was, could do nothing under such circumstances. Influence he had none, and power was equally wanting. Writing on the 11th of August from Cardiff to Prince Rupert at Bristol, he complained bitterly of the conduct of the inhabitants. He said "the County of Glamorgan is so unquiet as there is no good to be expected. Shall strive as far as I can to put things in order, which I despair of, because it is *power* to rule these people, and not

CHAP. VI.
1645.

[1] *Merc. Civicus*, No. 118, 28th August; and *The Kingdom's Weekly Intelligencer*, No. 114, 26th August.
[2] *Merc. Britannicus*, No. 98. (K. P. 226—15.)

entreaties with cap in hand to such as deserve the halter."[1] He did strive, but all his endeavours availed him little in the face of such manifest unfriendliness from all. From Newport, four days later, he wrote that the gentry of Brecknock were most of them inclined to be neutral and to join with the strongest party, which made it difficult for him to engage them to join together to relieve Hereford. The County of Monmouth was equally implacable. Nothing could be done. His commission to levy forces in Wales completely failed. His presence there seems to have only irritated people all the more. He summoned a meeting of the inhabitants of Monmouthshire, Glamorganshire, and the other counties of South Wales, at Abergavenny. A large assembly gathered. Sir Jacob desired them to join him to go against the Scots. Again they demanded the removal of English officers from the command of the garrisons in Wales. But this demand he thought too hard, and seeing that no good was likely to come of any further negotiations with the people, he called upon those who were for the Parliament to stand by themselves, and those that were for the King to stand by themselves. Upon which Sir Trevor Williams, of Llangibby, who hitherto had been for the King, stood forth and told him that "they came for both King and Parliament, and not to divide between them, as they perceived his intention was." Thereupon most of the company dispersed, leaving poor Sir Jacob utterly baffled.[2] The consequence was that the Parliament cause made great strides. The people every-

---

[1] Warburton's Prince Rupert, i., 527.
[2] *The Kingdom's Weekly Intelligencer*, No. 117 (K. P. 225—13.)

where clubbed for their self-protection, and these club-men, feeling their strength, soon began to show it. They set about the removal from command of officers who had become obnoxious to them. Cardiff Castle had been placed under Sir Richard Basset; though a countryman, he gave no satisfaction. Early in September Colonel Herbert, with his regiment, aided by the Glamorganshire club-men, appeared before it. The town and castle were soon evacuated, Sir Richard Basset being allowed to march out with his 200 men.[1] Col. Herbert took possession thereof, and found in the castle 16 pieces of ordnance, 10 barrels of gunpowder, about 400 arms, and good store of bullet, match, ammunition, and provisions. Col. Herbert's next design was the reduction of the garrison at Swansea, and this also was presently accomplished.

The Parliamentary newspapers at this time were teeming with allusions to this change of feeling in South Wales. Vaunting references were made to the King's failure at Cardiff to raise an army. "Could he get no recruits in Wales? Could not his Majesty's orations (which were eloquent enough) prevail nothing on the people? Could Digby's warrants draw no more into the sad and fatal list, although they used and abused the authority of the King? The King now complains of Wales and of the hearts of the people there, which, he says, are as hard and rocky as the country. Wales is at length grown wise and happy. It was as full of corrupt and malignant blood, which being now let (like a ruinous body after a long fever) it begins to recover into health and

---

[1] *Perfect Occurrences*, the 40th week (K. P., large 4to., 19—19.)

strength."[1] This crowing prevailed immensely. The loyalty of the Welsh, their great help in all times to his cause, were put down to ignorance; and this change in South Wales was attributed to a better and clearer understanding of the quarrel between the King and the Parliament. Hitherto it was said they understood nothing of the real issue; the people had been misled and deceived. But now all was changed, and "at length the *moles* have eyes."[2] South Wales in this respect was better off than North Wales. The dawn of a better day had not reached the mountainous recesses of the northern division of the Principality. Ignorance still led the people to the King's side. Nothing but education would show them their folly: it was urgently necessary that they should be "educated," and it was for this purpose ordered by the Parliament "that a declaration be drawn up and sent into North Wales to inform them aright of the Parliament," which was deemed by *Mercurius Britannicus* "very seasonable for Wales." The service of a writer acquainted with the country and its people was called into vogue, and a pamphlet was written for the edification of the Northwalians, and dispersed all over the six counties. And whether it was due to the persuasive eloquence of that writer, or to other causes which we shall presently investigate, the sympathies of those in the North became very soon changed, and Charles lost even there his power, as we have seen he had done in the South, to a very marked degree. The Parliament became more assiduous with respect to Wales.

---

[1] *The Parliament's Post*, No. 15, August 19.
[2] *Merc. Britannicus*, No 94.

Hitherto the Principality had not much engaged the attention of the Assembly at Westminster, and their newly-kindled desire to cultivate the Welsh was highly approved of by the Parliamentary press of London.[1] When Laugharne's letter relating his victory on Colby Moor was read in the House, his prayer for supplies was answered by an unanimous vote. His wife happened to be in Town at this time, and they also voted an allowance of £10 a week to her during her stay in London,[2] an act which the *Moderate Intelligencer* commends as "a very good work."[3]

Charles was very dispirited when he got to Oxford. All hopes of joining Montrose in the North had, at least for a time, vanished. But he had not been there more than a couple of days when intelligence reached him of the important triumphs which Montrose had obtained over the Covenanters at Kilsyth, in the Lowlands. The royal cause for the moment was prosperous beyond expectation in Scotland. The King's despondency gave way. With the small force which still attended upon him he quitted the city, with the intention to raise the siege of Hereford, judging that the besiegers, being reduced by Leslie's absence, would be somewhat disheartened at the news which had given him such encouragement. And he was not mistaken; for the Scots, either hearing of his approach, or called away to the assistance of their defeated brethren in the North, raised the siege, and a day before the King arrived at Hereford he heard that they

---

[1] *Weekly Account*, No. 34, Aug. 26.
[2] *Scottish Dove*, No. 96.
[3] *Ibid*, No. 26, for August 28.

CHAP. VI. 1645.

were marching hurriedly northwards. The siege of Hereford, in which the Scots had been engaged for over a month, was thus unsuccessful. Charles, if he had any real energy left in him, would doubtless have pursued the retreating Scots, as he indeed was urged to do. But at this time Bristol, the greatest of the King's strongholds in the West, was in great danger, being invested by Fairfax, who had swept everything before him on his way thither. Oliver Cromwell also was with Fairfax before Bristol. Prince Rupert had, as we have seen, undertaken the defence of that city, and had taken with him for that purpose a great number of Welshmen. Charles now thought the best thing that could be done would be to render some succour to Bristol. Hereford was reached on the 4th September. Charles, however, was not prepared to start at once upon his journey to Bristol. He wanted some assistance from the West: assistance which never came, and which had it come would probably have been too late. The charms of Raglan once more seduced the King. Quitting Hereford he came thither on Sunday, the 7th, and wasted a fortnight of the most valuable time. Instead of acting as a wise man, Charles whiled away the time listlessly, discussing the merits of sects with the Popish Marquis and his insane chaplain, Bailey; and very probably also discussing the secret projects with the Irish Catholics, which were being carried on at this very time by the Lord Herbert, then Earl of Glamorgan, the eldest son of the Marquis. On his arrival at Raglan, Charles dispatched Sir Marmaduke Langdale and Sir Jacob Astley, with horse and foot out of Monmouth,

Raglan, and Chepstow, to parley with the "Peace Army," as the dissatisfied party in Glamorganshire called themselves. Astley was in no mood to parley, or to "treat cap in hand with such as deserve the halter"; and the Peace Army, seeing his resolution to fight, and withal being raw, undisciplined troops, promised to lay down their arms and to supply the King with some money. This promise, however, was never kept; for in a few days they received ammunition by sea, and "these rogues hearing afterwards of the loss of Bristol joined with the Pembrokeshire forces."[1] Langdale marched to Brecon. What he did there I know not.

We have already seen that the County of Monmouth had been backward in aiding the King to relieve Hereford. In this respect its conduct was similar to that of Glamorganshire and Brecknockshire. There was perhaps less excuse for Monmouthshire, seeing it was on the borders of Herefordshire, and a common danger might have induced them to be a little more forward in the King's service. In a great measure this backwardness was due to the influence of some four or five individuals, who, whether they were tired of the war, displeased with the King's officers, jealous of the Marquis of Worcester, or antagonistic to Papistry, did their best to thwart the King's object. Charles was not the man to forget his enemies. From Raglan, attended with his guards, he goes on the 11th of September to Abergavenny,—his "business" being to commit five of the "chief hinderers." Our author[2] is not very precise as to

[1] Symonds' Diary, Harl. MSS., 911.
[2] Symonds.

these men;—what with his neglecting to give their residences, and omitting even the name of one of them, it is difficult to discover who these were. One, however, and the foremost, was Sir Trevor Williams of Llangibby, a gentleman destined hereafter to play an equivocal part, and whose conduct, strange to say, afterwards came to be questioned by Oliver Cromwell. The others designated were: Mr. Morgan, of T———; Mr. Herbert, of Colebrook; Mr. Baker of, I do not know where, and Mr. ———, I do not know who, for Symonds tells us not. This "business" Charles managed, I believe, very badly;—at any rate, he was rated by the old Marquis for his kindness in letting Sir Trevor Williams out on bail.[1] Probably, at the very hour on that Thursday afternoon when Charles was holding court over the "hinderers" at Abergavenny, Prince Rupert was marching out of Bristol, having been compelled to surrender that important garrison into the hands of the redoubtable Fairfax and Cromwell, after a struggle which lasted some eight days. This was one of the greatest blows which the King could have received; and it pained him all the more because he had fully calculated upon its holding out indefinitely;—at any rate, for a

[1] Cox's History of Monmouthshire. Sir Edward Walker gives the following version of the business at Abergavenny:—"And now the people of Monmouth began to show themselves, being animated by Morgan of Mahan [Machen], Herbert of Colebrook, and others, who coloured their disaffection and design of revolt under pretences of dislike of Popery and hatred to the House of Worcester; but the true cause was, they were creatures of the House of Pembroke, and consequently rebels from the beginning. Yet, to prevent their doing any more mischief, their persons were secured, and so was Sir Trevor Williams, but he, at the instance of the Lord Charles Somerset, and others, was presently discharged, though this obligation made him not at all honester, either to the King's cause or that family."—*Historical Discourses*, Ed 1705, p. 141.

long time. Indeed, Rupert himself had written to him to say that they would be able to hold out four months at least.

It was on the following Sunday, the 14th, that this distressing news reached Charles. It was no good any longer to stay at Raglan. His affairs in the West were utterly ruined. He needs must therefore move elsewhere. Whither? First of all, at any rate, to Hereford, which he reached in the evening. It was a gloomy Sunday for the King. Digby was with him, and so were others, but Digby's voice was chiefly listened to now. Digby's hatred of Rupert has been before alluded to; but Charles's great respect for the valour of his nephew had hitherto shielded him from feeling the full effect of this enmity. Now, however, when Rupert was overwhelmed with adversity, Digby had full scope to poison Charles's mind. And he did so. That very evening the King wrote a most severe letter to the unfortunate Prince, sending him a pass that he may go and seek his subsistence "somewhere beyond the seas." That very night he wrote another letter to Oxford, whither the Prince was gone, escorted by Fairfax's musketeers, to order the Council to demand back his commissions, and to displace and arrest Rupert's bosom friend, "honest Will Legge"—Col. William Legge, the Governor of Oxford. That same evening another hand was busily tracing a letter at Bristol for the Parliament. It was Oliver Cromwell's, rendering a glowing account of the taking of "so famous a city." Not a full account; but such as "wherein he that runs may read. That all this is none other than the work of God—he must be a very atheist that doth not acknowledge it." How different things must have looked to these two persons on that calm autumn evening;—to the one gazing exultingly on the fair city he had won, all looked hopeful;—to the other, wearily riding along the dusty roads of Monmouthshire and Herefordshire, everything must have appeared gloomy and desperate. But the contrast was not yet complete.

On the morrow—Monday, the 15th September—Charles intended to leave Hereford. He even set out thence, but owing to Gerard's horse not coming up, he returned, accompanied by Prince Maurice, Gerard, and others. On his return he found a letter from Montrose, giving an account of his "thorough victory in Scotland."

This news was doubtless encouraging to its recipients, and many plans were erected upon the foundation which it laid—one of them being to join Montrose in the North; and on the way to render some help to the faithful City of Chester, which once more was in a state of siege. With this end in view Charles quitted Hereford, and intended to make his first station at Worcester. This, however, proved to be impracticable, for the enemy, under Col. Poyntz, who had been ordered by the Parliament to watch the King's movements, was in the neighbourhood—a very "*leo in itinere*," as Manley in his *Iter Carolinum* states. On hearing that Poyntz had been marching all night in the direction of Worcester, the project was abandoned. Returning in the direction of Hereford, starting as early as six o'clock in the morning, then turning north-westwards, and passing by Weobley, the Royalist army trudged wearily along the rough and uneven country roads, and at midnight broke the eternal stillness of the couple of streets which then constituted Presteign. Weary march from six o'clock in the morning till midnight! The *Iter* states that the King halted at the house of a Mr. Andrews there, but a note in the old parish register of Presteign states that he slept at the Lower Heath, the residence of Mr. Nicholas Taylor.[1] His Majesty doubtless wanted rest, and if he did sleep there two nights it would not have been at all an extravagant halt to make. But no such rest fell to his lot, for early next morning they were again on the march—right over the mountains to Newtown. They had been told it was only ten miles, but to them it looked more like twenty; and so it was. A wild barren district, and "except in the first three miles we saw never a house or a church," says Symonds. Fairly exhausted, they halted for two days, recruiting their strength. Mr. Price's house, of Newtown Hall, seems to have been the head-quarters here. On Sunday, the 21st, again over the mountains, not quite so rugged, and somewhat less barren, passing by Sir Arthur Blayney's house at Gregynog, a trifle out of the way; but he was a firm Royalist—High-Sheriff, too, for last year — until they came to Llanfyllin, having dinner on the way at Plasucha, the house of "Price the Papist." Monday saw them again on the march: more mountains to climb, more valleys to descend. Tired as they were, the beauties of this district on that autumn day must have been lost to these weary sojourners as they marched to Chirk Castle. Here Sir John Watts

[1] Rees's South Wales, p. 892.

was still Governor. Almost surrounded on all sides by the garrisons of the enemy—and an enemy, too, who wanted to recover possession of his own property, this brave soldier held out in his strong fortress. News from Oxford reached them here. Poor Will Legge was in prison, and Rupert shorn of his honours. News from Chester also, that the enemy under Brereton had gained the outworks, and were in a fair way of gaining the city. What made this all the more galling was that the outworks appear to have been gained through the treachery of some officers. It was some consolation, however, to know that both officers—a captain and a lieutenant—were apprehended. The city was in great peril. Lord Byron could hardly manage single-handed to stem the tide of adversity, which had set in. Watts was therefore ordered by the King to send word to Byron to hold out a little longer—twenty-four hours. Early next morning the whole company quitted Chirk for Chester; indeed, a considerable party had marched all night for Holt Castle, on the Dee, where Sir Richard Lloyd—he of Wrexham, the King's Attorney-General for North Wales,—commanded. This detachment was under the command of Sir Marmaduke Langdale. From here it was intended to attack the besiegers before Chester. Charles went by another route, and that evening reached the city, which does not seem to have been invested. The guards were placed in the street to watch Sir Francis Gamul's house, where he slept that night—probably fearing some mishap, and to secure against an alarm.

Poyntz, with his Yorkshire horse, of whose movements the Royal party seem to have been entirely ignorant, was too sharp for them. By a shorter way he had already arrived at Whitchurch, intending to proceed to the assistance of the party before the walls of Chester. From Whitchurch he sent a letter to one Jones (some time a student at Lincoln's Inn), who commanded the horse that besieged the city, informing him that he was coming to their assistance. This letter was intercepted by Sir Richard Lloyd. It had never been anticipated that they would have to meet Poyntz; but now that they knew his intentions, it was deemed advisable to assume the offensive, and to give him an attack. Not a word was sent to inform the King of this resolution; but Langdale rushed on recklessly, came upon Poyntz between the Dee and Beeston Castle, and drove him well back, but did not rout him.

In all probability if the soldiers within the city had acted in concert with Langdale, the victory would have been on their side; but for want of intelligence, Gerard and those who were with the King remained idle in Chester, ignorant of what was going on. Not so the besiegers. They were requested to fall out to the assistance of Pointz. Langdale now found himself between two fires, and the day was lost to him. The Royalists were completely routed and put to flight. In every direction they scattered and sought safety. They were vigorously pursued, and in the chase many brave men fell—more were taken prisoners. Being informed at the eleventh hour of what was going on, Charles placed himself on the walls, and Gerard and those who had accompanied the King to the city sallied out. They did all they could to retrieve the fortunes of the day. But it was too late. And Charles must have been sick at heart as he gazed from the Phœnix Tower on the utter defeat of his only hope, upon Rowton Heath, on the 24th of September. Gerard and Langdale were both wounded in the fight. Many officers were taken prisoners: the very flower of that army. Among these was Colonel Sir Henry Stradling. Nearly a thousand soldiers were made prisoners; while over three hundred officers and soldiers were killed on the King's side alone.[1] Even worse news reached the King the next morning. Montrose, who but the other day appeared as the conqueror of all Scotland, had been a few days before irretrievably defeated at Philip Haugh, by David Leslie, on his way back from Hereford. When the news reached Chester Montrose's power was gone; beaten by his enemies, deserted by his friends, he was now an outcast—a fugitive. So, too, was Charles himself, in one sense. Three years before, to the very day, amid the shouting of thousands, the ringing of bells, the firing of guns, with civic pageant and military pomp, Charles had first entered the quaint old city—full of hope, full of pride. In the interval mighty events had happened: disaster upon disaster had followed him;—separated from his wife and children, bereft of the councils of good men, his was a sad outlook that night in the small rooms of Sir Francis Gamul's house, if he scanned the future by the light of the

---

[1] "The King's forces totally routed on Rowton Heath, &c." (K. P. 227—18.) See vol. ii., Document lxxxi., p. 272. Also Symonds' Diary, Harl. MSS.

past. "Uneasy lies the head that wears a crown": Charles's pillow that night bore a sorrowful head upon it.

Next morning came, and with it new plans. Chester itself was considered to be in danger—at any rate, it was of no use for the King to remain there. At ten o'clock he quitted it; and giving a passing call at Hawarden Castle, governed by Sir Wm. Neale, the King, with about 500 horse (which was all that had got within the city walls after the the battle), reached Denbigh that night. Denbigh Castle had throughout been a firm garrison for the King. Sir Edward Walker, who seems to have attended his Majesty on these sad marches, says it was "one of the strongest and noblest places I ever saw." The Governor was William Salesbury, of whom the same authority truly says, that "under the cover of a countryman he had more experience, courage, and loyalty, than many that made far greater stress." Old "Hosanau Gleision"—blue stockings—was the affectionate name by which he was known to his countrymen: an upright honourable man this General Salesbury. Right glad he must have been to welcome the Sovereign to whose cause both he and his had contributed freely, both in their persons and property;—right sorry, too, at the plight his "sacred Majesty" was in. Here the King remained the greater part of four days—awaiting the rallying of his dispersed army. At length, when they did meet together at a rendezvous some three miles from Denbigh, they were counted and numbered some 2,400 strong. Moreover, they were somewhat elated on that occasion by the intelligence that Prince Maurice, with nearly a thousand horse, was on his way to them—was even then at Chirk Castle. Some illusory hopes of Montrose even appear to have been occasioned by some false news.

But what to do, or whither to go, were questions surrounded with difficulties. "Old Blue Stockings" is said to have been afraid that the King would remain at Denbigh, which would make that district probably the battle-field between the two parties. At one time it was thought the best thing to do would be for the King to retire to Anglesey, and there fix his winter quarters. There were, however, weighty reasons against its adoption. That county was not undivided in its loyalty. The billeting of an army upon the inhabitants would increase the disaffection. Besides, it was felt that it would be indiscreet for the King to isolate himself, when he had many strong garrisons in England such as Oxford, Newark, Hereford, Worcester, and Chester. Worcester appears to have been the favourite by all the King's counsellors except Digby. He dreaded meeting Prince Rupert, whose downfall he had effected, and he knew well enough that the Prince would insist upon seeing the King to justify his conduct, and that this could be easily done at a place commanded by Prince Maurice. Digby's advice prevailed. The idea of Worcester was abandoned and Newark fixed upon. This was not finally settled upon until they had reached Bridgnorth, in Shropshire, on Tuesday the last day of September. Denbigh had been quitted on the previous Sunday, and the route thence lay by Ruthin, which was visited in passing, the castle there being garrisoned by the King. Chirk was reached in the evening, and the appearance there of Prince Maurice with a company of horse, numbering between 600 and 700,—the remnant of his own troop, and of that of Prince Rupert, which had survived the fall of Bristol,— must have been a little reassuring. By stealthy march,—for they were now in the country of the enemy,—leaving Oswestry, where Col. Mytton's head-quarters were, on the left, they reached the rural parishes of Llandisilio and Llandenis. Here the army encamped on the Monday night—the chiefs finding rest in some of the houses around.[1] Early the next day they were again in motion. Shrewsbury had to be passed as cautiously as possible. Three or four times they were alarmed by parties of horse from that garrison: probably foraging parties. No mischief was done beyond some stray shots, resulting in the death of a few only. Late at night, weary and footsore, Bridgnorth was reached, and there it was finally decided to settle for the winter at Newark. When the King reached Newark fresh troubles awaited him. Rupert was there, favoured by Sir Richard Willis, the Governor. He entered into the King's presence unbid, and insisted on having an opportunity to justify his conduct at Bristol. The King consented to calling a Council of War. This Council, after a few

CHAP. VI.

1645.

---

[1] Tradition still speaks of Charles's visit to the parish of Llandisilio, and in a way which certainly is not in keeping with that domestic morality which distinguished the King from his profligate son—the second Charles. The King's visit is said to have resulted in the birth of an illegitimate child, in a house which has ever since been called "The City," for the reason that a Prince of Blood Royal was born there. Near to it is a field still called the "Prince's Field." This offshoot of the House of Stuart was surnamed Prince, and until a late period a family of that name continued to live in the parish. The last of them died within living memory, and it is said that they possessed that Italian style of beauty which distinguished the Stuart family. See *Bye Gones*, Feb. 18, 1874: a local "Notes and Queries," for Wales, published at Oswestry, and conducted by Mr. Askew Roberts in a very able manner.

hours' sitting, declared that the Prince had not been deficient in courage or fidelity. This, however, did not satisfy the Prince, but the King would do no more. Charles was very angry with Willis, who entertained Rupert, and resolved to remove him from the governorship, and acquainted him of it. That very day, when Charles was at dinner, Sir Richard Willis, the two Princes, Charles Gerard, and some of the officers of the garrison, entered abruptly. All took Willis's part. Gerard said it was a plot of Digby's, and called Digby a traitor, asserting his readiness to prove it. The King asked Willis to step aside with him, but he refused, saying he had received a public injury, and expected a public satisfaction. Mad with anger, Charles ordered them to quit his presence and never to come near him again. They did so, and the next day applied to the Parliament for passes to go beyond the sea, which were granted. This standing by his friend and benefactor when adversity was upon him is the only noble trait I have been able to discover in Gerard's character. Digby would not face Rupert. Before coming to Newark he volunteered to go to the assistance of Montrose in the North. He left the King, taking with him nearly all the horse, and was utterly routed at Sherborne. He thereupon fled to Ireland.

Meanwhile, Major-General Laugharne was busy in Pembrokeshire. After his victory on Colby Moor, on the 25th of August, the strength of the enemy being broken, he found his task less arduous than it had hitherto been. The two Royalist Major-Generals—Stradling and Egerton—had retired to Carmarthen. Behind them, in Pembrokeshire, they left only three garrisons, viz., Carew, Manorbier, and Picton Castles. Both Carew and Manorbier were taken about the beginning of September, there being taken in them about 400 prisoners and arms. Mere passing allusions to them are made in the newspapers,[1] and I have not been able to discover who had been left in command in either fortress.[2] But Picton Castle was not so easily acquired. The garrison there was stronger, and it did not succumb until after a siege of nearly three weeks' duration. Some hopes of relief appear to have encouraged those within to hold out to the last. Major-Generals Stradling and Egerton did all they could to levy forces in Carmarthenshire, and expected that the Counties of Brecknock, Radnor, and some part of Cardigan, would join them.[3] But nothing could be done in the altered state of these counties; and no help coming, Picton Castle was yielded to Laugharne on the 20th of September.[4] By this the whole of Pembrokeshire was cleared of Royalists. Laugharne informs the Parliament thereof in a letter from Haverfordwest on the 25th, and requests that some money be granted to him. The House is extremely pleased with the news, and £2,000 is voted to him out of the Excise. More-

---

[1] *Merc. Britannicus*, No. 97; *The Kingdom's Weekly Intelligencer*, No. 117.

[2] That Manorbier Castle was besieged in the Civil War time is clear enough from the newspapers of the time, and is confirmed by certain discoveries made recently by J. R. Cobb, Esq., who has been rendering a portion of the castle habitable. In front of the present ancient gate house, and completely blocking access to it, Mr. Cobb came across a work consisting of an eight-foot bank of earth, cased in front with a five-foot wall, and in the inside with a three-foot wall, having all the appearance of a Vauban fortification for guns. Bolts or slugs of lead, five inches long by five-eighths of an inch in diameter, have been disinterred.

[3] *A Diary or an Exact Journal*, No. 71. (K. P. 227—7.)

[4] *Scottish Dove*, No. 101.

over, "for an encouragement and gratuity to him," the House ordered that the Slebech Estate, in Pembrokeshire, the property of John Barlow, "who is and hath been long in arms against the Parliament," should be granted to him.[1] This is afterwards done, but it takes some time to mature. "Thanksgiving" was to be given in all the churches in London on the next Lord's Day "for the happy success of our forces in clearing the County of Pembroke."

The Carmarthenshire Royalists, amongst whom Stradling and Egerton had sought refuge, were alarmed at the success of Laugharne, and not being very enthusiastic in their loyalty, were anxious to avert bloodshed and ruin. Even while Laugharne was before Carew, on the 5th of September, they sent him a letter signed by fourteen of them, most of them being Commissioners of Array for the County of Carmarthen, asking him to name commissioners to negotiate a treaty with commissioners to be nominated by them. This letter was not answered until the 25th, a few days after the taking of Picton Castle. On condition of their delivering to them the scattered horse of the enemy yet in Carmarthenshire, the Committee for Pembrokeshire were willing to engage for the safety of any four gentlemen to come to Haverfordwest with their attendants. For the 2nd of October a meeting of the county had been convened to consider what should be done, and to empower representatives to treat with Laugharne, but the "country met not." Laugharne now prepared to enter the county. By the 10th of October he had reached

[1] *Perfect Diurnal*, No. 115. (K. P. 19-20.)

St. Clears. His advance precipitated matters. Four of the commissioners, writing to him on that day from Llangyndeyrn, unreservedly declare themselves for the Parliament, promising to aid "with our lives and fortunes in anything that may conduce to the Parliament's service."[1] These entered Carmarthen that very day at the head of some 1,500 club-men. The townsmen accorded them ready welcome, and on the morrow the principal inhabitants and the gentry, headed by the Mayor, declare themselves in the same way, and request to be received into the Parliament's protection. Major-General Stradling and Colonel Lovelace, the Governor, were dismissed, and that night they departed the town with their soldiers. Laugharne the same day, marching from St. Clears, appeared before the town with a force of 600 horse and 2,000 foot. By 11 o'clock that night everything was concluded, and the next morning the conquerors made their entry. Laugharne "restrained plunder and used the country with all lenity," which attached to him the people in great numbers.[2] On the 2nd of November Public Thanksgiving was given for the capture of Carmarthen. The few horse under Lovelace and Stradling went to Newcastle-Emlyn, which remained in the hands of the Royalists, and strengthened the garrison there. Upon Col. James Lewes, of Coedmore, devolved the task of reducing this place, which, with Aberystwith, were the only garrisons for the King

[1] These were Edward Vaughan of Golden Grove; Henry Middleton of Middleton Hall; John Vaughan of Plasgwyn; and John Vaughan of Llanelly (?).

[2] "Major-General Laugharne's Letter, &c. Printed for Edward Husbands, October 28th, 1645." (K. P. 231—15.) See vol. ii., Document lxxxii., p. 273.

CHAP. VI.
1645.

that were left in the three counties.[1] Both sustained protracted sieges.

Laugharne now pushed forward into Glamorganshire. There the aspect of affairs was entirely changed. The people were unanimously for the Parliament. Cardiff had been wrested from the Royalists by Colonel Herbert, of Colebrook, and Swansea for once breathed freely. Having but little to do here the active Major-General pushed his way into Breconshire, a county which had hitherto escaped wonderfully from the ravages of the war. The great majority of the gentry here, like elsewhere in in Wales, were favourable to the King. Herbert Price, of the Priory, Member for the Borough, took up arms zealously for the King, and was disabled from sitting in Parliament. John Jeffreys of Abercynrig, Lewis Lloyd of Wernos, Edward Games, of Buckland, and others, were also conspicuous Royalists. When ill-luck attended the fortunes of their Sovereign, the enthusiasm of many of them waned, and they were not loth, when the opportunity presented itself, to propitiate the party which fortune favoured. Laugharne reached Brecon, and was well received. The castle, it appears, held out under Col. Turbervil Morgan, the deputy-governor there; but not long, and in a very short time, the entire county was reduced.[2] On the 17th of November the county was assessed in £120 weekly. Several Brecknockshire names were added to the Committee of Gloucester; and on the 23rd, thirty-four of the leading men of the county attached their names to a declaration offering, "in conscience of their

[1] *Perfect Passages*, No. 61.
[2] *Perfect Passages*, No. 58.

loyalty and not by terror or constraint," to submit themselves, their lives and fortunes, to the service of the Parliament, "being fully satisfied that the Parliament then sitting at Westminster was the lawful Parliament of England, and the Supreme Court of Judicature." The very fact of their stating that they made the declaration voluntarily, and not by constraint, in my opinion throws a doubt upon their sincerity, and the after-conduct of some of them confirms that doubt. Herbert Price and John Jeffreys were away at the time. I do not think either of them would have signed the declaration if they had been in the county. Laugharne sent this declaration, accompanied with other papers, to the Parliament. They are read there with satisfaction on the 5th of December, and the Speaker is ordered to write a letter to the Major-General for him to acquaint the signatories of the good acceptance by the House of their declaration.[1] Laugharne thereupon returns to Haverfordwest. Newcastle-Emlyn and Aberystwith still held out. "The extreme hardness of the frosty weather" at Haverfordwest detains Laugharne there. Col. Lewes, however, manages to obtain possession of Newcastle about the middle of December,[2] and does what he can to secure that part of the county.[3]

In Monmouthshire also the arms of the Parliament were equally victorious. Chepstow had been for a long time in the hands of the Royalists, and of the castle there one Col. Fitzmorris was the Governor. Col. Morgan, the Governor of Gloucester,

---

[1] *Commons' Journals*, iv., 365.
[2] *Perfect Passages*, No. 61.
[3] *Perfect Occurrences*, No. 8, 1645–6.

himself a Monmouthshire man, now that his hands were tolerably free in the West, crossed the Severn with some 300 horse and about 400 foot, of whom a portion had been contributed by Colonel Fleetwood, the Governor of Bristol; and proceeded towards Chepstow. The town made no resistance; but from the castle, in reply to the summons which was sent in, a refusal to yield was the answer. Batteries were made, and with mortar-pieces a breach in the wall was effected; and on Saturday, the 11th of October, the castle was yielded, and the men therein made prisoners, to the number of about sixty, among them being the Governor, three lieutenant-colonels and majors, and six captains. Thirty horses, seventeen pieces of ordnance, three hundred arms, and ten barrels of gunpowder, with other provisions of war, also changed hands.[1]

Charles was deservedly blamed by the aged Marquis of Worcester for letting Sir Trevor Williams out on bail; and what that nobleman predicted was soon fulfilled. Sir Trevor now became one of the most active partisans for the Parliament in the County of Monmouth. He headed the club-men there, and it was his influence that decided their course of action. With that violent zeal which invariably characterizes a renegade he was eager for a conflict. And at the head of some 1,500 men raised out of the Counties of Glamorgan and Monmouth, he decided suddenly to besiege Monmouth. In this he was joined by Col. Morgan, the Governor of Gloucester. The latter had a strength of about

[1] *Perfect Diurnal*, No. 116, and *Perfect Occurrences* for the 43 d week (K. P. 20—3 and 5.)

1,500 horse and foot, and Sir Trevor Williams commanded a body of 1,500 foot and 200 horse. They soon acquired the town, but the castle held out for three days—Henry Lunsford acting as Governor in the absence of his brother Sir Thomas Lunsford. Seeing preparations made for blowing up the fortress, the Governor demanded a parley, and the castle was thereupon surrendered, the officers being allowed to march away with their horses and arms. All the arms therein, comprising seven guns, four sling pieces, 300 muskets, 600 pikes, with the ammunition and provisions, became the property of the victors. This was on the 24th of October. The following Saturday Col. Morgan returned to Gloucester, leaving the Castle in the custody of Capt. Forster with only 100 men, and the town in the charge of Sir Trevor Williams. The countrymen, which constituted Sir Trevor's forces, did not intend to follow the profession of arms, and they were influenced by some Royalists in the town to return home, which they did that same night, "every man to his own home, leaving the town destitute of strength." Seeing the danger he was in, Williams asked Forster to help him in keeping the town. Failing in that, he sent to the Governor of Gloucester; and to Col. Kyrle, who was in the Forest of Dean. These at once sent the necessary aid, and thereby secured the town. Those who were suspected to be against the Parliament were on the following Monday ordered to depart the town upon pain of death, whereupon divers families were put out.[1]

[1]. King's Pamphlets, 231—14 and 232—19. See also vol. ii., Document lxxxiii. A. and B.

If we look into North Wales we find there that since the King's defeat on Rowton Heath, and his wanderings there had ended in his march for Newark, the power and spirit of the Royalists had been in a great measure broken. About the beginning of September Sir Thomas Myddelton was recalled by the House of Commons to occupy the seat from which he had been absent so long, and his command was transferred to his brother Sir William Myddelton, who thereupon became extremely busy in suppressing the Royalists in these parts. Marching from Welshpool on the 3rd September he came to Bala. Lord Byron and Sir Edmund Verney had collected there a force of some 1,500 men, and had established garrisons in the neighbourhood: one at Caergai, and another at Llandrysilio.[1] On Sir William's arrival before Bala the enemy ran away to Denbigh, leaving Caergai and Llandrysilio but meanly garrisoned. Against these the Parliamentarians directed their steps. The former was evacuated on their approach. They demolished it to the ground. They also found the latter deserted, and they pulled down the steeple of the church, which had been the stronghold of the enemy, so far that it could not again be used as a garrison. They pursued them to Denbigh, and scattered most of them, by which means Sir William hoped that "that country was quite settled."[2] Some of the Merionethshire people were however not so easily to be put down. Mr. Price, of Rhiwlas, was an unbending Royalist. He spent a lot of money for clothing for the soldiers, which,

---

[1] I have not been able to discover this place. Perhaps it was Llandrillo.
[2] His letter from Red Castle, 4th September. *City Scout*, No. 8.

until he found men ready to wear them, he placed with his tenants to be privately kept. The man entrusted to carry the clothes discovered it to the Parliamentarians, which caused Capt. Evan Vaughan to march one night from Abermachnant to Penllyn, where he discovered the clothes and much money. Captain John Nanney endeavoured to raise some soldiers at Dolgelly towards the close of the year. Captain Edward Vaughan, "a well-affected gentleman in Merionethshire," having intelligence of it, stealthily proceeded to Dolgelly, which he reached by three in the morning of the 31st of December. There he surprised Nanney and his lieutenant, one David Lloyd, and took prisoners some soldiers whom they had got together, with some thirty or forty horse. Only one man was killed in this fray.[1]

In the meantime Brereton was gradually drawing tighter the besieging lines around Chester. While the King was yet in North Wales Lord Byron thought it would be able to hold out six weeks. The King was very anxious to raise the siege, but with news of the disaster which had befallen Montrose in the North his power to do so was gone, and he quitted Wales without being able to offer any aid. Some hope of help from Ireland, where the Earl of Glamorgan had made peace with the Catholics, inspirited the besieged to bear privations and to hold out a little longer. Some Irish forces landed in Anglesey, and were collected together at Denbigh, under the command of Sir William Vaughan, whilom the Governor of

[1] Mostyn, or Penbedw MSS., in *Cambrian Quarterly Magazine*, vol. i.; also *Perfect Diurnal*, No. 131.

Shrawardine Castle, Salop. These intended to act in concert with forces from England, under the command of Sir Jacob Astley, and to bear upon the besiegers from front and rear. Astley's forces were, however, as yet in embryo, and he had not even reached Ludlow; and Brereton, having intelligence of the gathering at Denbigh, and having sufficient strength for the purpose, dispatched Colonel Michael Jones and Adjutant Lothian, with a force of 1,400 horse and 1,000 foot, "the cream of all those parts of the kingdom," to Denbigh. The Royalists were reported to be stronger in point of numbers, but were actually weaker, being 1,700 horse and about 400 foot. On Thursday, the 30th of October, the Parliament forces reached Mold; the next day Ruthin, where Colonel Mytton, who was in possession of the town, though not of the castle, joined them. On Saturday the hostile forces met in conflict. The fighting was sustained for a long time. The day for a time was doubtful, but ultimately the Royalists were defeated. Some one hundred of them were slain, and about four hundred taken prisoners, including some officers and men of quality. The loss on the Parliament side was slight. The vanquished retreated to Conway, and were pursued for about eight miles.[1] This was a terrible blow to the besieged Chester. Help was now almost beyond expectation, and the position of the city was becoming very serious. The six weeks were passed. The city was encircled, no supplies of food could be got, and what

---

[1] "A true relation of a great victory obtained by the Parliament Forces, &c., near Denbigh." (K. P. 232—14.) See vol. ii., Document lxxxiv., p. 282.

was in the city was nearly all consumed. The outskirts had been burnt down, and the inhabitants of those unfortunate places had crowded into the city, adding to the misery and want which had become almost universal. Already some breaches had been made in the walls, and beds had been requisitioned to fill in the gaps.¹ The outlying garrisons of the Royalists were one by one reduced. Beeston Castle was yielded on the 5th of November, and the few men who were in the garrison were permitted to march to Denbigh. Hawarden Castle also fell into the hands of the Parliamentarians. Once more a miserable Christmas was experienced at Chester—far more miserable, far more wretched, than any known there before. Of food and fuel there was scarcely any left. Leather and animals were freely consumed; and yet the place held out with a deadly desperation.

Another great blow which the Royalists sustained towards the close of this year was the loss of Hereford, which was surprised by Col. Birch and Col. Morgan on the 18th of December. To that city many of the most powerful Royalists of the district and several men of note had gone, deeming it safe in their hands. That city, from the beginning of the war, had been a stronghold of the Royalists. It is true, just on the eve of the battle of Edghill, Lord St. John obtained possession of it for the Parliament without any blood being shed or any effort at resistance; but the Parliamentarians soon evacuated it, and it was left entirely in the hands of the Royalists, under the command of Sir William Coningsby. When Waller made his victorious

¹ Lord Byron's Orders, 23rd October, in Harl. MSS., 2135, fol. 82.

CHAP. VI.
1645.

march to the West and destroyed the power of the House of Worcester before Gloucester, he presented himself before Hereford, and it was yielded to him upon conditions.[1] Waller, however, as we have already shown, soon quitted it, and it fell once more back into the hands of the Cavaliers. Col. Mynne was then appointed Governor of the city. Col. Mynne was slain at Red Marley by General Massey's men, and Prince Rupert then appointed Col. Barnabas Scudamore the Governor.[2] Under Scudamore the neighbourhood of the city and the county was drained of men and money, to such an extent as to create intense dissatisfaction; and the countrymen appeared in a hostile attitude before its walls, demanding a redress of their grievance. Rupert was then in Chester, and he had to hasten back to quell the countrymen, which he did. Early in the autumn of this year, the Scots, under the Earl of Leven, laid siege to the city, and continued for some time before the walls, and were on the eve of reducing it when ill-tidings from the North called them away, and Charles entered the city as its saviour.[3] Towards the end of this year the question of reducing Hereford was discussed by the Committee of both Kingdoms, and on the 5th of December, Col. Birch, a Lancashire man, who had been "formerly a carrier, now a colonel,"[4] and who had distinguished himself at the defence of Bristol, before it was surrendered by Fiennes to Rupert, was authorised to draw 1,000 foot and his horse, and by the aid of the Worcester-

[1] *Ante*, p. 153.
[2] Symonds' Diary, Harl MSS., 911.
[3] Rushworth's Historical Collections.
[4] Walker's History of Independency.

shire force, and that under the command of Col. Morgan, the Governor of Gloucester, to use all means to take the city. Col. Birch was then at Bristol. He quitted Bristol and Bath on the 6th, and came to Gloucester to confer with Col. Morgan and Sir John Brydges, of Wilton Castle, Hereford. These gave him very little encouragement at first, but allowed his men to quarter at Gloucester, whilst he went to see whether he could not by some means accomplish his object. Coming to Newington, he there obtained much important information from two officers of the King's who had thrown down their command, resenting some ill-treatment they had received, and were eager to be revenged. The plan they proposed was explained to Col. Morgan, who adopted it at once, and who, though "sick of an ague," marched out with him. The upshot was that the city was surprised, and a host of eminent Cavaliers and Royalists were taken prisoners. Among these were Sir Thomas Lunsford, once Lieutenant of the Tower; Sir Marmaduke Lloyd, Chief Justice of the Great Sessions for Radnor, Brecon, and Glamorgan; and his son, Sir Francis Lloyd, Comptroller of the King's Household; Sir John Stepney, late M.P. for Haverfordwest; Sir Richard Basset of Beaupre; Sir Philip Jones of Llanarth; Sir Edward Morgan of Pencoed, Mon.; Lieut.-Colonel Herbert Price of Brecknock; Lieut.-Colonel Jeffreys of Abercynrig, Brecon; and most prominent of all Judge Jenkins. This happened on the 18th of December. By the 24th, the castle was also taken, and the city settled in order and quietness. The Governor, Col. Barnabas Scudamore, with some fifty others, took advantage of the ice on the Wye, and escaped.

CHAP. VI.
1645.

CHAPTER VII.

1646.

State of affairs at commencement of year—Siege and surrender of Chester—Siege of Aberystwith—Revolt of Carne, the High Sheriff of Glamorganshire—His defeat by Major-General Laugharne—Laugharne's rewards—Some Pembrokeshire difficulties—Col. Mytton takes Ruthin Castle, and lays siege to the other garrisons in North Wales—Surrender of Aberystwith Castle—Town and Castle of Carnarvon yields to Col. Mytton—Anglesey reduced, and Beaumaris surrendered—The King quits Oxford and gives himself up to the Scotch—Orders all garrisons to yield as soon as possible—Siege of Raglan Castle—Sir Thomas Fairfax appears before it and takes it—The Archbishop of York turns round to the Parliament and assists at the storming of the town of Conway—Col. Salesbury yields Denbigh Castle—And Sir John Owen delivers up Conway Castle to Major-General Mytton—Retrospect of Imperial and other affairs—Harlech Castle, the last to hold out, is surrendered in March, 1647.

THE year 1646 opened with anything but a bright prospect for the Royalists. Since his return to Oxford in November the King had been very anxious to come to some terms with the Parliament. But the Parliament was not so anxious to come to terms with the King. It no longer consisted of those who had remained at Westminster when the King sought the arbitration of the sword, and when many seats were left empty by men who threw in their lot with their Sovereign. In the autumn of 1645 these seats were formally declared empty, and writs were issued for fresh elections. Most of the men who were sent up to fill the vacancies were men who had distinguished themselves as supporters of the cause of Parliament, and who looked with anything but favour upon any proposals from the King. Among these may be named Fairfax, Ireton, Fleetwood, Ludlow, and Hutchinson. The King offered to come himself to Westminster to treat in person with the Parliament. The Scots did all they could to prevail upon the Parliament to accede to this; but the Independents were now too strong there, and they could afford even to refuse the request of their allies. Moreover the King was, as it were, in their hands. They could expose his duplicity and his intrigues in such a way as would discredit him in the eyes of all the people, for they had proofs of the treaty of alliance which the King, through the Earl of Glamorgan, had made with the Irish rebels. Under this treaty 10,000 of the Irish were to land soon at Chester, under the Earl of Glamorgan. Charles for this aid had promised to allow the Catholics full liberty of their worship, the repeal of the penal laws against them, and that they should continue in possession of the churches and lands which they by force had occupied. A copy of the treaty and many letters relating to it had been found in the carriage of the Archbishop of Tuam, one of the rebel leaders who was slain under the walls of Sligo. They were sent to the Committee of the two Kingdoms, late in October; but they were not disclosed until it became necessary, as it did now, to throw discredit upon the King. Early in January of this year they were laid before Parliament, and were at once published. And now Charles, utterly disconcerted, was guilty of conduct the most mean and cowardly. He denied that he gave any power to the Earl to treat with the rebels, and disowned him publicly; but at the

CHAP. VII.
1646.

same time privately gave him every encouragement, and released him from prison, into which the more scrupulous Ormond had thrust him when the storm broke and the intrigue was exposed. No one, however, believed Charles now. He had deceived the people too long already; and once more the question of peace was set aside.

The Royalists had only two bodies of soldiers in the field, one in Cornwall, under Lord Hopton, and the other in the Marches of Wales, under Sir Jacob Astley, intended for the relief of Chester.

That city, since the departure of the King after his defeat on Rowton Heath in September, had been under a state of siege. Early in October it was encircled by Brereton; the suburbs were burnt and pulled down, so as to afford no shelter to the enemy, and the effects of being cut off from communication with the outside world soon began to be felt within the walls. Lord Byron wrote to the King, when the latter was at Denbigh, early in October, that he would be able to hold out about six weeks. Charles then hoped to be able to send some assistance to Lord Byron, but he had to quit Wales without more than enough to guard himself. Some aid was expected from Ireland. The Marquis of Ormond had been labouring hard to help in this matter; but it was not so easy to do now as it was when the disbanded English army had to be sent away from Ireland. When Lord Digby quitted the King, before his arrival at Newark, he went to Ireland, and there tried to raise some forces to relieve Chester. He was, however, by no means successful. Colonel Roger Mostyn also had gone over there to try his hand at recruiting. But they expected more from Ireland than was really forthcoming. In fact, the old Archbishop of York, conning over matters at Conway, came to the conclusion that "there is no relying upon these Irish forces for this service." The Royalists in North Wales exercised whatever influence or power remained to them to collect men to aid in the relief of Chester. Colonel Gilbert Byron was at the head of some 500 or 600 men in Carnarvonshire. Colonel Mostyn landed from Ireland with an additional "piece of a regiment," about 160 men, and would be able to raise in his own county some 200 more. Sir William Vaughan, whose defeat near Denbigh I have already alluded to, had by this time recovered from the effects of that disaster, and by the beginning of the year was at the head of some 1,500 horse and foot at High Ercal, in Shropshire, where he expected to be joined by Lord Astley, with the main supply from Oxford and Worcester. But the condition of the besieged was daily getting worse, and while these ill-concerted measures for relief were being digested, Brereton was drawing closer his lines round the ill-fated city, and famine and want was beginning to help him within. The sufferings of the city were intense. Fuel was scarce, and food also. The misery had been much increased by the overcrowding of the place with the unfortunate people who had to quit the suburbs and seek safety within the walls. By the 10th of January Lord Byron began to despair. Brereton had been for some time in communication with him and with Charles Walley, the Mayor; but Lord Byron was loth to give up while there was the slightest hope of relief. Famine was his greatest enemy. All the meat had been consumed, even to the cats and dogs, and of corn there was very little left. On the 14th of January Byron issued his warrant to certain officers and civilians[1] to inquire how much corn remained unconsumed in the city. That very day search was made in the different wards, and the returns, which are yet preserved, if really true, show a state of destitution quite fearful to contemplate. The returns give the names of the various householders, with the number of their families, and of the soldiers billeted upon them, and of the quantity of corn, meal, beans, or bread they had. From a cursory glance Eastgate and St. Bridget's wards were the worst off. In the former there were about one hundred and sixty families, of whom over a hundred had "no corn." These families comprised about nine hundred persons, besides about one hundred and fifty soldiers. In the Bishop's kitchen, though there were twenty-four in the family, there was no corn. Other houses with two and three in the family were reduced to "one great loaf."[2] Lord Astley and Sir William Vaughan at length united their forces, and "lay hovering about Bridgnorth," and their intention was to further strengthen themselves by joining with the Welsh forces under Lord St. Paul and Colonel Gilbert Byron, and those Irish who had come over under Colonel Mostyn, and those

[1] These were Lieut.-Col. Henry Leigh, Lieut.-Col. John Robinson, Lieut.-Col. Peter Griffith, Sergeant-Major Thropp; Hugh Wilbraham, Peter Leicester, Esquires; Capt. Edmund Persall, Edward Aldcock, and Richard Malory; Mr. Ald. Holmes, sen., Mr. Hunford Phillips, Mr. Ald. Holm, jun., Mr. Richard Byrd, and Mr. Edward Hulton.

[2] In the Harl. MSS., 2135, f. 109, &c., these returns are all preserved, and are not destitute of considerable interest. They form a perfect census of the population of the city.

who had been sent over by Lord Digby, and who had just landed at Beaumaris. Brereton, however, had timely warning of the scheme. So he sent Col. Mytton to intercept the progress of Lord St. Paul. Mytton reached Ruthin on Saturday, the 24th of January. He got possession of the town, and the enemy beat a hasty retreat to Denbigh and to Conway. By this means the last hopes of Lord Byron were dashed to pieces. Astley and Vaughan, for some reason or other, dared not venture upon the relief, and withdrew themselves towards Worcester. The besieged, now hopeless of relief, were anxious to give in. How they held out so long with such a scarcity of provisions is a marvel. On the 30th of January Lord Byron sent out his commissioners to treat with Brereton.[1] The first day nothing was concluded upon. They were very anxious to have until the 2nd of February to decide, but Brereton pressed them to an earlier settlement, whereupon it was decided to yield upon honourable conditions, so as to prevent the plunder of the city, which could not have been prevented if it had been taken by storm. The articles for the surrender bear date the 1st of February, and were signed by the twelve commissioners appointed to treat on either side, and confirmed by Lord Byron. The conditions were liberal to a degree. Lord Byron and the officers, and all nobles, gentlemen, and soldiers, were allowed to march to Conway, and to be protected on their way thither for five

CHAP. VII.
1646.

[1] Each side had twelve Commissioners. For Lord Byron the chief were Sir Edmund Verney, Lieut.-Col. Robinson, Lieut.-Col. Peter Griffith, Lieut.-Col. Henry Leigh, and Aldermen Blease and Ince. For Brereton, Colonels John Boothe, John Bowyer, Duckenfield, Michael Jones, John Carter, and Adjutant Lothian, were the most prominent.

days. The Welsh officers and soldiers were at liberty to return to their homes. The officers were allowed, according to their degree, to take away each a sum of money—the chief of them to be allowed to take their servants and horses. The women to have their apparel, the town to be preserved from plunder, and the citizens to be protected in their persons and goods, and freedom of trade to be permitted; and the city, with the fort, and all the arms and ammunition, to be delivered to Sir William Brereton by Tuesday, the 3rd of February. Here we shall part with Sir William Brereton. So long as we have known him he has shown himself a very able officer, and worthy of the success which attended all his actions. His next actions are in England, for as soon as he settled Chester he set out in pursuit of Sir William Vaughan and Sir Jacob Astley, and at Stow in the Wolds, in Gloucestershire, on the 22nd of March, broke up their army, took Lord Astley prisoner, and destroyed the only force which remained to the King, for Sir Ralph Hopton had surrendered himself to Fairfax in Cornwall eight days before. Brereton after that, crowned with glory, returned to Parliament, not however to rest on his laurels, for he raised higher and higher, and when Cromwell attained power his services to the State were not forgotten.

South Wales by this time was nearly all reduced to the obedience of the Parliament. Cardiff and Swansea had given in, and the castles there were respectively governed by Col. Prichard of Llancayach, and Col. Philip Jones of Swansea. The County of Brecon had yielded humble submission to the Parliament. Carmarthen and Pembroke were cleared of Royalists, and in Cardiganshire the garrison at Aberystwith Castle alone held out, under Col. Richard Whitley. A siege was laid to it early in November. Major-General Laugharne had too much to do in superintending the general settlement of affairs in South Wales to attend to the siege personally. Col. Rice Powell was entrusted with the command. In this he was helped by Col. John Jones of Nanteos, and it is said that even Mr. John Vaughan of Trawscoed, who had hitherto been a firm, though not very active Royalist, deemed it proper to try and make peace with the Parliament at the price of assisting in the taking of Aberystwith Castle.[1] Weeks and weeks passed and the capture of the castle appeared as distant as ever. In the meantime the besiegers pillaged the adjacent country in every direction. From an old chronicler I extract the following:—

"About the 8th of December Col. Jones of Nanteos, and about twenty soldiers, came by night to Peniarth, and there took Lewis Owen of Peniarth and Mr. Francis Herbert of Dolguog (who did there sojourn for fear of the Parliamenteers) in their beds, and carried them to Cardiganshire."

"Jan. 2nd. Cardiganshire men came over to Merionethshire, as far as Barmouth, and on Saturday night, being the 3rd, plundered that village, and so went away in their boats."[2]

These depredatory raids occasioned some remonstrances from the inhabitants to Major-General

[1] *Cambrian Register*, vol. i., p. 164.
[2] *Cambrian Quarterly Magazine*, i., Mostyn MSS.

Laugharne, whose answer was couched in the following words:—

"These are to certify, whom it may concern, that what inroads were by my soldiers made in Montgomery and Merioneddshires were without orders and command from me, and was done in my absence. Therefore, I desire a free and usual intercourse and correspondence to be carried on between the counties of my association and the said Counties of Montgomery and Merionedd: promising that if hereafter any of my men commit the like offences they shall be exactly punished according to the law of war.

"ROWLAND LAUGHARNE.
"Dated 4th February, 1645-6."

While Laugharne was before Aberystwith, fresh troubles were gathering in Glamorganshire. The House of Raglan, though very much crippled by the loss of Monmouth and Chepstow, and by the turning round of Sir Trevor Williams at the head of the club-men, was not yet put down. It is true the Earl of Glamorgan was absent in Ireland, but the old Marquis had powerful allies in Sir Charles Kemeys and Sir Philip Jones of Llanarth. The last-named had lost his house, and the Parliamentarians intended to place a garrison in it; but owing to frequent alarms they had to defer this till a more fitting opportunity arrived. The Governor of Gloucester was, however, on the alert; and Sir Trevor Williams was very active. To distract the latter the Royalists, by some means or other, had induced the High-Sheriff of Glamorganshire, Mr. Edward Carne of Ewenny to revolt from his obedience to the Parliament. Carne, as we have seen, had been in the preceding autumn among the most active in resisting the demands of the King. He also had been the chief man among those of the gentry who invited Major-General Laugharne to enter Glamorganshire, and had materially assisted in reducing that county. For his conduct on these occasions, probably, he was in the November following made high-sheriff. It is difficult to account for his turning round so soon. Whether he was disappointed or not at having only the shrievalty bestowed upon him, while Mr. Bushey Mansel was appointed Commander-in-Chief of Glamorganshire, and Colonel Prichard was made Governor of Cardiff, and Colonel Philip Jones made Governor of Swansea, I have no means of ascertaining. Some such disappointment alone can account for such instability. Under colour of putting the county in a posture of defence, he and some other gentlemen called a general muster, and by means of a declaration which they published, so fooled the people that they were resolved to venture their ruin in the prosecution thereof. Others he forced to serve under him; and having plundered the county to some extent, they appeared before Cardiff, and summoned Colonel Prichard to surrender to them the town and castle. Prichard, who had with him but a small body of men, withdrew to the castle, which he stored with such provisions and ammunition as he could find, determined to hold it out to the last. The Governor, also, sent for aid to England, and to Major-General Laugharne. Aid was sent from England by sea, and Laugharne, once more leaving the siege of Aberystwith to the care of Colonel Rice Powell, marched directly to the relief of Cardiff with about 250 of his own horse and foot, and some others who had volunteered to aid him. In the meantime the enemy had summoned the castle, but had only received a flat denial. The Raglan forces, under Sir Charles Kemeys, by this time had joined the Glamorganshire forces, commanded by Carne. Laugharne found a party of them upon a heath within a mile of the town, prepared for fight. The Royalists were routed, and pursued for some six miles in the direction of Raglan. Their foot forces were nearly all either killed or taken. Laugharne thereby relieved the castle, and was admitted into it. His men, eager for further victories, sallied out too soon, and had the worst of it. His own brother, who was a lieutenant-colonel, was taken prisoner, and a few others; the rest made their way back to the castle. Night parted the combatants, and the fighting was renewed in the morning, and "with such cheerfulness" on the part of the Parliament soldiers that they totally routed their enemies, chasing them for about seven miles. In both actions the Royalists lost 250 men, and 800 more were made prisoners, comprising several officers. Another account calls it "a very bloody fight," and asserts that 2,000 were either killed or taken. "Carne himself," says this authority, "stayed not to keep them together, but, like a vagabond, ran up and down, bemoaning himself, and glad he was that he had a nimble horse, not to charge, but to fly with." Thus ended this revolt in Glamorganshire. The power of the House of Raglan was further weakened. Sir Charles

Kemeys had but few left of the body he set out with, and even these he was in great danger of losing, for Colonel Morgan of Gloucester and Sir Trevor Williams intended to cut off his retreat.[1]

Laugharne at once communicated his success to the Parliament. His letter of the 21st of February, from Cardiff, was read at Westminster on the 28th. His services were approved of, and a letter of thanks ordered to be sent to him. He was, moreover, appointed Commander-in-Chief of the forces in Glamorganshire, as well as of the three western counties. A thousand pounds were ordered to be paid over to Mr. Arthur Owen, out the Excise, to provide horse and men for him, and an ordinance was passed for making a grant to Laugharne in fee of the beautiful estate of Slebech, which John Barlow had forfeited through his opposition to the Parliament. This matter had been once before discussed in the House. Now it was carried into effect, and the grant was issued under the Great Seal on the 4th day of March following. "The great mercy" of his success "over the revolted forces of the enemy at Cardiff," was also to be the subject of Thanksgiving.[2] On the 3rd of March, Laugharne, Sir. Trevor Williams, and the Governor of Gloucester, were requested to take speedy means for the settlement of the counties of South Wales; and some fresh names were added

---

[1] See "A great overthrow given to the King's forces in Wales, &c." (K. P. 249—8); Vol. ii., Document lxxxix., p. 298, and Laugharne's Letter, in a pamphlet entitled "Two letters sent to the Honourable W. Lenthall, Esq., &c." (K. P. 249—17.)

[2] Commons' Journals, iv., 457—8. The grant of Slebech is given in full in the appendix to Fenton's Pembrokeshire.

to the Committee of Gloucester and the eastern counties of South Wales.

A few days before, some troubles in Pembrokeshire had been under discussion in the House of Commons. But the difficulties are so vaguely alluded to in the minutes as to be incapable to me of solution. Poyer is in custody. Sir Richard Philipps and others arrested for debt incurred in the service of the State. Votes of money to secure their discharge and for clothing the army. A portion of the debt of one David Parry to Judge Jenkins, ordered to be paid to Sir Richard Philipps, and the other part to Arthur Owen. Difficulties evidently arising from irregularity of payments, and indiscretion of some friends of the Parliament in that county in pledging their personal security;—troubles now attempted to be removed and justice done.[1]

With the loss of Chester the King's power in North Wales was virtually annihilated. Several towns, it is true, remained in the hands of his adherents, and several old castles continued to be garrisoned for him. Sir William Brereton, who had been assiduous in the service of the Parliament in Cheshire, and had from the commencement of the war rendered them most material assistance, now quitted that county; and leaving North Wales to be reduced by Mytton, who had recently been promoted to the position of Major-General, went in pursuit of one of the two main bodies of the Royalists, which still kept up and which was under the command of Lord Astley and Sir William Vaughan. This he completely routed at Stow in the Wolds, in Gloucestershire, on the

[1] Commons' Journals, iv., 444.

22nd of March, after which he went to London to attend to his duties as a Member of Parliament.

Major-General Mytton had still ample work before him. There was a garrison at Ruthin Castle. The town we have already seen him in possession of. There was a small garrison at Holt Castle, under the command of Sir Richard Lloyd. Flint Castle was in the hands of the Royalists. A strong garrison, under Colonel William Salesbury, maintained Denbigh Castle. To Carnarvon Castle Lord Byron had gone on the fall of Chester. The Town and Castle of Conway, now under the command of Sir John Owen, held out for the King. Lord Bulkeley maintained a strong force at Beaumaris, and the Island of Anglesey as yet was purely Royalist, and Harlech Castle was safe in the keeping of Colonel William Owen of Brogyntyn, the brother of Sir John Owen. The reduction of these was a work of time. But Mytton was not in the least degree dismayed at the prospect. His own tact and military skill had hitherto won for him many a hard-fought battle. His men were veterans in the field, and inured to the hardships incidental to active service; while aiding him were able and trustworthy officers, among these being his son-in-law, Col. Roger Pope; and Col. John Jones, who afterwards was one of those who sat as the King's Judges, and who signed the warrant for the King's execution. Lieutenant-Colonels Carter and Twistleton, Capt. Richard Price, and Capt. Simkies, also were experienced officers.

Ruthin Castle was the first to fall in: this fact, however, reflects no discredit on the Royalists who had charge of that fortress. Mytton confessed that

CHAP. VII.
1646.

it had cost him more time and ammunition than he expected when he first laid siege to it. And it was dearly won. The besieged struggled stoutly for victory. "There hath never been a day since," says the Major-General, "but they sallied out constantly twice or thrice a day." Many lives were thus sacrificed, and much powder and match consumed. At length, however, the Parliament soldiers erected batteries for cannons to play upon it, and dug mines all round the fortress. When these mines were ready to be sprung, Mr. John Reynolds, the Deputy-Governor of the castle, who was in command, sought a parley and agreed to yield up the fortress on condition of his own liberty and the liberty of the soldiers, other than the Irish, who were barred by ordinance of Parliament. On the 8th day of April the articles for the surrender were duly signed by Mr. Robert Fogge, Mytton's chaplain, and Capt. Edward Thelwall, on behalf of the Major-General, of the one part, and the Deputy-Governor of the other part. Parliament was informed of this victory by Mytton, who dispatched Lieut.-Colonel Thomas Mason with the intelligence. Mason for his trouble was voted twenty pounds; and, moreover, on the recommendation of Mytton, who spoke of him as a "faithful, active, and godly gentleman, the most knowing man in his profession that we have in these parts, having been a soldier above twenty years, and lost his command in Ireland because he refused to bear arms against the Parliament," he was appointed governor of that castle, to hold it on behalf of the Parliament.[1]

[1] "A letter to the Speaker of the House of Commons, concerning the surrender of Ruthin Castle, &c." (K. P. 257—9.) See also vol. ii., Document xc., p. 301, and the Commons' Journals, April 15th.

And the Marches.

CHAP. VII.
1646.

While Mytton lay before Ruthin, a small body of his soldiers were attempting to capture Holt Castle, naturally a very strong fortress; but which had in it only a small garrison, commanded by Sir Richard Lloyd of Ecclusham, near Wrexham: he who entertained the King on his visit to the latter place in 1643. Mytton, immediately after the fall of Chester, sent a detachment to that place, consisting of some of his own men and some of the Cheshire Firelocks. Through some misunderstanding or other the Cheshire Firelocks were withdrawn from the town, leaving Mytton's men, who numbered less than the garrison, in a position of considerable weakness.[1] Whitelock, in his Memoirs, generally correct, states that the place was surrendered in April, the Governor being allowed to go beyond the sea with £300, and his lady to enjoy his lands, which amounted to about £300 a-year.[2] But a letter, written six weeks after the capture of Ruthin, preserved in the King's Pamphlets,[3] written by Capt. Richard Price, Lieut.-Col. Mason, and Lieut.-Col. Twistleton, states—"Holt hath been besieged ever since the taking of Chester. It is a very strong place. Starving is the only way that we can use against that place." I have not been able to fix satisfactorily the date when this fortress was surrendered.

The north-western counties of North Wales had hitherto escaped from the worst ravages of war. They had not been battle-fields. They had certainly been very much drained of men and money

---

[1] *Ibid.*
[2] Whitelock's Memoirs, 231.
[3] King's Pamphlets, 264—1. Vol. ii., Document xcii.

CHAP. VII.
1646.

for the King. Prince Rupert and Prince Maurice, Lord Byron and Lord Capel, had levied heavy contributions upon them. But the Commissioners of Array for most of the counties of North Wales had been not very forward to exact these demands, and the country had been somewhat better off in consequence than if they had been entirely swept over by military despots. Lord Byron speaks very slightingly of the Commissioners of Array. I do not, however, place too much importance on his evidence, for his style of writing was ever violent. Now, however, that the King's power at Chester had been destroyed, Denbigh, Carnarvon, and Anglesey were destined to experience some of the evils of war.

Immediately after the surrender of Ruthin, siege was laid to the Castle of Denbigh, where Colonel Salesbury held supreme command. A very brave man and loyal was this Colonel Salesbury—"a very wilful man," his adversaries called him. The castle had in its situation all the advantages for strength that any stronghold could have. Moreover, there were in it some five hundred able fighting men, and many of the gentry had sought refuge within its walls. Summons after summons was sent in, but the answer was always the same—an unflinching refusal to surrender; and for months the siege continued. The besiegers were in hopes to deprive those within of the benefits of a well in Goblin's Tower. There was only one other well within the walls, and that always dried up in the summer. Goblin's Tower, however, was not taken. The summer came and went, and the drought notwithstanding, Salesbury maintained his hold.

While this was going on Carnarvon Castle was also besieged. The Major-General himself conducted this siege, for it was deemed a most important garrison. Moreover, it was to this castle that Lord Byron and his chief officers went when they quitted Chester. Flint Castle, too, was under siege. On the 22nd of May, at midnight, it was deserted by a large party. Several of them went over to the Parliament forces at Hawarden, some went to Chester, and such as were Welshmen went to their homes. On the 23rd the flag of defiance was taken down, and shortly afterwards the place was surrendered.[1] Of all the garrisons in North Wales, Conway, Rhyddlan, and Harlech Castles alone remained free from a siege towards the end of June.

The siege of Carnarvon was all this time making very slow progress. The besiegers, however, had plenty to look after, for those within allowed them very little rest. Lord Byron appears to have assumed the command of the garrison, and he did all in his power to harass the enemy. They made two desperate sallies, but on both occasions were beaten back, with an aggregate loss of about thirty men. Mytton himself appears to have been in some danger at the second sally. He received considerable assistance from the country in conducting this siege. Notably, Col. Thomas Glynne, of Glynllifon, the brother of Sir John Glynne, Recorder of London, and Sir William Williams, of Vaenol, rendered material service.[2] On the

[1] King's Pamphlets, 264—1. *Perfect Occurrences* for 5th June. (K. P. 24—6.)
[2] King's Pamphlets, 264—1.

the 4th day of June, in answer to the second summons, Lord Byron agreed to capitulate. Six commissioners were chosen to draw up the articles, there being for Lord Byron, Cols. Edward Vere, John Vane, and Disney; for Mytton, Col. Thomas Glynne, Col. John Carter, and Major Zanchy. Lord Byron, and all officers in the commission, gentlemen of quality, and their servants, were to have freedom to go to their homes, and were allowed three months, either to make their peace with the Parliament, or go beyond the seas; the inferior officers and soldiers were permitted to go to Worcester, but if that city was besieged, then they were to have freedom to disperse to their homes. The town was saved from plunder. Sir William Byron, Colonel John Robinson, Colonel Shakerley, Archdeacon Price, and others named, were also to have the benefit of the articles.[1] One of the old newspapers of the period[2] gave it out that there were three bishops in the garrison,—viz., Hereford, Chester, and Bangor; but I have seen no confirmation of this statement.

During the progress of the siege of Carnarvon Castle, some negotiations had been carried on between General Mytton and the Royalists in Anglesey. To pave the way for a friendlier feeling the latter had abstained from rendering any assistance to the garrison at Carnarvon. At their request Mytton sent Col. Pope, Col. John Jones, and one Thomas Edwards, with propositions to treat with

---

[1] "The taking of Carnarvon, &c. Printed by Jane Coe, June 11, 1646." (K. P. 264—17.) Also vol. ii., Document xciii., p. 309.
[2] *Perfect Occurrences*, 24th week.

them for the surrender of the Island and the Castle of Beaumaris. Beaumaris, from nearly the commencement of the war, had been garrisoned for the the King by Lord Bulkeley of Baronhill. The place had been of very great convenience to land troops and ammunition from Ireland, and the Marquis of Ormond, the Archbishop of York, and Lord Bulkeley, had been making the most of it to advance the King's cause for a long time. Now, however, no fresh consignments of men from Ireland were forthcoming, and like all other places it had to change hands. The inhabitants of Anglesey had the prudence to submit before they were compelled to do so by the sword. On the 14th of June, at Beaumaris Castle, articles were signed on behalf of Col. Richard Bulkeley, the governor of the castle, and the rest of the country gentlemen there assembled, whereby they gave up the castle and promised to make their peace with the Parliament within four months. The signatories to these articles were the above-named commissioners on behalf of General Mytton, and Lieut.-Colonel John Robinson, Dr. Robert Price, and Major David Lloyd, for the Governor, Col. Bulkeley.[1]

The Parliament was duly informed of these important successes. Mytton was appointed Governor of Beaumaris Castle and the Isle of Anglesey. Col. Thomas Glynne had a letter of thanks voted to him for his good service in assisting in reducing North Wales, and a sum of £3,000 was ordered to be raised for Mytton out of the estates of delinquents in North Wales.[2]

---

[1] *Perfect Occurrences*, 26th week, 1646. (K. P. 24–14.) Vol. ii., Document xciv.

[2] Commons' Journals. Date 25th June, 1646.

There now remained only four garrisons for the King in the whole of North Wales, viz.: Conway, Denbigh, Rhyddlan, and Harlech. These were all under siege; but they held out for some time. Here we shall, therefore, leave them to look at affairs in South Wales.

Ever since the failure of the attempt of certain renegades in Glamorganshire, at the instigation of the House of Raglan, to seize upon Cardiff, Col. Morgan, the Governor of Gloucester, and Sir Trevor Williams, had been extremely vigilant in watching Raglan Castle, and eager for its reduction. But Raglan was a very secure place, and a stronghold of considerable importance. All that boundless wealth could do had been done for its security; and the inventive genius of the Earl of Glamorgan, who has been claimed as the discoverer of steam power, had contributed very materially to this end. Deep moats surrounded it, which could be filled with water at any time, and ammunition could scarcely fail them during a siege, seeing that they had a powder mill within the walls, which was capable of making a barrel a day. Every preparation had also been made to enable its inmates to sustain that siege which now appeared to all to be inevitable. The garrison had been increased in strength, ample stores had been brought in, and deeming it the safest place from the enemy, a large number of those of the leading inhabitants of the county who still remained loyal to the King had quitted their own homes to seek shelter within its strong walls. Along with these were many who had held important commissions in the Royalist armies which lately had been destroyed. Colonel

Morgan and Sir Trevor Williams, however, did not begin to draw their lines round the castle until they had heard of the defeat of Lord Astley's force by Brereton at Stow in the Wolds, to which I have already referred. When they heard that, they knew that the sole enemy with whom they would have to contend were those who had been collected together within the fortress. So they made their preparations accordingly. It is true, the aged Marquis relied to a certain extent on aid from Ireland, which his son was trying to bring over. He was even told that they had arrived, and were on their way to the rescue. This induced him to write to the Governor of Chepstow, and the Committee for Monmouthshire, expressing a hope that bloodshed might be avoided. He was "content to live a quiet neighbour amongst them," if reparation was made to him, and he was allowed to have his rents which they had taken from him, without which he could not live. To this the Committee for the County sent a reply, characterising the news of the landing of the Irish as a "pretty Jesuitical invention," and attributing to the Marquis the ruin of the county and all its sufferings.[1] Major-General Laugharne, now that Aberystwith Castle had been surrendered to Colonel Rice Powell, had reduced all South Wales, and was free to proceed to the aid of Colonel Morgan in Monmouthshire, which he did accordingly, having, moreover, received frequent importunities to do so. These solicitations were coupled with a promise to raise contributions for

CHAP. VII.

1646.

[1] *Perfect Diurnal*, No. 156. (K. P. 24—11.) The signatures to the Committee's letter were—Henry Herbert, Charles Katchmey, Thomas Hughes, Rice Williams, Edward Morgan, Roger Williams, Wm. Herbert, and Wm. Blethyn.

the support of the soldiers. Laugharne, with some 600 horse and foot, entered Monmouthshire, and was quartered at Abergavenny. Matters at this time were making very slow progress. Laugharne found that he had nothing to do, and also that the promised contributions were not forthcoming; in fact, as he complained, he and his men were lying idle at Abergavenny "without any manner of encouragement." It is true, his men carried away some 300 head of cattle from under the very walls of Raglan; but he was forced to quarter his men on the county, which gave dissatisfaction to all concerned. The people grumbled. So did his men. He remonstrated with the Committee, and also represented the state of affairs to Parliament, and was "wearily waiting" some improvement.[1] His men at last grew mutinous, which probably induced the Committee to pay them, on the 10th June, £1,500 arrears, and a further sum of £500 as a sop to prevent further mutiny, upon which they quitted the county and returned to Pembrokeshire.[2]

Meanwhile Col. Morgan was drawing his lines tighter around the garrison. On the 3rd day of June he sent in his first summons. To that the Marquis refused to accede, saying he would not yield the castle without having the King's own authority for so doing. A lengthy negotiation took place after that between the two parties. Being charged with ruining the county by keeping the garrison, the Marquis replied that "the true reason" for his keeping forces was not in defiance of the

[1] See Laugharne's letter, dated Abergavenny, 25th May, in *Perfect Occurrences* for 5th June. (K. P. 24—6.)
[2] *Perfect Occurrences*, 26th week. *Ibid.*

Parliament, but for his own preservation. Summons after summons was sent. Colonel Morgan did all in his power to prevail on the Marquis to give in; but all his persuasions proved fruitless. Constant sallies were made from within, and those in the leaguer had hard duties to perform. On the 28th of June Colonel Morgan once more attempted to prevail on the Marquis to yield. Two reasons for his speedy yielding were given—the one was that it would soon be futile to hold out much longer, seeing that Sir Thomas Fairfax, having, as Colonel Morgan truly stated, "finished his work over the Kingdom," was on his march towards Raglan; the other was an order from the King himself, addressed to the Governors of Oxford, Worcester, and all other garrisons in the Kingdom, requiring them upon honourable conditions to quit the garrisons and to disband all the forces under their command. It should be here stated that the King, after the defeat of Astley, in Gloucestershire, and Hopton, in Cornwall, was besieged at Oxford. Feeling that resistance was no longer of avail, and still not anxious to yield himself up to Fairfax, who commanded the siege, the King made his escape from Oxford; and after having travelled through the country in the guise of a servant, had given himself up to the Scotch, in whose custody he remained until he was carried away by the army. On the 10th of June he signed the above warrant, which was dated from Newcastle, and addressed to the Governors of Oxford, Worcester, Lichfield, and Wallingford, and all other commanders, &c. Colonel Morgan sent a copy of this warrant with his summons—a true copy "upon the faith and honour of a soldier." The old Marquis, however, does not seem to have been inclined to place too much reliance on such honour; and because the King had omitted even as much as to name Raglan in his warrant, he asked for "leave to suspend his belief," asserting that no man could make him think so "unworthily of his Majesty." Doubtless the Marquis, who had sacrificed so much for the King, expected at least to have some acknowledgment, and would have been amply satisfied if Raglan had been only named in the warrant. However, it was quite true. Charles did forget the great service which the Marquis had been to his cause. Colonel Morgan, being still anxious to induce the Marquis to give in before he should be compelled to do so by Fairfax, offered him permission to send an officer to Oxford to verify the King's warrant. To this the Marquis would not listen. July passed, and still the besieged made no signs of giving in. Early in August Fairfax himself came, and on the 7th he sent in his first summons. A "dilatory" answer was sent, and the next day the Marquis wrote to Fairfax "a calm letter," acknowledging his respect for the General's family, and his long acquaintance with his grandfather, and at the same time asked to have propositions sent in to him. These were sent at once. Fair conditions enough were offered for the soldiery. As to the Marquis himself, he was to submit to the mercy of the Parliament. Some doubts as to whether the Parliament would confirm Fairfax's terms occasioned some slight hitch in the negotiation. These being removed, the Marquis sent out a drum on the 13th, desiring leave to send out commissioners to treat for the capitulation; and a safe conduct was given. Meanwhile every preparation had been made to reduce the place—to take it even by storm if necessary. The lines had been drawn tighter, mortar pieces of great power, carrying grenade balls of twelve inches diameter, were placed at advantageous positions, and trenches had been dug under the superintendence of Fairfax's chief engineer, Capt. Hooper. The terms which were sent in, in respect of the soldiers, were of a favourable kind, but the Marquis himself was to be at the disposal of the Parliament, who had already placed him high in the list of persons who were excepted from pardon. Of course, the aged Marquis struggled hard to obtain better terms, and it does seem harsh that they were denied to a man whose age was already eighty-four years. On the 15th the commissioners representing both parties met at one Mr. Oates's house, about a mile and a half from Raglan. The conditions were there discussed and adopted; and it was then arranged to yield up the castle to Sir Thomas Fairfax on Wednesday, the 19th of August. All the officers, gentlemen, and soldiers of the garrison, numbering about 500, were to be permitted to march out of the garrison, with their horses and arms, colours flying, drums beating, trumpets sounding, match lighted at both ends, bullets in their mouths, each soldier with twelve charges of powder, bag and baggage, and to go to any place within ten miles of the garrison, where they were to deliver up their arms to the use of the Parliament, and where the soldiers were to be disbanded. All to have benefit of articles except such as had been excepted by Parliament—the Marquis alone being of this category. Three months were allowed the officers and gentlemen to make peace with the Parliament, or to go beyond the seas, for which purpose they were to have passes granted to them. Sick and wounded to remain in the castle until recovery. Thus fell Raglan Castle, after a close siege of over three months—having held out some months longer than any English garrison. Among those who surrendered there were no less than six colonels, three majors, thirty-two captains, sixteen lieutenants, many inferior officers, and a large sprinkling of gentlemen of quality, and several ladies. Though the siege had been of such long continuance, the besieged do not appear to have suffered much inconvenience, beyond being kept within the limit of the garrison; for when the castle was yielded up, there was in it a great store of corn and malt, wine of all sorts, and beer. The horses appear to have been the greatest sufferers. For want of hay many of them had been starved out, and the rest were almost worthless; they were in such extremity as to be forced to eat their own halters.[1]

South Wales and the Marches were now entirely in the hands of the Parliament. Not a garrison remained to the King. Laugharne in the West, Colonel Morgan in the East, Brereton and Mytton in the Marches, had carried everything before them,

[1] Details of the siege of Raglan may be found in "A letter to the Hon. W. Lenthal, &c., from Col. Morgan, &c." (K. P. 266—16): "An exact and true relation of the messages, &c., between Sir T. Fairfax and the Marquis of Worcester, &c." (K. P. 274—18); "A letter from his Excellency's Quarters, &c." (K. P. 275—13); *Perfect Diurnal*, No. 160, and *Perfect Occurrences*, 35th week (K. P. 24—46). See vol. ii., Document xcv. A. B. C. and D.; also Coxe's Monmouthshire, and Williams's ditto.

and the whole of that part of the country was now in a fair way of being settled in their obedience to the Parliament. In the whole of England also there remained not a single garrison unsubdued. The King himself was a prisoner, carried hither and thither by the Scotch.

In North Wales, however, a few more castles remained unreduced. Our survey of that district extended up to the middle of June, when Anglesey was reduced. At that date, Conway and Denbigh, Rhyddlan and Harlech, held out. Of these the town of Conway was the first to fall. Hitherto that town, chiefly through the influence of John Williams, Archbishop of York, had been loyal to the King. The castle had been repaired and strengthened entirely at his own expense, as well as the walls of the town. The Archbishop throughout the continuance of the troubles had been zealous to promote the King's interest. His correspondence with the Marquis of Ormond, Lord Digby, Lord Byron, Lord Bulkeley, and others, bear sufficient testimony to his fidelity and zeal. He had, moreover, spent quite a fortune in the royal cause. Conway soon became the head-quarters of the Royalist clergy. From Yorkshire and from every part of Wales they flocked thither. And the Archbishop came to be looked upon, and he looked upon himself, as the rightful governor of the town and castle. Prince Rupert, however, appointed Sir John Owen, of Cleneney, to the governorship of the town and castle, in the face of the Bishop's protestations, and much to his disgust and annoyance. This is not the only instance of this kind of indiscretion on the part of the Prince which

I have had to record. This, however, was a barefaced act of injustice, for the King himself, before Rupert even had received his own commission, "had upon high and dear considerations passed over unto me," says the Archbishop, "and my assigns [the castle], which from bear walls I have repaired, victualled, and ammunitioned at my own charges."[1] A man endowed with a spirit less soaring and ambitious than that of the Archbishop, would have been soured by conduct such as that. For Rupert and Sir John Owen Dr. Williams had no affection after this. Of the latter he never failed to speak contemptuously, characterising him as one of the sharks and children of fortune, who know not how to subsist but by license and imposture.[2] Still the old Archbishop continued faithful to the King, and while Chester was under siege, exerted himself to promote steps for its relief. But now, when the King himself had given in, and he saw that his Sovereign could no longer be benefited by further resistance, and, moreover, being anxious to save his native town from utter ruin, he was not above going over to the other side, so as to conciliate his enemies by assisting Col. Mytton in reducing the Town and Castle of Conway. His advice in a Council of War, held to consider the reduction of the town, was of great service to Mytton; and by means of it the town was taken by storm on the 18th of August. The conduct of the Archbishop of York on this occasion has been severely condemned by

[1] See his letter to Lord Digby, dated Conway, 13th April, 1645. State Pap. Dom., Charles I., vol. 319, § 270. Vol. ii. of this work, Document lxxiv., p. 243.
[2] *Ibid.*

writers of a Royalist bias, and all kinds of strictures have been passed on his character. I admit, however, that after serious consideration of all the circumstances, I do not agree with his censurers. All his acts during the war, and while there remained the slightest hope for the King, show him to have been thoroughly and zealously loyal, and throughout he evinced the greatest regard and solicitude for his Sovereign. The King's power was now, however, entirely gone. None but a fool could expect any good from holding out an insignificant and almost solitary garrison in the wilds of North Wales, when the King himself was a prisoner, his officers and advisers beyond the seas, and when the continuance of strife could have no other result than the ruin of the town or neighbourhood. Dr. Williams had served his King well, and was anxious even now to do so; he was also naturally anxious to save from ruin a town in which he had friends and property, and which was governed by a man to whom he owed anything but gratitude. This quarrel between him and Sir John Owen certainly gives an appearance of malignity to the Archbishop's conduct; but I am fully persuaded that higher considerations were dominant in his mind when he offered his council to Mytton, and that his conduct would have been the same if the governor had been another than his implacable foe. The next we hear of him is in November, when Colonel Mytton, writing to the Parliament, recommends the Archbishop to the protection of the House, and that he may enjoy the remainder of his estate free from sequestration, which was assented to on his taking the Negative Oath and the National League and Covenant.¹ This he probably took, and he was afterwards useful in maintaining order and peace in North Wales, taking a great interest in everything, as had been his habit: even writing to Oliver Cromwell, whom he had known, Carlyle surmises, when Bishop of Lincoln. Cromwell's letter to him bears date 1st September, 1647, and was written from Putney:—

"MY LORD,—Your advices will be seriously considered by us. [The army had then obtained the ascendancy over the Parliament.] We shall endeavour, to our uttermost, so to settle the affairs of North Wales as to the best of our understandings does most conduce to the public good thereof, and of the whole; and that without private respect, or to the satisfaction of any humour—which has been too much practised on the occasion of our troubles. The drover you mentioned will be secured, as far as we are able, in his affairs, if he come to ask it. Your kinsman shall be very welcome. I shall study to serve him *for kindred's sake*; among whom let not be forgotten, my lord, your cousin and servant,

"OLIVER CROMWELL."²

This letter is of the greatest possible interest, as it shows that Cromwell was conscious of his Welsh ancestry, and was proud to own it. The Archbishop was permitted to live at Conway during the remainder of his life, which was not long, for he died in January, 1649:—of a broken heart, it is said, for the fate of the King.³

---

[1] Commons' Journals, under date 21st January, 1646-7.
[2] Carlyle's Cromwell, Letter xlv.
[3] Hachet's Life of Williams.

Conway Castle still held out, and it was not surrendered by Sir John Owen until the 18th November.

In the meantime, Denbigh Castle also had been yielded to Mytton. It was surrendered on the 26th October. The town of Denbigh had since April been in the possession of the Parliamentarians, and the castle was summoned as early as the 17th of April; but Colonel Salesbury, to whom frequent allusion has before been made, was too ardent and loyal a soldier to show the white feather until compelled to do so. Another summons was sent to him on the 24th June, and he was informed at the same time that Carnarvon Castle had been taken, and the whole Island of Anglesey reduced. Salesbury's reply was, that what Anglesey and Carnarvon had done did not concern him. Siege was therefore laid to the castle, the management of it being entrusted to Sir William Myddelton. Col. Salesbury asked leave to send to the King, of whose flight to the Scots he had been informed, to ask his pleasure. Mytton, however, at first declined to grant this, on the ground that it had been denied to those who had commanded the garrisons of Raglan, Oxford, and elsewhere. But, whether with the consent of Mytton or not, Salesbury despatched Eubule Thelwall to the King, to inform his Majesty that "this castle hath now for several months been closely besieged." The King thanked the loyal governor for his "constancie," and promised whenever it should please God to enable him to show his thankfulness to his friends he would particularly remember him. On hearing from the King, Salesbury delivered up the castle to Mytton.[1]

[1] *Perfect Diurnal*, No. 171. Parry's Royal Progresses, pp. 373—379.

Holt Castle, the surrender of which, on the authority of Whitelock, I have placed in April,[1] was not then surrendered. It held out for many more months. Sir Richard Lloyd, whose name was among those who were to be excepted from pardon, was doubtless unwilling to throw himself upon the mercy of the Parliament. Colonel Carter had the management of the siege, which he found rather a difficult task, for many sallies were made by those from within, and relief obtained, which protracted the struggle very considerably. Towards the end of October, however, it was capitulated, whether on the terms mentioned by Whitelock or not, I have not been able to discover.

A notable fact, that the two last fortresses in England or Wales which were held for the King, were under the governorship of two brothers. Conway, governed by Sir John Owen, was, as I have before stated, surrendered to Mytton on the 18th of November; but Harlech Castle, of which Col. William Owen of Brogyntyn, was the Governor, was not delivered up to the Parliament before the 13th of March, 1647, and even then only on very honourable conditions. Colonel Owen in this was assisted by Sir Arthur Blayney and one Captain William Edwards of Chirk, and some other local gentlemen. The Civil War was now at an end—the King had been defeated and the Parliament victorious. But victory is not always attended with success. Internal dissensions soon began to disturb the peace, and after a short time more blood was spilt.

[1] *Ante*, p. 363.

CHAPTER VIII.

1647—1648.

The end of the Civil War—Attempts to disband the Army—Differences between the Army and the Parliament—Remonstrance against the Eleven Members—Fresh Revolt of Royalists in Glamorganshire suppressed by Major-General Laugharne—Disposal of the Welsh Armies—Royalist intrigues—General reaction in favour of the King—Col. Poyer heads an insurrection in Wales—Establishes himself at Pembroke Castle—Rises the country—Declares for the King—Is joined by Laugharne, Powell, the Stradlings, and others—Col. Horton, sent to repress the revolt, takes Brecon—Fights Poyer in Carmarthenshire—His correspondence with Laugharne—Obtains a great victory at St. Fagans—Poyer and Laugharne retreat to Pembroke—Tenby is fortified—Oliver Cromwell is sent to Wales—Chepstow is taken—Passes through Glamorganshire and takes Carmarthen—Tenby is reduced—Siege of Pembroke and its surrender—Poyer, Laugharne, and Powell sent prisoners to the Tower—Sentenced to Death—Poyer is executed—Insurrection in North Wales—Denbighshire, Flintshire, and Montgomeryshire, remain faithful to the Parliament—Sir John Owen defeated—Lord Byron routed—End of second Civil War.

SINCE the 5th day of May, 1646, the King had remained at the head-quarters of the Scottish army at Newcastle. Every influence was there brought to bear upon him to induce him to adopt the Covenant, and to convert him to Presbyterianism. Proposals from Parliament to form the basis of a Treaty of Peace were sent him in July. To these he replied by merely demanding that he should be received in London to treat personally with the Parliament. But this could not be seriously entertained by the Parliament. During the autumn of that year the great questions which troubled Parliament were the desirability of getting rid of the Scotch forces which occupied the North of England, and the disposal of the King's person. At this time the struggle for supremacy between Presbyterians and the Independents added much to the difficulties of the situation. The latter bore no good-will towards the Scotch, but at the same time felt that their retirement was absolutely necessary, and that this could not be done without paying them. The Scotch demanded three-quarters of a million. This was considered preposterous. Ultimately the sum of £400,000 was voted as the maximum sum which would be paid to them: one-half to be paid down, and the other half at the expiration of two years. This was accepted by the Scotch. Then came the question of the disposal of the King's person. The Independents evidently did not mean to pay the Scotch so large a sum, and to leave in their power the person of the King, which might work their own ruin. This question embarrassed very much the English leaders of Presbyterianism. They could not afford to quarrel with the Scots, and they thought that if the King was delivered over to the hands of the Parliament, they would be able to dispose of the army, wherein consisted the strength of the Independents, and their only dread. Difficulties innumerable arose; but a treaty was ultimately signed, regulating the retirement of the Scottish army. On the 1st of January, 1647, thirty-six carts arrived at York from London, conveying the first moiety of the indemnity; and within three weeks it was paid over, but not before the Scottish Parliament had consented to surrender the King to the English Parliament, which justified Charles's expression when the English Commissioners appointed to receive him arrived at Newcastle on the 22nd of January—"I am sold and bought." On the 9th of February the King quitted Newcastle, and, after travelling slowly, reached Holmby Castle on the 16th.

And now that the person of the King was in the hands of the Parliament, the Presbyterians there, who formed a majority of the House, lost no time before they commenced their long-intended attack on the army;—their greatest dread being Cromwell, who was an open foe to their intolerance in religious matters, who was at the head of the Independent party, and whose popularity in the army was beyond question. Ireland was sadly in want of soldiers, and the Parliament voted that 12,000 men be sent over there under the command of Skippon and Massey; and that the rest of the army be disbanded. But the army was not inclined to accept such terms, and insisted on being paid all arrears of pay, to be indemnified for acts done in war, and clear discharge, instead of being sent over to Ireland, except under their old commanders. Skippon and Massey, it should be observed, were Presbyterians,—the latter a very strict one, indeed,—and the army of Fairfax and Cromwell was not inclined to serve under them. This demur of the army called forth a severe and an unjust rebuke from the Parliament, who, hearing that the army was preparing a petition, voted all who should have a hand in the promotion of such petition to be "enemies of the State, disturbers of the peace," felt by all to be "a blot of ignominy,"—a vote which afterwards had to be cancelled from the records of Parliament, where asterisks still fill its place.[1] The army at this time was stationed at Saffron Walden. Two Parliamentary deputations were sent down to try and effect an agreement, but failed to do so. Cromwell himself in May attempted it, but the army was not in a mood to alter its demands. Preparations were made, therefore, for the forcible disbanding of the army—every precaution being taken that this resolution should not be known. But the secret oozed out, and the plot was frustrated. On the 5th of June, by a skilful manœuvre, the King, who had in the meantime continued to reside at Holmby, was carried away thence by Cornet Joyce, and brought to the army. The Presbyterians were never in such a plight before. A meeting between the army and commissioners appointed by the Parliament, on Triploe Heath, on the 10th June, having resulted in a further demand of justice from the army, the latter moved on to St. Albans to the terror of the Parliament and of the City of London. The struggle between the two powers had now became intense. Covering London, the army was in a position to insist on their demands, to which they added another, viz., that eleven members of the House, who had been the chief enemies of the army, should be impeached, and in the meantime expelled the House. The House was loth to give way, the army advanced, the shops of London were shut, and the difficulty not settled until the eleven accused members had "asked leave to retire for six months," and had hidden themselves. These eleven members were looked upon as the

[1] Commons' Journals, March 29th, 1647.

cause of all these troubles. Holles was at the head of them. General Massey, Sir Wm. Lewis, and Mr. Recorder Glynn, were amongst their number. Of Massey we have often spoken before. Sir William Lewis was of Llangorse, in the County of Brecon, and at this time was Member for Petersfield. John Glynn was of Glynllivon, in the County of Carnarvon, and Recorder of London. Lewis and Glynn were charged with having, in excess of their powers as members of a Committee appointed to consider the propositions for the settling of Wales, ordered the Committees for Sequestration to forbear all proceedings against the inhabitants of the Principality, whereby all that had borne arms against the Parliament, all disaffected and scandalous ministers, who, in their sermons, had reviled the Parliament, calling them rebels and traitors, and not only incensing the people against the Parliament, but taking up arms and leading their parishioners in arms against the Parliament, and many other desperate delinquents were freed from sequestration. To this charge both gave a denial, adding that the only order they gave had a reference to Carmarthenshire only. Sir William Lewis was also charged with having protected many notorious delinquents, viz., Lord Carbery and others in Carmarthenshire; Mr. Carew and others in Glamorganshire; Mr. Morgan, late knight of the shire, Mr. John Herbert, and others, in Brecknockshire; Mr. Gwyn, Mr. Lewis, and others, in Radnorshire; by freeing them from composition, and that he had encouraged some of them to continue true to the King;—that he had put in the Commission of the Peace several who had been Commissioners of Array, viz., his brother

Thomas Lewis, Mr. Gwyn, Mr. C. Walwyn, Mr. Meredith Lewis, Mr. Edward Williams, and many others, while those who had been faithful to the Parliament had been overlooked;—that he had appointed his kinsman, Edward Williams, to be solicitor for sequestrations, and by fraud had procured his own son to be chosen burgess for Brecon. Lewis was further charged with having caused the personal estate of Col. Herbert Price (Governor of Brecknock for the King) to be restored unto him without any satisfaction to the State, and had caused his real estate, worth £300 a year, to be let to a friend of Price, for the use of Price's wife, at only £50 a year, contrary to the orders of Parliament. Sir William denied these allegations. As for the Earl of Carbery, he had only moved in the House to make good Major-General Laugharne's promises to the Earl. As to Mr. Carew of Glamorgan, and Mr. Herbert of Brecknock, he had only moved that their fines should be ascertained according to the rules of the House. And for Mr. Herbert, he had done nothing in his behalf since Mr. Rumsey had preferred charges against him, and he was still a prisoner in Ely House. To Mr. Morgan he had only been civil in the way of an old acquaintance, and as a countryman. As to Mr. Gwyn and Mr. Lewis, of Radnorshire, between whom were certain disputes, and who were highly spoken of by Laugharne and Col. Birch, as having furthered the reducing of that county, he had moved that their disputes be referred to the Committee of Gloucester. With regard to the justices of the peace, he had nominated the fittest men he knew. They might have done some questionable things when the King had forces there; but of his brother, Thomas Lewis, he could safely say that in his fidelity to the Parliament he had suffered as much as any of double his fortune. He was even carried prisoner by Sir Wm. Vaughan to Ludlow, and not released until he had paid a ransome of eight score pounds. His son had been chosen burgess by the unanimous assent of the burgesses of Brecon. As to Col. Price's property, he had, on the petition of Mrs. Price, showing her sad condition, written to the Committee to allow her a fifth of her husband's estate, according to ordinance of Parliament, and to restore her wearing apparel, which had been taken from her. These charges were not investigated by Parliament, because the accused members removed the difficulty by going abroad.

The army ultimately won their point. They were not disbanded, nor did they go over to Ireland. Having marched into the city with boughs of laurel in their hats, their supremacy was complete. The army settled at Putney, and the King was lodged at Hampton Court.

Taking advantage of these distractions, some active Royalists in Glamorganshire attempted to raise an insurrection and to seize Cardiff. In this they were, it is said, instigated by Judge Jenkins, who was at this time a prisoner in the Tower, where he had been placed on his capture at the surprise of Hereford. Nothing daunted by the reverse of fortune, this valiant old man was as enthusiastic as ever. Pamphlet after pamphlet issued from his pen while a prisoner there, all breathing the most ardent loyalty for his Sovereign, but utterly repudiating the acts of the Parliament. For these contempts he was brought to the Bar of the House, where certain charges were read against him. He denied the right of Parliament to try him, and refused to answer the charges. Moreover, he would not appear before them uncovered; not out of any disrespect to them, he said, as a body of gentlemen, but because he could not admit their status as a Parliament. He was sent back to the Tower; and, probably, the proceedings against him would have been continued but for the outbreak of the second Civil War, which caused him, for a time, to be forgotten; and he remained in the Tower. When the Parliament had once more its hands clear, his case was mentioned, and he was ordered to be taken back to Wales, and there to be tried for treason at the sessions in his own county. It has been said that he was tried and sentenced to death, and that he heard the sentence with composure, and expressed his resolve to go to the scaffold with the Bible under one arm and *Magna Charta* under the other; but I have not been able to discover any official account of this trial. It is clear he was not executed, for he died after the Restoration a disappointed man.

Immediately on hearing that the King had been brought to the army, the principal Royalists in Glamorganshire gathered together, and resolved to take advantage of the distraction to rise for the King. The ringleaders were Sir Richard Bassett, Sir Edward Thomas, Sir Thomas Not, Sir Charles Kemeys, the Stradlings, and others. They summoned the whole county, sending out their warrants to the constables of every hundred to summon all able-bodied men to meet at Cowbridge. These warrants were dated the 13th of June. By the 15th they had mustered over 1,000 strong, and had formed their head-quarters at Llandaff, whence they sent by a lady a message to Col. Prichard, the Governor of Cardiff, calling upon him to yield up the castle to them. At the same time, fearing the power of Major-General Laugharne, who at this time was at Carmarthen, they wrote to him, explaining that their chief reason for meeting was to save themselves from the action of the Parliamentary Committee of the county, by whom their property had been heavily taxed, and hoping that Laugharne would assist them. From Saint Lythan's Down they again wrote to Laugharne, reiterating that their proceedings were "meant only for the vindication of our estates and liberties from the unjust and arbitrary disposition of Committees here." Laugharne, however, made no answer, but instantly set out to repress them. Colonel Prichard also remained firm, and demanded upon what authority they had disturbed the peace of the county; whereupon, on the 17th, from Llandaff, they sent a notice to the Governor, threatening, in case he resisted, he "must appear before the world to be guilty of the blood which shall be shed." But the timely appearance of Laugharne at Cardiff saved bloodshed, and scattered the dissatisfied party. They had actually got together between 1,500 and 2,000 men, but on the approach of Laugharne these deserted their leaders, who, thereupon, took to flight: most of them to turn up again in the role of insurrectionists.[1]

[1] King's Pamphlets, 318—5 and 820—9. Vol. ii., Document xcix.

In London, too, about this time there prevailed the wildest excitement. The City was Presbyterian to the core, and could not tamely submit to the Independent ascendancy which had just been established. Petitions were signed to secure the King's return to London. The Parliament was compelled by the mobs which assembled to vote for his return. The army thereupon drew nearer London. Over sixty members, including the Speakers of the two Houses, sought safety from the violence of the mob at head-quarters. Nothing daunted by this secession, and desperate perhaps with fear, the Presbyterian element of which again the Parliament was composed,—strengthened, too, by the eleven members, who now resumed their seats,—tried to secure the City. Massey, Waller, and others, were ordered to raise regiments for its defence with all speed. Men were easily found and money easily raised. The King was formally invited to return to London. Fairfax and Cromwell, however, frustrated this design by entering London. Fairfax went first. The City cowed again at his appearance, sent out its Lord Mayor and its Council to receive him. The Presbyterian leaders fled, and the members who had sought refuge with the army were again installed in their seats. A day or two after, Cromwell entered the City at the head of the army and marched through it,—an imposing spectacle,—and once more the triumph of the army was complete.

Now, however, arose serious difficulties within the army itself. Satiated with victories, proud of their successes, and conscious of their power, they were not backward in setting forth demands and pretensions which astonished even some of their leaders. They were dissatisfied at the conduct of their leaders, Cromwell especially, in negotiating with the King. Cromwell and Ireton were, I think, sincere in their efforts in trying to effect a peace with the King, and it was not until Charles's duplicity had been proved beyond a doubt, that they broke off their negotiations with him. I do not, however, believe the vulgar stories promulgated by his enemies, that Cromwell truckled with the King for the sake of having a mere garter bestowed upon him. Surely, if peace were established through his efforts he deserved some share in the Government, some high position in the State; but that he looked upon garters as objects to be sought for is quite inconsistent with his character. When he found out that the King was not to be relied upon, he lost no time to denounce him. Speaking soon after from his place in the House he said, "The King is a man of great sense, great talents, but so full of dissimulation, so false, that there is no trusting him. While he is protesting his love for peace, he is treating underhand with the Scottish Commissioners to plunge the nation into another war."

In the meantime, the King had fled to the Isle of Wight; but instead of finding freedom, he found himself a prisoner in Carisbrook Castle, of which Col. Hammond was the Governor. The disunion in the army meanwhile had been extending. They demanded many reforms, the most prominent being that they should put down Monarchy and establish a Republic, and that the King should be called to trial. And on the 3rd of January, 1648, Sir Thomas

Wroth proposed in the House of Commons "to lay the King by and settle the kingdom without him"; to have the country governed by any means, "so it be not by kings or devils." Cromwell supported the motion, and gave his opinion of the King's duplicity, which I have quoted. The discussion before had been warm, but after Cromwell sat down no one spoke, and the motion was carried by 141 against 92. The next day it was sent to the Lords, who adjourned the debate twice, but on the 15th adopted it.

This action of the Parliament created the deepest sensation throughout the land. From every part of the country came protests and rumours of plots. Everywhere men were heard crying "God save the King." Tumults occurred even at the very door of the Parliament, which caused Whitehall and the Tower to be occupied by troops, and the army once more to march through London. The discontent, however, increased. The Royalists were all one in their desire to see the King restored to power; and thousands of others, tired of the warring squabbles of the Parliament, and anxious to be eased of the burdens imposed on them through the necessity of maintaining a large standing army, were not disinclined for some accommodation with the King. The Scots, too, were preparing to raise forces for the same purpose, and a portion of the navy had revolted. Riots and tumults were of frequent occurrence. But the greatest defection of any was that which occurred in South Wales.

That country having been finally reduced to the obedience of the Parliament, it was thought there was no longer any necessity to charge the counties with the expense of supporting so large a body of armed men; orders were therefore issued for the disbanding thereof, retaining merely some small garrisons at Cardiff, Swansea, Carmarthen, and Pembroke. Some arrears were due to the officers and soldiers, and of course it was only fair that they should be paid for the valuable services they had rendered. The Parliament appointed committees for several districts, who were to superintend the disbanding; and these were empowered to pay a portion of the arrears in hard cash, and to give debentures for the balance. Pursuant to this authority they summoned the garrisons to meet at some central places, such as Carmarthen and Swansea. But under pretence of insisting on being paid the full amount of their arrears, Col. Poyer, who had hitherto been of the greatest service to the Parliament, revolted. Some suspicion of his intention to do so had evidently reached head quarters, for Fairfax sent down one Col. Fleming to replace Poyer in the governorship of the Castle of Pembroke; and Ludlow says that the suspicion against Laugharne was so great that he had been cast into prison.[1] Clarendon states the cause of dissatisfaction on the part of Laugharne and Poyer to have been, that they had been thought less of than Col. Mytton, and had not been rewarded according to their merits. How Laugharne could feel dissatisfied I cannot understand, for the Parliament had granted to him a most valuable estate in his native county; and Poyer's promotions and emoluments from his various offices and appointments must have also been very considerable. Clarendon

[1] Ludlow's Memoirs, i., 247.

further suggests that Laugharne, Poyer, and Col. Rice Powell, on discussing their supposed grievances, resolved to take the opportunity of the Scotch coming in to declare for the King in the Presbyterian interest. But Laugharne, who was not infected with the freaks of Poyer and Powell, would not declare himself until he first of all sent a competent agent to Paris to inform the Prince of what they determined, and of what their wants consisted, which, if not relieved, they would not be able to pursue their purpose; and desiring to receive orders for the time of their declaring, and assurance that they should receive sufficient supplies to carry out their object. Lord Jermyn sent him a promise under his hand that he should not fail of receiving all the things he had desired before he could be pressed by the enemy, and therefore conjured him and his friends to declare forthwith for the King, which he assured them would be of singular benefit and advantage to his Majesty's service, since upon the first notice of their having declared the Scottish army would be ready to march into England, and the Royalists would everywhere rise in arms.[1] There can be no doubt whatever of the truth of this allegation, which clearly shows that Poyer, in refusing to disband on the pretext of non-payment of arrears, was guilty of gross perfidy. The appearance of Col. Fleming, whom Fairfax had sent down to supplant him in the government of that town and castle, hastened the crisis, and occasioned hostilities to break out before matters were quite ripe, and before any of the help promised by Jermyn could have arrived, even if the promise had been made

[1] Clarendon's Rebellion, iv., 379, 380.

in all sincerity, which Clarendon appears to question, for he states "they were never thought of after."[1]

The 1st of March was the day fixed in Cardiganshire for the disbanding of the forces. The committee, consisting of Col. James Phillips of the Priory, Thomas Lloyd of Llanllyr, the High-Sheriff, and others, summoned a meeting of the troops on that day at Lampeter. In answer to that summons, Col. Lewis of Coedmore, Capt. Jones of Nanteos, Capt. Lloyd, Capt. Vaughan, Capt. Read, Capt. Sloeman (? Stedman), and several other officers of Col. Lewis's regiment, with their troops, assembled at Lampeter, and accepted the payment offered them, whereby the county was cleared of free quarter and other impositions. Poyer was summoned about the same time by Fleming to deliver up the Castle of Pembroke. His refusal to disband had already raised a suspicion as to his fidelity. And Fleming called upon him to surrender the castle in twelve hours, or to be proclaimed a rebel and traitor. Poyer, however, refused to surrender, and instead of sending the key he sent certain propositions in his own favour and in that of his soldiers. Not that he was hopeful or even anxious that they should be granted, for instead of waiting for a reply he fired several guns upon the town, battered several houses, wounding, too, several men. Fleming consulted some of the neighbouring gentry, and on their advice promised Poyer a sum of £200, and that he and his soldiers should have the same terms as all others who had been disbanded, and that the many actions

[1] *Ibid, ante.*

pending against him on the part of some of the county gentlemen, whom he is accused of having plundered, should be stayed. But these terms Poyer refused to accept. So he strengthened his position, attacked Col. Fleming, Roger Lort, John Lort, Griffith White, and others, at Henllan, Castlemartin, and nearly captured them. They, however, managed to get away on board ship; whereupon Poyer grew bolder, summoned the county, caused musters to take place at the town of Pembroke, and assessed the neighbouring parishes. Laugharne and Powell as yet made no motion, and at a meeting held at Carmarthen, Poyer's actions were repudiated by several officers who had served under Laugharne; who denied the aspersions cast upon them, that they had attempted to seize the Treasurers appointed to pay the soldiers on their disbanding, and that they intended to fortify Tenby against the Parliament. Notwithstanding this declaration, most of the men who attached their signatures to it went over soon after to the rebels. Fleming having failed in his mission, and Poyer having not only set him at defiance, but also an ordinance of the Parliament of the 4th of March, calling upon him, under the pain of being declared a traitor, to surrender the castle according to the directions of Sir Thomas Fairfax, the latter sent Col. Horton to suppress the insurrection, and to carry out the disbanding of the army in these parts. Fairfax also ordered Col. Reade, at Bristol, to hasten the march of two companies of Col. Overton's regiment, to assist in the reducing of Pembroke Castle. Horton lost no time in pushing forward, and early in April he established himself at Brecon, having first of all dispersed a small garrison which had been brought together there by some of the very men who had in November, 1645, out of their own motion, declared the Parliament to be the sole lawful authority in the Kingdom. Mr. Games appears to have been the leader of the movement, and he with some ten more men were made prisoners. Horton on his way thither had been of some service in Glamorganshire, in assisting the Commissioners at Cardiff in their work of disbanding some of Laugharne's forces. One of the demands of the officers was, that they should all be disbanded together, but Fairfax would not allow this, and required that they should be disbanded troop by troop, and company by company;[1] but Horton managed to remove this objection in some instances, and it was arranged that some more troops should be disbanded on Swansea Sands.[2] This, however, was not carried out. Laugharne in the meantime declared himself against the Parliament. Horton was indisposed at this time; but sacrificing all personal considerations, he exerted himself manfully. He had a difficult task to accomplish, for the insurrection was fast becoming general. All the disaffected, whether actuated by a loyalty towards their Sovereign, or a dislike to the heavy assessments which Parliament had imposed upon them, appeared in arms. Poyer and Powell had now openly declared for the King. The former, though discountenanced by the gentlemen of his own neighbourhood, was daily making additions to his forces, and the latter

CHAP. VIII.
1648.

[1] Rushworth, pt. 4, vol. ii., 1036.
[2] *Ibid*, 1051.

had established himself at Carmarthen, where he was in considerable force. In Glamorganshire the old spirit which had given birth to the revolt of the preceding autumn now broke forth with greater energy than ever, and the Stradlings of St. Donats, ever constant in their fidelity to the King, appeared at the head of the movement there, and aided by many other considerable persons. The Royalists of Brecon, though deprived of the assistance of some ten of their leading men, who had been taken prisoners by Horton, were by no means put down, and joining with some Radnorshire men, were bent on raising forces to harass Horton. Monmouthshire at first was tolerably quiet, the old Marquis of Worcester was in prison, and his son, the Earl of Glamorgan, beyond the sea; but Sir Charles Kemeys soon threw himself into the insurrection, and by a stratagem Chepstow Castle was taken possession of by Sir Nicholas Kemeys. Col. Morgan, formerly the Parliamentary Governor of Gloucester, now made his appearance as a Royalist, and there is reason to believe that Sir Trevor Williams, whom we have already seen in different lights, now resolved himself once more into a Royalist, and was partly instrumental in the surprisal of Chepstow. The three western counties, where the insurrection first broke out, were not so universally tainted with the spirit of insurrection. Poyer was not very popular in his own neighbourhood, where he was probably looked upon as an upstart, so that among the better class of persons he had not a large following. The Earl of Carbery discountenanced this second attempt at civil war, and his influence in Carmarthenshire neutralised many who otherwise would have gone headlong into the fray. In Cardiganshire we have already seen that the troops quartered there raised no objection to being disbanded, and all the officers remained true to the Parliament, and soon became active in assisting Horton. Some rumours that Sir Richard Pryse of Gogerddan was raising troops to assist Poyer reached Carmarthen, and a statement to that effect was transmitted in a letter thence to London;[1] but I am inclined to doubt it, as in another place it is stated that he refused to join,[2] and, moreover, was busy the other way, in conjunction with Capt. Thomas Evans.[3] And this is more likely to be the truth, for since 1646 he had been in the House of Commons as Member for the County of Cardigan, and his son was afterwards such a thorough supporter of Cromwell as to be chosen by the latter as one of the six who represented Wales in Cromwell's Little Parliament.

Poyer, having driven Fleming away from Pembroke, now ventured to take the field. On the 9th of April he mustered the County of Pembroke on Colby Moor. There he was joined by many of Laugharne's soldiers, who had been disbanded, and the poor inhabitants of the county dared not to disobey his summons.[4] The next day he appeared at Carmarthen, where he was joined by Powell. Pushing their way thence they reached Lampeter, in Cardiganshire, on the 12th, where they probably expected further recruits. Altogether it was said

---

[1] "News from the North, &c." (K. P. 360—26.)
[2] King's Pamphlets, 365—2. See vol. ii., Document cv.
[3] *Perfect Diurnal*, No. 68.
[4] Rushworth, p. 1065.

they mustered between three and four thousand strong. Horton, being informed of these movements and anxious to nip the evil in the bud, set out from Brecon at the head of his own regiment, and some 200 dragoons out of the county. He was further strengthened by the Cardiganshire forces to the number of some thirty companies of horse and foot, well-armed, and commanded by Col. Lewes, Capt. Jones, Capt. Read, Capt. Griffiths, and Capt. Vaughan. Thomas Lloyd, the High-Sheriff, and the rest of the Commissioners, were there, too, and Colonel Fleming was also of Horton's party. Poyer retreated towards Carmarthen on their approach, and ordered all the bridges across the Towy to be cut down and the passages to be protected; so that when Horton came to Pontargothi, he found the bridge cut down and the passage defended by some of Poyer's men. Finding himself at this disadvantage, Horton made for another passage, whereupon Poyer and Powell retreated a little further, but were followed by Horton. The Welsh occupied a hill, which gave them so great an advantage, that Horton, acting on the advice of his officers, hesitated to attack them. Several sharp skirmishes took place between them, but without any great result. Col. Fleming, ordered to make for a pass in the rear of their army, dispersed those who had charge of the pass, but was opposed by some of Powell's men, under the command of Major Roach. The latter was worsted, but Fleming, pursuing them too far in the rout, fell into an ambush, and his party was dispersed. He, with some one hundred more of his men, sought refuge in a church, which they hoped to be able to maintain until relief should come from Horton, who was only four miles off; but the Welsh made most of the chance, took possession of the church, and Fleming, either by an accident or intentionally, let his pistol off, and was killed in the church. Carlyle says the name of "this pass" is not given. None of the old newspapers give sufficiently minute information as to the locality, but in an old MSS. in the Mostyn Collection,[1] it is said that Col. Fleming shot himself in the church of Llandilo-fawr: a statement which so far agrees with our authorities, that the fight was on the banks of the Towy. In these several skirmishes, extending over some three or four days, the advantage was probably on the side of the Parliament, and many prisoners were made, who were afterwards exchanged. The insurrectionists had on their hats a blue and white ribbon, with the motto—"We long to see our King."

Poyer fell back towards Carmarthen, and Horton proceeded to Swansea and Neath, where he expected to be reinforced by Col. Okey, who had been sent to his assistance by General Fairfax. Swansea was at this time safe enough in the hands of the Parliament, under the governorship of Col. Philip Jones, who had been untiring in his zeal to maintain order and to suppress the revolt. Horton, being short of ammunition, returned to Brecknock, which he reached after a tedious journey over barren mountains, where they had great difficulty in finding food for the horses. Other difficulties which he suffered on his marchings arose from the antipathy of the people towards the Parliament

[1] *Cambrian Quarterly Magazine*, vol. i., p. 60.

forces. Wherever they appeared the people quitted their homes, taking with them whatever they could, and driving before them their cattle to seek refuge in the woods and mountains. The smiths everywhere disappeared, having previously cut their bellows, pulled down their smithies, and made all their materials unserviceable, so that there neither was a horse-shoe to be had, nor a place to make it, "if you would give 40s. to have a horse shod." Moreover, the insurrection was spreading—men constantly poured in, swelling the ranks of Poyer and Powell. Even from London and from Chester they flocked to their ranks, and Carmarthen became full of these rowdies. The state of the country from a Parliamentary view was as bad as it could be. Horton was too weak to combat with the insurrection, and constant messages were sent to London asking for aid; and pending this the whole country was rising. The great majority of the gentry were for the King, and they led "the common people which way they please."[1]

Meanwhile, the influence of Poyer's action was spreading throughout all England. The Royalists everywhere were astir, instigated by agents from beyond the sea. And the Scotch Parliament had resolved to raise an army of forty thousand for the invasion of England. The difficulties in London were very serious. The Parliament, split up into two parties, were at a dead lock, and the City, brimful of Presbyterianism, could scarcely be cowed into silence by the presence of the army. The many representations from Wales fully opened the

---

[1] Horton's letter from St. Fagans, 6th May. See vol. ii, Document cviii. A., p. 361.

eyes of Cromwell, and others, to the seriousness of their position. It was felt by them that unless the insurrection was put down with an iron hand all they had fought for at such vast sacrifices would be lost, and they themselves irretrievably ruined. It was also felt that the greatest present danger was threatened from Wales, and it was then decided that Cromwell himself should proceed thither. On the 1st of May Fairfax informed the Speaker of the House of Commons that he had sent Cromwell to Wales, with a suitable body of forces, to quell the insurrection there. And on the 3rd of May the valiant Lieutenant-General, with his small force, consisting of five regiments,—two of horse, being his own and Col. Thornhaugh's, and three of foot, being those of Col. Pride, Col. Ewer, and Col. Dean,—set out on his journey, and the next we hear of him is his arrival at Monmouth. When Poyer had intelligence that Cromwell was designed against him, he said that he would be the first man to charge against the *Ironsides*: that if Cromwell had a back of steel and a breast of iron, he durst and would encounter with him.[1]

Horton's difficulties in the meantime, instead of abating, were increasing. Accompanied by Colonel Philip Jones from Swansea, he arrived at Brecon to replenish himself with ammunition, and to prepare to go against the enemy in Pembrokeshire. At the same time he issued an address to the Welsh, informing them of the cause of his marching into Wales, but this was printed in English and was of no use. Moreover, it could not be

CHAP VIII.
1648.

[1] Sand's letter from Carmarthen, 3rd May. (K. P. 365—6.) See vol. ii., Document cvii.

anywhere published, especially in Carmarthenshire, where everybody was in arms. In fact, they were rising everywhere; if suppressed in one place, they appeared somewhere else. And at the very time Horton was preparing to march into Pembrokeshire, news reached him (May 1) that the enemy had pushed into Glamorganshire, were even then at Swansea and Neath,[1] and bent upon taking Cardiff, if possible, by tempting Colonel Prichard and Mr. Bushey Mansell to come in unto them; if not, by force. This necessitated a speedy march towards Cardiff. The roads were rough over the mountains, and the weather was very unseasonable; but there was no help for it, and the journey had to be made, and quickly. On Thursday, the 4th of May, they crossed the Taff at Llandaff, about a mile above Cardiff, and encamped at St. Fagans, on the river Ely. The enemy had already advanced as far as St. Nicholas, and intended quartering at St. Fagans the very same night. Major-General Laugharne now appeared officially at the head of the insurrection; and writing from St. Nicholas on the 4th of May, he questions Horton's authority to appear in the counties of his association, strikingly unmindful that it was occasioned by his own disobedience.[2] On Friday, the 5th, they withdrew from St. Nicholas and established themselves at Penmark, Llancarvan, and Fonmon. Both parties maintained their position throughout Saturday; but on Sunday the rebels again approached to St. Nicholas, which was a position of some advantage. This was clearly under-

---

[1] Rushworth, vol. ii., p. 1103.
[2] "A declaration by Major-General Laugharne, &c." (K. P. 366—8.) See vol. ii., Document cviii. B.

stood to show an intention to fight, and during that Sunday night preparations were made for the conflict, which was inevitable. Horton's forces were very little over 3,000, while his opponents mustered a force of nearly 8,000. With daybreak next morning commenced the struggle—the attack being made by the rebels with a forlorn of foot, which was resisted by a small body of horse, and Colonel Okey's own troop of dragoons. From hedge to hedge, from close to close, and over a little brook the latter drove their enemies, until they came to a bridge, where their principal strength lay. The fight now became general, both sides contesting every inch of ground with the utmost gallantry. The strength of the Parliament forces lay in their horse —their opponents being especially weak in that respect, not being 500 in the aggregate. Of the fight I shall here give no details, referring the reader to several well-known letters on the subject[1] from Col. Horton and Col. Okey. The Parliament forces were entirely victorious. Over 3,000 prisoners were taken, comprising some dozen field officers, 24 captains, 30 lieutenants, 28 ensigns, &c. Some 50 officers were slain, one of them being Laugharne's brother, Lieut.-Col. Thomas Laugharne. No less than 150 soldiers were slain on one side only. Laugharne himself was wounded. Those who were not made prisoners escaped, and made their way as fast as they could to Pembroke and Tenby, leaving Horton master of the situation in Glamorganshire. Eleven of the principal officers were taken on board the *Admiral Crowther*, where a Council of War was held, and they were con-

---

[1] For one of these, see vol. ii., Document cix.

demned to die. These were—Major-General Stradling, Major Phillips, Capt. Thomas Matthews, Capt. Wm. Button, Mr. Miles Matthews, Lieut.-Colonel Hopkin Popkins, Lieut.-Col. Thomas Morgan, Col. Arthur Harries, Captain Edward Walker, Captain Richard Cradock, and Lieut.-Colonel Lewis Thomas. Three were at once shot to death and one hanged. Whether the rest suffered I do not know.[1] A most terrible fight this. The waters of the pretty Ely ran deep in blood, and the widows in Glamorganshire were many. The Royalist newspapers tried to underrate this victory—calling it a mock victory.

Cromwell was now far advanced in his march into Wales. On the 10th of May he had reached Monmouth. Here intelligence came of the great victory of St. Fagans, which must have been of great encouragement to him. The 11th they proceeded to Chepstow, where Sir Nicholas Kemeys had placed a garrison. They found the walls of the town lined with musketry, but Colonel Pride's men fell on so desperately that the gate was soon taken, and also the town. A retreat was made to the castle, which was a strong place. Cromwell had no time to essay the siege, so leaving Colonel Ewer in charge of it, he set out on his journey for the West, and on the 15th he was at Cardiff.[2] While there false rumours reached him, that Laugharne and Powell had quarrelled, that Powell had been run through by Laugharne, and that the latter had gone North. News also came that Carmarthen had been quitted by the enemy, that Horton was before Tenby,

---

[1] *Moderate Intelligencer*, No 166. (K. P. 368—9.)
[2] *Commons' Journals*, v., 566, sub. dat. 20th May.

before which were also the *Bonadventure* and the *Expedition* ready to attack it from the sea.¹ Pushing forward with as little delay as possible, and calling on the way at Swansea and at Carmarthen, now deserted by the rebels, Cromwell appeared before Pembroke about the 24th of May.

When Cromwell took his departure from London at the head of his invincible Ironsides, and accompanied by regiments as distinguished and as brave, he doubtless calculated on meeting the enemy in open field, where it is only natural to suppose that the advantage would be with his veteran soldiers —elated with their high prestige—men who had faced death a hundred times, and who knew not defeat. But the battle of St. Fagans had utterly demoralized the enemy—the majority of them being club-men had dispersed to their own homes, while the few troops that held together with the officers and gentry sought shelter in Tenby and Pembroke. Col. Rice Powell held Tenby with a force of between 500 and 600, while Laugharne and Poyer made good their retreat at Pembroke, at the head of a more considerable party. Cromwell left the reduction of Tenby to Colonel Horton, who had established himself there before his arrival, while he reserved his own strength for Pembroke. Horton had pursued the enemy in their retreat with the greatest energy. As early as the 14th May he had settled down before Tenby, and on that day he attempted to storm the town, but was repulsed. Another attack upon an outwork was more successful, resulting in the capture of about thirty of the besieged, which made those within more anxious

¹ *Perfect Occurrences*, No. 73. (K. P. 33—31.)

to surrender. And on the 31st of May, being unable to hold out any longer, Powell sent out a "humble suit" to Horton, and so threw up the die, agreeing to surrender the castle, with all arms and ammunition, to Lieut.-General Cromwell, to the use of the Parliament, and yielding himself and the other officers, to the number of nearly forty, "prisoners at mercy." Among these were Col. Edward Kemeys, Col. Donnell, formerly Governor of Swansea, Captains Beal and Addis, who had first of all taken possession of Tenby at the beginning of the revolt, notwithstanding their declaration of their willingness to disband.[1]

Chepstow Castle had in the meantime been captured by Col. Ewer, whom Cromwell had left behind. Having obtained some guns from Gloucester, Ewer planted them against the castle, rased the battlements of the towers, and disabled the guns of the fortress, and on the 25th of May made a breach in the wall. Upon this some of the besieged soldiers tried to run out, and "Esquire" Lewis (of St. Pierre, I think,) appeared on the walls, and appealed to some gentlemen of the county who were there, professing to be ready to yield to mercy. Ewer, however, insisted on treating with Sir Nicholas Kemeys alone. The latter refused to yield unless he and his men were allowed to march out of the castle; but Ewer would grant no other terms than that he should submit to mercy, which Kemeys swore he would not do. The soldiers thereupon deserted him, and Ewer's troop rushed in, took possession of the castle, and in the fray

---

[1] "Exceeding good news from South Wales, &c.," and "Two great victories, &c." (K. P. 870—27 and 23.) See also vol. ii., Document cxiii.

Sir Nicholas Kemeys fell. Officers and soldiers to the number of 120 were made prisoners, among the former being "Esquire" Lewis, and the representatives of several other Monmouthshire families.[1]

In South Wales Pembroke alone now held out. North Wales was also somewhat agitated with the spirit of insurrection; but it did not prevail to anything like the extent it did in South Wales, nor did it assume any approximate importance. Indeed, three counties had openly declared their fidelity to the Parliament, and their readiness to assist in the suppression of the insurrection. At a meeting of the principal inhabitants of Flintshire and Denbighshire, held at Wrexham on the 9th of May, resolutions were come to for the defence of those counties against any that should be in arms against the Parliament — the management of Denbighshire affairs to be entrusted to Sir Thomas Myddelton, the High-Sheriff, Mr. Simon Thelwall, and Lieut.-Colonel Twistleton, while the same authority for Flintshire was vested in Col. Thomas Ravenscroft, Col. John Addersley, Mr. John Salesbury of Bathgrage, and Capt. Luke Lloyd. Ruthin and Rhyddlan Castles were to be rendered untenable.[2] And a numerously signed declaration of the principal inhabitants of Montgomeryshire, dated the 20th of May, manifested the adherence of that county to the Parliament.[3] But in Carnarvonshire the restless spirit of Sir John Owen was once more roused, and he

---

[1] "A full relation of the taking of Chepstow Castle, &c." (K. P. 369—6.) See vol. ii., Document cxii., p. 875.

[2] "A Resolution of the Sheriffs, &c., of Flint and Denbigh." (K. P. 367—16.) See also vol. ii., Document cx.

[3] *Perfect Diurnall*, No. 252. See vol. ii., Document cxi., p. 373.

got together so strong a party that Col. Mytton and William Lloyd, the High-Sheriff of the county, were forced for their security to repair to Carnarvon. And on the 3rd June Mytton sallied out at the head of a small force, and met the enemy some three miles outside the town. The High-Sheriff ventured so far that he was wounded and taken prisoner. The treatment of the High-Sheriff was cruel in the extreme—one of the worst features in the whole insurrection. He was carried about from place to place, his wounds undressed, and when he could no longer be carried on horseback he was conveyed on a litter, and jostled about so violently that death soon came to his relief. Hearing of these doings, Col. Twistleton out of Denbigh, and Col. Carter out of Conway, issued out to suppress Sir John Owen. In this they had the assistance of some of Col. Jones's troop, some volunteers, and a detachment sent from Chester. On Monday, the 5th, they met on the plain near the seaside, between Aber and Bangor. The Royalists were routed, several of their officers slain, and Sir John Owen himself taken prisoner.[1] He was carried to Denbigh Castle, where, notwithstanding a futile attempt was made to rescue him by Major Dobben, Capt. Parry, Capt. Chambres, and others,[2] he remained until he was removed to the Tower, there to be tried and sentenced to death. The sentence, however, was not carried out—his importunities for his life having saved him from that extremity.

[1] "A narrative, with letters, presented by Capt. Taylor to the House of Commons, &c." (K. P. 371—8.) Also vol. ii., Document cxiv.

[2] "Denbigh Castle surprised by the King." (K. P. 376—4.) Vol. ii., Document cxv.

Peace was for a time restored in North Wales, but difficulties soon arose in Anglesey, where the royalist proclivities of Lord Bulkeley and Lord Byron caused the county to be fined seven thousand pounds.[1]

To return to Pembroke. That place was now undergoing a regular and a close siege. Cromwell had an arduous task to perform, since he said he had "a very desperate enemy" to contend with, "who, being put out of all hope of mercy, are resolved to endure to the uttermost extremity." Had they been the common people there would be some hope of them, but "very many of them were gentlemen of quality and men thoroughly resolved." He was, besides, in a hostile country, for though a good many came in to him, and the gentry of Pembrokeshire, who had not engaged themselves in the insurrection, afforded him every assistance in their power, yet the country generally was very restless, requiring the most strict guard. "The country, since we sat down before this place, have made two or three insurrections, and are ready to do it every day, so that with looking to them, and disposing of our horse to that end, and to get us in provisions, without which we should starve, this country, being so miserably exhausted and so poor, and we having no money to buy victuals. Indeed, whatever may be thought, it is a mercy we have been able to keep our men together in the midst of such necessity, the sustenance of the foot for the most part being but bread and water."[2] More-

CHAP. VIII.
1648.

---

[1] Parry's Royal Progresses.
[2] "Denbigh Castle surprised for the King." (K. P. 376—4.) Vol. ii., Document cxv.

over, they had no guns of sufficient calibre to assault the place effectually. Swift messengers were sent to Gloucester for guns; and no time was there lost in despatching them, but the vessel stranded at Berkley, as if the very elements themselves were conspiring against the Lieutenant-General and the "faithful." The place could not be taken "without fit instruments for battering." The few small guns and culverins which he had were not fit for such a purpose. What use could be made of them was done with the aid of the shells and shot cast "in the iron furnaces of the County of Carmarthen," which were duly forwarded to Cromwell by his "noble friends the Committee of Carmarthen," doing therein "a very special service to the State."¹ An attempt to storm the town proved futile—the ladders were too short, and those within too active, in which some of his brave soldiers fell, though he was confident the enemy lost more.² Later on several other attempts were made to capture the town. Once the besiegers scaled the walls, entered the town, drove the enemy up to the very castle walls; but Major Laugharne—recovered from his wounds at St. Fagans—came in the rear and forced them to quit the town, with a loss of about thirty. This assault was made by Col. Horton and Col. Okey.³

The enemy within were now reduced to great straits; their provisions nearly exhausted, which made it very difficult for Poyer to keep his men

---

¹ Cromwell's letter of the 9th June. Vol. ii., Document cxvi A., p. 387.
² His letter to the Speaker of the House of Commons, 14th June. Vol. ii., Document cxvi. B.
³ "A great and bloody fight at Pembroke, &c. (K. P. 375—35.) Vol. ii., p. 395.

from deserting. The latter was hopeful of some relief. Probably they thought that Lord Jermyn's promise would be fulfilled, or that the Scotch would appear to the rescue. So hopeful were they, that they believed a salute fired by Cromwell's orders, on his hearing of some good news from Kent, to have been a warning that Prince Charles and the revolted ships were come to their relief. Hoping, in fact, against hope.

Cromwell meanwhile was assiduous in his labour, as "willing to fight for the liberties of England as he ever did formerly." He had the whole of South Wales under his eye. Some intelligence having reached him as to the originator of the "stratagem" by which Chepstow Castle had been surprised by Kemeys; in fact, "that Sir Trevor Williams was the malignant who set on foot the plot," orders were given to Col. Thomas Saunders, then at Brecon, to seize him, as well as Morgan, the High-Sheriff of Monmouthshire. Williams, being the more dangerous man by far, was to be seized first. This would require great tact, "for he was a man full of craft and subtlety, very bold and resolute,"—rather a favourite, too, by his neighbours, all of them malignant.[1] Of Richard Herbert of St. Julian's "secret practices against the public advantage," Cromwell, too, had trustworthy report, which causeth the latter to indict him "a plain warning" not to conceal or abet either of the two men named above, or "I will cause your treasonable nest to be burnt about your ears"[2]—a warning which, I think, proved effectual. The Scots by this time

[1] Cromwell's letter 17th June. Vol. ii., Document cxvi. c.
[2] *Ibid*, 18th June. Vol. ii., Document cxvi. D.

414 Civil War in Wales

CHAP. VIII.
1648.

had entered England. To starve out Pembroke Cromwell had more than sufficient men. He, therefore, sent a few horse and dragoons towards the North, by way of Chester, where their assistance was somewhat required to appease tumults, and thence to Leeds.[1]

The besieged at Pembroke were becoming more and more uncomfortable. Famine and distress began to tell upon the troops, some of whom could hardly be prevented from open mutiny. At length, about the 1st of July, the long-looked-for guns from Wallingford and Gloucester came down the Severn, and were safely landed at Milford Haven; and forthwith the batteries were completed and the guns planted. The sufferings of the besieged must have been very great; their water supply had been cut off, and they had to depend on what rain water they could secure and a little biscuit. Cromwell,—a generous enemy,—believing that the common people and soldiers were but "a seduced, ignorant people," was really sorry for their distress, and sent on the 10th of July, at four o'clock, his last summons to Col. Poyer, which, inasmuch as it is not given in Carlyle's, I transcribe here:—

"SIR,—I have (together with my Council of War) renewed my propositions, [and] I thought fit to send them to you with these alterations, which, if submitted unto, I shall make good. I have considered your condition, and my own duty; and (without threatening) must tell you that if (for the sake of some) this offer be refused, and *thereby misery and ruin befall the poor soldiers and people with you*, I know where to charge the blood you

[1] *Ibid.* 28th June, *ante.*

spill. I expect your answer within these two hours. In case this offer be refused, send no more to me about this subject. I rest your servant,

"OL. CROMWELL."

The next day, being the 11th of July, unable to hold out any longer, Poyer accepted the conditions offered, and surrendered the town and castle to Oliver Cromwell. Seeing the desperate game they had played, the blood they had caused to be shed, and the danger in which they had involved the country, the propositions cannot be looked upon otherwise than as fair and even generous. Laugharne, Poyer, Col. Humphrey Matthews, Capt. William Bowen, and David Poyer, were to be at the mercy of the Parliament;—persons who had formally served the country in "a very good cause; but being now apostatised, I did rather make election of them than of those who had always been for the King, judging their iniquity double because they have sinned against so much light and against so many evidences of Divine Providence, going along with and prospering a just Cause in the management of which they themselves had a share." Of those who had been always for the King, the leaders were within six weeks to quit the kingdom and to remain in exile for two years. These were Sir Charles Kemeys, Sir Henry Stradling, Mr. Miles Bulton, Major Prichard, Lieut.-Colonels Stradling, Laugharne, and Brabazon, Mr. Gamage, Majors Butler, Francis Lewis, Matthews, Harnish, Captains Roach, Jones, Hugh, Bowen, and Thomas Watts, and Lieutenant Young. All the rest, submitting to the authority of the Parliament, were at liberty to go to their respective homes there to live quietly. The town was not to be plundered, and the townsmen were to be protected from violence.

Cromwell had now completed his mission. He had effectually put down a most stubborn enemy, and had rid the country of all elements of danger. He did not like the Castle of Haverfordwest to be capable of being possessed by ill-affected persons, so he got the Commissioners of the County to order its demolition. This order was dated the day next after the fall of Pembroke, and to prevent any misapprehension Cromwell added to the order in his own hand, "If a speedy course be not taken to fulfil the commands of this warrant, I shall be necessitated to consider of settling a garrison." The Mayor and Corporation at once obeyed, and set workmen about it; but the work being so difficult without powder to blow it up, that it would exhaust a "huge" sum of money, and take a long time, they asked the Lieutenant-General for some powder, and that the whole county should join them in the work, bearing a share in the expense. On the 14th Cromwell, by his warrant, authorised the municipal authorities to call for their assistance the inhabitants of all the hundreds of the county. The castle, however, still stands, though shorn somewhat of its glory. But it caused no further trouble.

Cromwell had no time to lose, for the Scots had already invaded England. Leaving behind him in South Wales Col. Horton and his regiment of horse, a troop of dragoons, and two companies out of Col. Pride's and Col. Deane's regiments, he set out for the North, and by the same troops which a handful of men in Pembroke had occupied for full six weeks, he soon annihilated the Scotch army of forty thousand, and restored peace to the kingdom. Horton was rewarded for his services by a grant of the Slebech estate, which Laugharne had so foolishly forfeited.

Poyer, Laugharne, and Powell were sent up to the Tower, where they remained prisoners till the following spring. They were tried by Court Martial and sentenced to death. The authorities, far from being vindictive, and anxious to show as much leniency as possible, consented to carry out the sentence only in one instance. The prisoners were therefore allowed to draw lots for their lives. On two of the lots was written, "Life given by God," the third being a blank. A child drew the lots, and the fatal one fell to Col. Poyer, who, on the 21st of April, 1649, was shot at the Piazza, Covent Garden. He met his fate calmly, and died like a soldier. Laugharne and Powell were ordered to quit the country,—a vote for their banishment being passed by the Parliament. Col. Humphrey Mathews, imprisoned at Nottingham Castle, was released on composition, to the great disgust of Cromwell, who wrote to some Members a sharp remonstrance thereon. "Mathews," he said, "than whom this Cause we have fought for has not had a more dangerous enemy;—and he not guilty only of being an enemy, but he apostatised from your Cause and Quarrel; having been a Colonel, if not more, under you, and 'then' the desperatest promoter of the Welsh Rebellion amongst them all! And how near you were brought to ruin thereby, all men that know anything can tell;

and this man was taken away by composition, by what order I know not," to the "amazement" of Cromwell and his officers.[1]

The affairs of South Wales were now entrusted to safe hands—the leading supporters of the Parliament in the several counties. Of these the most prominent was Col. Philip Jones, the Governor of Swansea, and a native of that place, who had been a strenuous supporter of the Parliamentary cause, and had contributed much towards maintaining order in Glamorganshire when that county was full of discontented loyalists. At the battle of St. Fagans he evinced great courage and military tact, and Col. Horton freely acknowledges his indebtedness to him in that conflict. When Cromwell passed through Swansea, on his way to Ireland, in the spring of the next year, he was a guest of Col. Jones. In 1651 he suppressed a fresh revolt of the Royalists, and in 1653 was elected representative of Monmouthshire in the Little Parliament. In 1654 he was returned for the same county, and the next year he was elected both at Brecon and for the County of Glamorgan. Cromwell raised him to his Upper House, and appointed him Comptroller of his Household, which he held until Cromwell's death. He was one of those who pressed the crown upon Cromwell. Envied and hated by some of his neighbours, charges of a serious character were brought against him, but which he clearly repudiated, and which had no foundation whatever. In the meantime he amassed a considerable fortune, and purchased extensive estates in Glamorganshire at Fonmon, where his descendants

[1] Sloane MSS., 1519—94. Carlyle's Cromwell, Letter lxxxii.

now live, still maintaining the distinguished name of the Protector, a name which was given to Col. Jones's eldest son when Cromwell stood his godfather.[1]

Bushey Mansell, Commander-in-Chief of Glamorganshire, Major-General Dawkin of Kilvrough, in the same county, Sir Richard Pryse, the second Baronet of Gogerddan, Col. James Phillips of the Priory, Cardigan, and Capt. Thomas Evans of Peterwell, Cardiganshire, were also energetic supporters of the Parliament. Bushey Mansell, Sir Richard Pryse, and Col. James Phillips were of the six who represented Wales in the Little Parliament. Major-General Dawkin was Governor of Carmarthen, and as such suppressed an insurrection in Cardiganshire in 1651, when some attempts were made in various parts of the country to place Prince Charles on the throne. The leaders of the movement in Cardiganshire were Major Lewes, a brother of Sir John Lewes of Abernantbychan, Thomas Lloyd, Llanllyr, or Llanfair-Clydoge, Capt. Richard Jones, Mr. Reynold Jenkins, and Cornet Morgan Jenkins, the latter two, probably, of Pantyrlys, respecting whom there is a tradition that the motto of the Jenkinses of Cilbronau—"*Da yw ffon amddiffyniad*"—originated in a conflict during the Civil War.[2] In the conflict between them and Major-General Dawkin at "Llanbadarn," the insurrectionists were entirely routed,—twenty-eight being killed and about sixty made prisoners,—

CHAP. VIII.
1648.

[1] An interesting memoir of Col. Jones is given in Col. Francis's valuable work, the Charters of Swansea.
[2] Communicated to me by Mr. R. D. Jenkins of Cilbronau.

among the latter being Lloyd, Jones, and the two Jenkinses.[1]

The Parliament cause in the meantime had been entirely successful. The insurrection of 1648 had been completely put down; and in January, 1649, Charles I., King of England by "Divine Right," as some thought, was beheaded at Whitehall—a proof positive of the sovereignty of the People, and of the hollowness of Divine Right. Two Welsh Members sat on his trial and signed his death warrant, viz., Colonel John Jones, the Governor of Anglesey, and Thomas Wogan, Member for the Cardiganshire Boroughs. I am not called upon to justify or condemn the King's trial and its tragic issue; but I believe that the liberty of the subject and the privileges of Parliament have been all the more firmly established through being stained in Royal blood.

Of Wales during the Commonwealth, of its religious and political struggles, of its conduct at the Restoration, and of many other incidents of the Civil War, I should like to treat at length, but here space will not permit me; and the task, if ever taken up by me, must be at some future time.

[1] Tanner MSS. Carry's Memorials, ii., 279, and Francis's Charters of Swansea, 179.

END OF VOL. I.

MORGAN AND DAVIES, "WELSHMAN" OFFICE, CARMARTHEN.

CPSIA information can be obtained at www.ICGtesting.com
Printed in the USA
LVOW09*1800151214

418938LV00014B/297/P